The Chronic Pain Management Sourcebook

Also by David Drum:
  Making the Chemotherapy Decision
  The Type II Diabetes Sourcebook (with Terry Zierenberg)

The Chronic Pain Management Sourcebook

David Drum

Foreword by
MALIN DOLLINGER, M.D., F.A.C.P.

LOWELL HOUSE

LOS ANGELES

NTC/Contemporary Publishing Group

Library of Congress Cataloging-in-Publication Data

Drum, C. David
        The chronic pain management sourcebook / By David Drum.
            p.   cm.
        Includes bibliographical references and index.
        ISBN 0-7373-0101-5
        1. Chronic pain Popular works. 2.Chronic pain—Treatment.
3. Chronic pain—Alternative treatment. 4. Holistic medicine.
I. Title.
RB 127.D78 1999
616' .0472—dc21   99-21948
                                                                CIP

Text design: Jack Lanning

Published by Lowell House
A division of NTC/Contemporary Publishing Group, Inc.
4255 West Touhy Avenue, Lincolnwood, Illinois 60646-1975 U.S.A.
Printed in the United States of America
International Standard Book Number: 0-7373-0101-5
99 00 01 02 03 04 RRD 18 17 16 15 14 13 12 11 10 9 8 7 6 5 4 3 2 1

for Winona

Nothing in life is to be feared.
It is only to be understood.
— Marie Curie

Acknowledgments

The author would like to thank the following individuals within the medical community who provided useful information and timely advice: Malin Dollinger, M.D., John Wayne Cancer Center, Santa Monica, California; Paul Rosch, M.D., president, American Institute of Stress, Yonkers, New York; C. Norman Shealey, M.D., Shealy Institute, Springfield, Missouri; Ben Schwachman, M.D., Los Angeles; Leon G. Robb, M.D., Robb Pain Management Group, North Hollywood, California; Susan Adams, M.S., R.D., Nutritional Sciences Graduate Program, University of Washington, Seattle, Washington, for the American Dietetic Association; Debra A. Wolf, R.N., B.S.N., M.P.H., nursing supervisor, University of Washington Medical Center, Seattle, Washington; Mark Jensen, Ph.D., head statistician, University of Washington Medical Center; Denise Economu, R.N.; M.N., A.O.C.N., Cedars-Sinai Medical Center, Los Angeles; Gene Dedick, past regional director, Southern California region, American Chronic Pain Association. The author owes a special debt of thanks to the men and women with chronic pain who gave of their time and experience during personal interviews.

Contents

Foreword   xiii

CHAPTER I

About Chronic Pain   1

Unnecessary Suffering • Undertreatment and Overtreatment
Reasons for Hope • Emotional Turmoil • The Extent of Chronic Pain
About This Book • Achieving Good Health

CHAPTER 2

The Treatment of Chronic Pain   23

Acute Versus Chronic Pain • Body and Mind
The Importance of Accurate Diagnosis • Getting a Medical Assessment
Your Role in the Process • Doctor-Patient Communication
The Treatment of Pain

CHAPTER 3

Physical Pain   61

The Nervous System • Types of Pain • Causes of Pain
Major Categories of Pain Disorders

CHAPTER 4

The Mind   101

Power of the Mind • Breaking the Pain Cycle • Depression
How Therapy Helps • Family Support • Effective Communication
Sexual Activity

CHAPTER 5

Physical Conditioning   137

The Importance of Movement • Physical Unfitness • Fitness
Physical Therapy • The Benefits of Exercise
Skin Stimulation Techniques • TENS

CHAPTER 6

Nutrition   163

Eating Well • Good Nutrition • Obesity • Alcohol, Caffeine, and Tobacco

CHAPTER 7

Social Support   185
Support Groups • Spiritual Support

CHAPTER 8

Stress   199
The Symptoms of Stress • Stress as a Trigger • Different Strokes
A Good Night's Sleep • Brain Waves • Stress-Relieving Techniques
A Balanced Lifestyle

CHAPTER 9

Drugs   229
Reducing the Use of Drugs • Regular Doses • Long-Term Use
Taking Your Medicine • Specific Drugs That Relieve Pain
Other Drug Treatments

CHAPTER 10

Surgery   261
Implanted Drug Delivery Systems • Spinal Column Stimulation
Back and Spine Surgery • Joint Replacement • Coronary Artery Surgery
Sympathetic Blocks • Temporomandibular Joint (TMJ) Disorders
Ablative Surgeries

CHAPTER 11

Cancer Pain   281
The Undertreatment of Pain • Mitigating Pain • Drug Treatment
Doctor-Patient Communication • Types of Pain • Emotional Stress
A Difference in Perspective • Hospices

CHAPTER 12

Looking Ahead   301

APPENDIX

Resources   307
Medical Organizations Dealing with Pain
Information and Support for Specific Medical Conditions
Other Resources
Related Reading
Internet Sites

Glossary   325
Index   335

Foreword

Beginning with Eve, pain has been the universal fear of humankind. Whether it is a toothache (or the experience of having the problem fixed), the milder episodes of headache or backache, or the heroic experience of childbirth, every living person knows about pain. The consolation that it may call our attention to a problem that requires treatment is little solace for the afflicted.

Acute pain at least bears the promise of redemption. When the kidney stone is passed, when the child is born, when the incision heals, you will be well again . . . and pain-free. Chronic pain is a different and difficult challenge. For weeks, months, and often years, the suffering lingers, as does the sufferer. The pain may seem to outlast the disease, a final reminder of a good life gone awry. Chronic pain has many patterns and causes, but one thing that is always present is suffering. Early in my experience as a cancer doctor, I learned that pain takes precedence over everything else. If the pain cannot be controlled, it does not matter what marvelous deeds I might perform to cure the disease.

Where do you start on your journey to relief from chronic pain? You may spend days and weeks going from one doctor to another, from one pain clinic to another, trying this or that remedy, whether it is pills, shots, skin patches, heat or cold, nerve blocks, TENS units, or acupuncture. And indeed, you should not fail to get the best professional help you can.

But first, read this book. *The Chronic Pain Management Sourcebook* is an ideal place to start. David Drum has become the spokesperson for all of the pain relief professionals, whose wide spectrum of information has been merged into this useful book. He has created for you an easy-to-understand, well-written, comprehensive summary of everything you might wish to know—indeed, need to know—about chronic pain. He discusses the causes and patterns of chronic pain, the choices of treatment and management, the places, people, and clinics to consult, and the wide spectrum of treatment choices that you have. This thoroughly researched book also contains information on diet, physical conditioning, social support, and stress, and a helpful list of organiz- ations and places to seek additional information.

Pain is universal. This book will become the universal companion and friend to sufferers from chronic pain. It brings to everyday understanding the complex and technical aspects of this difficult branch of medicine. This information will be your key to enlightenment, to dealing with the problem, and to your relationship with the most important people in your life: your loved ones, your health care professionals, and yourself.

MALIN DOLLINGER, M.D., F.A.C.P.
Clinical Professor of Medicine
University of Southern California School of Medicine
Oncology Consultant, John Wayne Cancer Institute,
Santa Monica, California

The Chronic Pain Management Sourcebook

CHAPTER ONE

About Chronic Pain

∽ *Chronic pain is a complex condition that occurs in one out of every three families, but its worst effects can be controlled.*

When a tall, attractive woman whom we shall call Leslie escorted her daughter down the aisle to be married on a balmy October day, she considered that short walk a victory. Leslie has suffered from chronic pain for the past several years.

After suffering a work-related accident several years ago, Leslie, a single parent with three children, has had to deal with the effects of fibromyalgia, carpal tunnel syndrome, and other joint and soft tissue problems as well as a lawsuit that has yet to be resolved. When Leslie's daughter was planning her wedding, she had asked her mother to accompany her down the aisle "if you're able to walk." Leslie postponed surgery on her knees, but she admits it was nip and tuck right up until the time she walked her daughter down that aisle.

Leslie works out at a gym, attends a support group, and cooperates with her medical doctor to manage her pain problems. She has a sense of humor and a loving family. But Leslie admits, "Sometimes I feel like I'm not a productive member of society, and like I'm not needed. It's been very depressing for me."

For any person living with its debilitating effects, chronic pain is extraordinarily frustrating to experience and exquisitely painful to endure. For that person's loved ones, it is equally frustrating to witness. One's outlook on life is constantly tested. The physical and emotional suffering that accompanies chronic pain tries the body and the mind, and tests the limits of the spirit and the self. More than almost any other type of medical problem, chronic pain chips away at one's personal sense of self and at one's well-being on a day-to-day basis. Focusing only on pain and fearing that its effects cannot be controlled can slowly turn a normal person into a

PAIN WITHOUT SUFFERING

Education can help improve your ability to endure pain. According to the book *Pain and Disability*, edited by Marian Osterweis, you can tolerate even severe pain without suffering if you understand the following:

1. The source of the pain

2. That the pain is not dire

3. That the pain will end

4. That a means exists to control the pain

bitter, helpless invalid, unless that person makes a conscious decision to fight back.

Great advances in understanding how to treat chronic pain have been made over the past three decades. Although many medical conditions that cause chronic pain are not yet curable, the pain itself is more easily managed than ever before.

The experience of a person in chronic pain is similar to the experience of a nightmare, psychologist Lawrence LeShan has observed. LeShan has observed that all nightmares involve terrible things done to the dreamer and worse things threatened. In nightmares, the dreamer is helplessly under the control of outside forces and cannot predict when the nightmare will end. The person in pain is in the same formal situation, LeShan has said.

Chronic pain can throw your home life, your social life, your finances, and even your career askew. You may angrily shake your fist at God and ask, "Why me?" Or you may turn your own anger on yourself in an emotionally painful, seemingly endless depression. You may live in constant anxiety. You may feel helpless and alone, crying out for relief in the night. You may feel there's nothing that can be done to help you, and nothing you can ever possibly do to help yourself exit the nightmare.

By definition, *chronic pain* is pain that cannot be eradicated by medical treatment. Therefore, the challenge of managing chronic pain on a day-to-day basis falls on you.

You can achieve a substantial amount of control over chronic pain. But learning to live with chronic pain can be a long process, more like jogging from Boston to Philadelphia than running a 100-yard dash. It takes a continuing display of courage, patience, and determination to cope effectively with pain. Courage is required to face the fact that there may be no medical solution to the problem as yet. Patience is useful as you move through a learning process that may involve a great deal of time and persistent effort, a process that does not always yield immediate results. With determination, you can move forward. You can take your focus off the pain itself and focus on learning to live with it. You can reduce your level of pain, reduce your level of disability, and build up your mental and physical strength. You can vow that you will live your life as fully and as completely as possible by learning to use all the tools at your command.

Instead of giving in to a life of psychic defeat and disability, you can choose to make the best you can of your life, beginning today. Millions of men and women in the United States and Canada are successfully coping with chronic pain at this moment. You can live your life as a survivor, not a passive victim. If you resolve to endure, you can find the courage to change, to cope, and to help yourself. What the American Chronic Pain Association calls changing from a patient to a person involves a change in attitude, and ultimately a commitment to take action to help yourself.

Medical doctors can understand and treat acute pain. Chronic pain is different from acute or suddenly-appearing pain, and it is treated differently. Chronic pain is much more complex—it involves a more intimate and complicated mix of body, emotion, and mind. Physical unfitness, excessive drug use, painful emotions such as anxiety and depression, feelings of helplessness and guilt, negative social behavior, and even obsessive thoughts of suicide can accompany chronic pain.

Taking action on your own behalf increases your strength, builds self-confidence, and helps combat depression. If you choose to strengthen your body, your mind, and your spirit, you fortify your own will to endure and to live. By making a stubborn commitment to live your life as fully as possible and within realistic limits, you can rise toward life-affirming joy and laughter, rather than falling into the darkness of depression and despair.

UNNECESSARY SUFFERING

The *Concise Oxford Dictionary* defines *pain* as "suffering, distress of body and mind." The Latin word for pain, *poena,* implies both pain and punishment. Another word for pain, *dolor,* can be translated as "ache" or "anguish," meaning either physical or mental pain. Because pain envelops both body and mind, it has been called "the ultimate psychosomatic phenomenon."

Like suffering, pain is subjective. It is impossible to measure physical pain accurately even with the most sophisticated sensors and tests. Chronic pain may be the ultimate exercise in solitude and misery—a uniquely private experience, but one from which all instincts cry out for immediate relief.

Acute pain comes on suddenly, a symptom that vanishes when healing is complete. *Chronic* pain lasts much longer. Chronic pain is frequently defined as pain that persists more than six months after the onset of a medical problem, or as pain that persists after accepted medical treatments have failed to produce the desired result. In *The Management of Pain,* renowned pain specialist John J. Bonica, M.D., defines *chronic pain* as any pain that persists more than a month beyond the usual course of an acute injury, process, or disease. Dr. Bonica says chronic pain is associated with a "chronic pathological process that causes continuous pain or the pain recurs at intervals for months or years."

Chronic pain is different from short-term or acute pain in several ways. Richard A. Sternbach, a psychologist and director of the Pain Treatment Center at Scripps Clinic and Research Foundation in San Diego, California, observes that acute pain is a useful biological signal to the body that something is wrong, like an alarm signaling the brain that a fire has broken out somewhere in the body. Chronic pain, however, is a "false alarm" that continues to ring after the fire has been extinguished or brought under control as much as possible. It should be noted that so-called chronic *benign* pain, referred to as chronic pain in much of this book, is different from the chronic *malignant* pain that arises from cancer or during cancer treatment. The pain associated with cancer often is similar to acute pain, and because it is treated somewhat differently, it is addressed in a separate chapter in this book.

Over time, the experience of chronic benign pain grows complicated. According to the American Pain Society, it "may be associated with changes in personality, lifestyle, and functional ability and may be associated with symptoms and signs of depression, hopelessness, helplessness, loss of libido and weight and sleep disturbance." Unrelieved pain creates excruciating physical and mental stress. It disturbs the metabolism. It causes problems with blood clotting and water retention. Pain delays healing, produces hormone imbalances,

THE EXTENT OF PAIN

A Harris survey, published in 1985 as the Nuprin Pain Report, questioned Americans ages eighteen to sixty-five and found the following percentages of people who missed more than thirty days of work a year because of pain.

Type of Pain	Percent
Backache	13.9
Joint pain	13.8
Headache	13.3
Muscle pain	9.9
Stomach pain	4.0
Premenstrual pain	3.7
Dental pain	1.9
Other	2.0

impairs the immune system, and causes the gastrointestinal system to malfunction. Pain can decrease your ability to move around, and interfere with appetite and sleep. Strong pain-relieving drugs useful for the treatment of acute pain often become part of the problem by creating additional pain when used over long periods of time.

Chronic pain is widespread, touching one family in three. Dr. Bonica estimates that 25 to 30 percent of the U.S. population, and that of other industrialized nations, suffers from chronic pain. He estimates that between 50 and 75 percent of those who experience chronic pain are partially or totally disabled for a period of days, as in a headache; for weeks or months, as in reflex sympathetic dystrophy; or permanently, as in low back pain, arthritis, or cancer.

UNDERTREATMENT AND OVERTREATMENT

Treating chronic pain can be uncomfortable and frustrating for doctors, a few of whom blame the victim for lack of response to a particular treatment. Rather than spending a great deal of time on a very detailed physical examination, some doctors find it simpler to write a prescription, order up more tests, refer the patient to another doctor, or even dismiss a real complaint of pain as "all in your head." With chronic pain, medical treatment is at best only a part of the solution. In fact, overtreating or undertreating pain are both recognized problems.

Overtreatments, or treatments that do not work and are not effective, can harm or weaken the body, making it more difficult to endure pain, or creating more. Pain expert Marcia E. Bedard, Ph.D., says that patients with severe, unrelenting pain from permanent structural damage to their neurologic or musculoskeletal systems are "often subjected to expensive and unnecessary surgeries and other painful invasive procedures." Procedures such as multiple back surgeries frequently provide no benefit and don't cure back pain.

The undertreatment of pain is a different sort of problem. A prime example is pain associated with cancer, which usually can be relieved by powerful drugs such as morphine. These drugs are not always used, or used in amounts not adequate to control cancer pain. Although cancer is one of the most feared of all diseases, 90 to 95 percent of cancer pain now can be controlled by relatively simple means. But when pain-relieving drugs are underused, many people suffer horrible and unnecessary agonies that could be alleviated. In a 1995 report, the American Medical Association's Council on Scientific Affairs stated that pain was often undertreated because of a low priority on pain relief in the health care system, poor pain assessment, ignorance of pain management on the part of doctors and patients, exaggerated fears by doctors of opiate side effects and the possibility of addiction, and the reluctance of patients to report pain.

Discrimination by undertreatment is widespread, some experts say, especially among certain groups of chronic pain patients. According to some studies, at the greatest risk are women, racial and ethnic minorities, children, the elderly, workers' compensation patients, and previously disabled patients such as those who are deaf, blind, amputees, and polio survivors. Taken collectively, these groups constitute a majority of the people with chronic pain.

REASONS FOR HOPE

Although medical treatment continues to advance, doctors don't have all the answers to treating chronic benign pain. The presence of a degenerative disease like arthritis, for instance, can be accepted and dealt with only on its own terms since arthritis is among a number of diseases that cannot yet be cured.

In the field of health care, the treatment of chronic pain is gaining recognition as a distinct medical specialty, one that benefits from special training and knowledge. The American Society of Anesthesiologists' special certification in pain treatment is a step in that direction. Additional recognition has come from the formation of pain societies, composed of doctors and other pain treatment professionals, which have sprung up over the past several years.

Given the miracles accomplished by medical treatment on acute pain, many people with chronic pain naturally seek permanent and immediate relief from a system that seems able to cure most ailments with a shot, an operation, or an esoteric new treatment technique. Medicine is more sophisticated than ever before in the history of the world, but the assumption that doctors can cure anything is unfortunate. When pain becomes chronic, seeking medical treatment can be an exercise in frustration. Sometimes doctors can't find any reason why a patient's pain is continuing, and are therefore unable to treat it. Sometimes they can pinpoint a physical cause but are unable to cure the underlying condition. Sometimes they can control the pain, but they really don't understand exactly how what they are doing helps control the disease.

Over the past three decades, chronic pain itself has been recognized as a collection of symptoms composed of overlapping physical, mental, emotional, and social elements. Dr. Bonica is credited with introducing the idea of a "team approach" to treating chronic pain. In 1960, he helped organize the nation's first multidisciplinary pain center at the University of Washington in Seattle, the prototype for an estimated 1,200 pain care centers or clinics that now exist in the United States. About two hundred of these, specializing in chronic pain, have been accredited by the Commission of Rehabilitation Facilities in Tucson, Arizona. An estimated 3,000 medical doctors in the United States focus on pain management. Although many people benefit from programs at advanced pain treatment centers, the price of these treatments—as high as $30,000 for a four-week inpatient stay—is reportedly causing insurance companies to question their cost-effectiveness. And after any person completes a pain program, what is learned also must be continued at home.

The best treatment for chronic pain is multidisciplinary, and it involves the whole person, body and mind. This treatment is sometimes called holistic. Multidisciplinary treatment draws from many disciplines, including medicine, psychology, occupational therapy, exercise therapy, and nutrition therapy. More and more, chronic pain treatment utilizes cognitive and behavioral therapy, stress-relieving biofeedback, hypnosis, relaxation therapy, and therapies such as acupuncture and transcutaneous electrical nerve stimulation (TENS).

The boundaries of good medical treatment are expanding. A program begun by San Francisco physician Dean Ornish, M.D., uses a vegetarian diet, yoga, communications training, stress reduction, and support groups to treat heart disease successfully without drugs and surgery. In New York City, a program begun by John Sarno, M.D., helps many people with back and neck pain return to functional lives through a program of education, exercise, and stress relief rather than back surgery. On the lighter side, off-duty clowns from Ringling Brothers and Barnum & Bailey Circus wheel comedy carts around Morton Plant Hospital in Clearwater, Florida, one of many hospitals in the United States that utilize the healing benefits of humor.

By considering the whole person and blending the expertise of many disciplines, chronic pain may be better managed today than ever before.

EMOTIONAL TURMOIL

"Pain upsets and destroys the nature of the person who feels it," the Greek philosopher Aristotle wrote in *Nicomachean Ethics,* an observation that still holds true. Over time, unrelieved pain creates physical, psychological, and behavioral changes that diminish the quality of life.

Chronic pain can trigger a relentless chorus of emotionally painful feelings, including fear, hostility, anger, depression, resentment, irritation, loneliness, and a general feeling that one's life has spun hopelessly out of control. These roiling negative emotions can break apart relationships and marriages, and they can rip the enjoyment and sweetness from the experience of life. Anxiety and depression will increase pain. Depression and pain often work together, like an insidious team of horses, pulling you along a dark road almost against your will, unless you act to stop them.

The Robert Wood Johnson Foundation studied the circumstances surrounding more than 4,000 deaths and found that 40 percent of families said their loved ones experienced severe pain for practically all of their final days—stark evidence that pain is often undertreated. In a recent survey, 50 percent of chronic nonmalignant pain patients who did not experience adequate pain relief said they had considered suicide. When statistics like these are considered, some believe Western medicine is losing its compassion and its understanding of emotional suffering by focusing too exclusively on the simple physical aspects of pain.

Religion, philosophy, folklore, and literature have ascribed many meanings to pain. The earliest peoples apparently believed that pain was caused by the invasion of the body by evil spirits, and primitive shamans sought to drive these spirits away with masks, magic, and herbs. The ancient Greeks sought relief from pain by spending the night at the temple of Askelepios, the god of medicine. During the uncontrollable and virulent plagues that swept through the Middle

SOME STATISTICS

- 1 in 3 Americans suffers from some form of recurring pain.
- 1 of every 3 families contains a person who suffers from chronic pain.
- 4 out of 5 Americans have one severe headache a year.
- 1 in 5 Americans experiences migraines or other headaches.
- 1 in 7 Americans is affected by arthritis.
- Peptic ulcers affect 1 in 5 men in their lifetime.
- Peptic ulcers affect 1 in 10 women in their lifetime.

Ages, some Christians sought pain as a means to attain contact with the divine—walking down medieval streets, lashing themselves with whips in the hope that their pain and suffering would convince God to drive the plague away.

The best contemporary explanation of how pain actually works is Ronald Melzack and Patrick Wall's "gate control" theory. This theory postulates that the experience of pain has many distinct dimensions, including several that are psychological or emotional. In chronic pain treatment, these can be addressed to great benefit. Behavioral therapy has had remarkable successes since it was developed a little more than twenty years ago, and its use is widely accepted in pain programs. Cognitive therapy, also widely utilized, helps change destructive thought patterns, and it has been quite helpful for

EDUCATING YOURSELF

Finding out more about your particular medical problem and how to control it may help you understand and deal with your pain, or help you understand and explain your experience to a loved one. In addition to simply asking questions of your doctor, listed below are basic ways to begin learning about your medical problem.

- Informational handouts such as brochures, flyers, or videos, available at your doctor's office or hospital, are frequently the simplest educational materials, and a good place to begin educating yourself.

- National nonprofit or governmental organizations that exist to provide information on a particular problem, such as the Arthritis Foundation and the National Institutes of Health, are listed in the appendix at the back of this book. Many of these organizations provide brochures, videos, and other educational materials on request, and many have Web sites, magazines, or newsletters that provide current information on a regular basis.

many people with mild to moderate depression. Education, counseling, and support groups help great numbers of people address social and emotional issues, and to personally learn to combat the stress and anguish that accompany chronic pain. Even fine-tuning one's communication skills can help one cope with pain.

Laura S. Hitchcock, a psychologist and executive director of the National Chronic Pain Outreach Association, has written of a personal odyssey that began as she was helping

- Local organizations, hospitals, and clinics sometimes sponsor educational meetings where an expert on a particular aspect of your illness may speak and answer questions of interest to you.

- Books and magazines on health topics are available in public libraries and bookstores. Medical school and university libraries have medical textbooks, professional journals, and databases such as MEDLINE that may be searched for articles and books on particular topics. Nursing textbooks can provide explanations of complex medical or surgical procedures in simple language.

- Support groups for people with chronic pain are often a good source of local information. These groups sometimes invite experts to appear and address topics of interest to participants.

lift a kitchen sink out of a car trunk. She injured her back. Her first doctor recommended conservative treatments such as physical therapy, hot packs, ultrasound, and exercise for three months. When those failed, her doctor recommended back surgery. Instead, Hitchcock sought the advice of another medical doctor, a physiatrist, who designs physical therapy and rehabilitation programs. This specialist treated Hitchcock with gentle manipulation and mobilization, then suggested a program of gradual exercise, which eventually brought her to the point where she could live with her pain without undergoing surgery.

From her personal experience and her work with support groups, Hitchcock has learned a great deal about patients who experience chronic pain. She says chronic pain does not choose people because of their occupation, socioeconomic group, or premorbid mental health. "The topic of stigmatization and stereotyping is one that is raised repeatedly in the chronic pain support groups I have led as well as by pain patients in my practice," she wrote in *Pain Management*. "Patients are very pleased to find a health care professional who knows what it is like to live with daily pain. Chronic pain is an equal opportunity problem."

THE EXTENT OF CHRONIC PAIN

In the United States and other industrialized countries, the extent of chronic pain is enormous. C. David Tollison, Ph.D., director of the Center for Health and Occupational Services in Greenville, South Carolina, estimates that 75 million to 80 million Americans suffer from chronic handicapping pain, an estimate generally regarded as conservative. Included are 31 million people with low back pain, the most common cause of disability in persons under forty-five. Approximately 43 million Americans suffer from arthritis, according to the Arthritis Foundation, with 600,000 new cases diagnosed each year. An estimated 15 million Americans suffer migraine head-aches, with another 25 million suffering muscle contraction or tension headaches, Tollison estimates. Headaches affect an estimated 70 to 80 percent of the U.S. population at least once a month.

Chronic pain costs money. Within the United States, more than $4 billion is spent each year on painkilling drugs.

Of the $900 million spent on nonprescription drugs, an estimated $100 million is spent on aspirin. Lost workdays and medical treatments for chronic pain in the United States account for up to $65 billion to $75 billion per year, Tollison estimates, more than twice the cost attributed to alcoholism. According to a Harris survey conducted in 1985, 1.3 billion American workdays were lost because of back pain, 1 billion because of joint pain, and 600 million because of headache. In *Back Pain in the Workplace,* editor and pain specialist Wilbur E. Fordyce estimated that if present trends continue, they will bankrupt government disability programs.

At the moment, it is estimated that somewhere between 4 and 9 percent of the U.S. population between the ages of eigthteen and sixty-four is disabled. According to a 1980 report by the U.S. Department of Health Services, musculoskeletal conditions such as lower back pain, joint pain, arthritis, and rheumatism comprise the leading causes of disability for people in their working years. In one study, 36 percent of respondents with spinal cord injuries reported that it was the incidence of chronic pain rather than paralysis that kept them from working.

The treatment of pain is a particular concern for older people. An estimated four out of five people over the age of sixty-five have at least one chronic disease. More than half of those in the same age group have two existing chronic health problems. In a 1993 study, 70 percent of nursing home residents surveyed suffered chronic pain. In a study of 3,000 older residents in rural Iowa, 86 percent complained of some type of pain the previous year, and 59 percent had multiple pain complaints.

Many chronic pain patients see doctor after doctor in a frustrating cycle leading to little genuine relief. L. Douglas

Kennedy, M.D., of Pain Consultants of Lexington, Kentucky, estimates that most patients who are referred to pain specialists have been evaluated and treated by at least five other doctors.

Typically, Tollison wrote in *Pain Management,* chronic pain patients have suffered "several years of agony, have undergone two or more failed surgeries for pain relief, they are restricted in their jobs or unable to work, they take multiple medications, they experience chronic sleep disturbance, marital and family dysfunction, suffer depression and emotional distress, and are physically and psychologically depleted." While chronic illnesses such as cancer and heart disease can affect *quantity* of life by reducing life expectancy, Tollison observes that chronic pain is different because it interrupts life's *quality*.

Major breakthroughs in the treatment of chronic pain began about three decades ago. Whereas acute pain is properly viewed as a symptom, chronic pain is more correctly seen as a *syndrome* encompassing complex physical, mental, and social effects. This syndrome results in excessive pain and disability, but with effort, both can be reduced.

The great physician Albert Schweitzer once called pain "a more terrible lord of mankind than even death itself." When it comes to the treatment of chronic pain, this terrible lord's worst and most debilitating effects can be reduced and controlled.

ABOUT THIS BOOK

Many doctors say that educated patients are ultimately better patients because they have a realistic idea of what can be accomplished by medical treatments and support therapies, and what they reasonably may do to help themselves. This sourcebook is written for people who are seeking help in dealing with the experience of chronic pain. It also is written for family members and caregivers who seek to learn and to help their loved ones. In addition to case histories of people who are living successfully with chronic pain, this book contains basic health information designed to supplement what information you may receive from medical doctors, who should remain your primary source of information on your medical condition.

The first chapter provides a basic overview of the problem of chronic pain, including its prevalence and its cost to society.

Chapter 2 looks at the treatment of chronic pain, including some strategies used at major pain clinics, and describes how a pain specialist might diagnosis and assess pain.

Chapter 3 examines the biology of chronic pain—the mechanisms that help create pain in the nervous system, new thinking such as Melzack and Wall's "gate control" theory, and a survey of the major types of chronic pain, including back pain, arthritis, and headaches.

Chapter 4 looks at the emotional and psychological elements of pain, which are important aspects of chronic pain management.

Chapter 5 surveys the milder, more conservative types of medical treatment, including physical therapy, hot and cold treatments, TENS, and acupuncture. Highlighted is the role of exercise in reversing the excessive physical unfitness that often contributes to chronic pain.

Chapter 6 focuses on important quality-of-life issues such as nutrition and diet.

Chapter 7 examines the role of social support, including interactions with friends and family, and other factors such as support groups and spirituality, which can play a key role in good health.

Chapter 8 deals with stress, a major factor in many types of chronic pain. It includes a survey of stress-relieving treatments—relaxation therapy, visualization, and biofeedback, among others—useful in an overall strategy of pain control.

Chapter 9 lists some of the drugs used in the treatment of pain, and discusses how they may be most effectively employed.

Chapter 10 examines the surgeries that can be useful in some situations.

Chapter 11 looks at the special area of pain relief for cancer patients, whose pain is treated differently than other types of chronic pain.

Chapter 12 looks at a few new treatments on the horizon.

In addition, an appendix of resources is included at the back of this book. It lists helpful sources of additional information such as major pain organizations, Internet addresses, and books of interest. Also at the back of the book is a glossary defining pertinent terms used throughout this book and possibly in your treatment.

ACHIEVING GOOD HEALTH

The American Occupational Therapy Association defines *wellness* as a way of life that incorporates good health habits, including rest, exercise, nutrition, and supportive thought processes developed even in the presence of a disability such as chronic pain. The World Health Organization has defined *health* as "a state of complete physical, mental, and social well-being and not merely the absence of disease and infirmity."

The anthropologist Ashley Montagu defined *health* as "the ability to love, to work, to play, and to think soundly."

Ultimately, it is the author's wish that this book helps bring you information that allows you to move closer to a state of the best possible physical and mental health, with a reduced level of physical pain.

Although many strides forward have been made in its treatment over the past several years, chronic pain remains a nationwide problem, but with many aspects that may be productively addressed. You can take actions to lessen the excessive pain and disability that are part of the chronic pain syndrome. As explained in the next chapter, pain treatment is the province not only of medical doctors, but also of a team of specialists from many disciplines who can help you help yourself.

CHAPTER TWO

The Treatment of Chronic Pain

⌘ Understanding the diagnosis and treatment of chronic pain, and why it is different from acute pain.

Chronic pain should be approached and treated differently than acute pain. Because chronic pain often leads to excessive pain and disability, effective treatment should allow you to control it as much as possible and get on with the business of your life. A thorough assessment is important and usually is the first step in treatment by a good doctor, or a treatment team at a comprehensive pain treatment center. Over the long haul, dealing with chronic pain involves working not only with medical doctors, but also with specialists in related areas—physical therapists, psychologists, occupational therapists, and others who function as educators in teaching you ways to control your pain. In many respects, chronic pain is self-managed. After all is said and done, you must rely as much on yourself as on a medical doctor for control of pain's day-to-day effects.

From a strictly physical point of view, there are many reasons why people experience chronic pain. Chronic pain can arise from an injury or operation; from an illness such as arthritis or cancer; from muscle, joint, or tissue problems; or from an injury to the nervous system. Some chronic pain arises from an undiscoverable source or from a combination of factors that can't be determined with current medical technology.

Pain treatment specialist John J. Bonica, M.D., has observed that many doctors don't spend the time necessary to correctly diagnose the combination of factors that add up to chronic pain syndrome. "The inability (or unwillingness) of many health care professionals to spend several hours in the initial work-up of the patient is probably due to the pressure of their clinical practice and lack of interest in, and knowledge of, chronic pain syndrome. Consequently, a correct diagnosis is not made and the patient is started on a course of empirical therapy which usually ends up in drug toxicity and other iatrogenic complications, or in an endless series of hopefulness, disappointment, frustration and hopelessness," he wrote in *The Evaluation and Treatment of Chronic Pain*.

Some of this frustration comes because patients and doctors often don't distinguish between acute and chronic pain, and recognize that treatment strategies are quite different for each.

ACUTE VERSUS CHRONIC PAIN

On the surface, the difference between acute and chronic pain may seem to be a matter of time. Chronic pain is different because it lasts longer; however, other important distinctions can be made. These tell us a lot about our assumptions regarding what medical treatment can and can't do. In light of these differences, chronic pain must be approached and treated differently.

Most doctors and patients think of all pain as acute. Acute pain is a symptom, a useful warning signal from the body that something is awry. Acute pain signals an injury, such as an inflamed appendix, which the doctor dutifully tracks down and fixes or eliminates. The acute pain model is mechanistic—it looks at the body as a biochemical machine that is separate from the mind. An assumption is that medical problems are caused by external agents such as viruses or bacteria, or by a fall that breaks bones, and that treatment of symptoms will cure the underlying injury or disease process, and that will eliminate the pain. The doctor works by logically reducing the possibilities and then isolating and treating the symptom or set of symptoms responsible for the pain, which is presumed to be proportional to the injury. The acute pain model assumes that the pain signal is transmitted accurately from the site of the injury to the brain, where an identical pain sensation registers. Both the acute pain and its treatment are assumed to be short term. Both doctor and patient assume that once appropriate medical treatment takes place, healing will occur, and the pain will stop.

To see how the acute pain model works, imagine an attack of appendicitis. The patient comes to the doctor with pain, the doctor eliminates possibilities, isolates the problem, operates to remove the diseased appendix, and uses drugs to control infection and postsurgical pain during a short hospital stay. The patient who has undergone this treatment goes back to his life, more or less as good as new. In this case, it really doesn't matter how the patient perceives or reacts to the pain, since removing the appendix stops the pain in its tracks. The doctor's role in this medical drama is active, and the patient's role is passive. Both are satisfied with the results.

In healing this acute pain symptom, illness is seen as an outside force that invades the body. Disease is tracked down with logic and any number of expensive technological tests, and the demon of disease is tossed out by the doctor using good science. A sort of unspoken contract exists between doctor and patient, who both have roles to play in this drama of sickness and health. In 1958, sociologist Talcott Parsons described the role a sick person is expected to play in the American medical system. The rights and responsibilities of this role include:

1. The sick person can't be blamed for causing the illness.

2. The sick person is exempt from meeting normal role and task obligations.

3. The sick person doesn't like being sick, and has an obligation to try to "get well."

4. The sick person is obliged to seek medical treatment and cooperate with doctors who try to help him or her.

Playing the sick person's role is quite appropriate in the case of acute pain such as that found in appendicitis. People expect to be exempt from certain obligations when they are sick, but they also expect to return to normal life once the doctors fix the problem.

In our health care system, certain assumptions are made by both doctor and patient. Philip L. Gildenberg, M.D., Ph.D., and Richard A. DeVaul, M.D., have written in their book *The Chronic Pain Patient* that these assumptions include an obligation on the part of the patient to "do her job" and passively cooperate, and an assumption that the doctor will "do his job" and actively treat the patient to cure the pain. The patient often assumes good medical treatment means a complete cure; unfortunately, some people who experience chronic pain reject anything short of a return to their previous health status, which is often impossible. These high expectations cause some people to keep seeking medical solutions that don't exist.

As Richard Hanson and Kenneth Gerber point out in their excellent book, *Coping with Chronic Pain,* chronic pain contradicts many of the assumptions many of us make about acute pain: The pain is not temporary, medical treatment can't isolate and cure the problem, and treating the pain basically isn't the doctor's job. Therefore, the best stance is not one of passive recipient. Trying to play the normal sick person's role in a chronic pain situation often makes matters worse, since this role must be played for the rest of your life without the payoff of a medical cure. Treatments such as surgeries and painkilling drugs rarely provide a good long-term solution. Medical doctors often are frustrated by problems that are difficult to understand and define and frustrate every attempt to cure or control them. "Well, learn to live with it," doctors sometimes say, a remark that seems cruel. Busy doctors often don't have time even to explain to the patient exactly how this advice is to be followed.

In the end, chronic pain that cannot be adequately controlled by a medical treatment must be managed at home. The notion of self-management means that the patient handles most of the treatment alone, using the tools and coping techniques that he or she has learned to control it.

BODY AND MIND

Chronic pain involves the mind, body, and spirit. Even the common idea that pain always originates at the site of the injury or disease is false. In chronic pain, the central nervous system and the mind are intimately involved in amplifying or diminishing the pain signals. Emotional and mental factors frequently make chronic pain worse.

Because chronic pain goes on without cessation, it impacts every aspect of your life. Emotional or psychological problems can multiply in the wake of unrelieved pain. These often are part of a pain cycle that brings hope that medical treatment will relieve pain, and disappointment when treatment is not successful. Depression and anxiety, fairly common emotional states for the pain sufferer, enhance pain and create unnecessary disability. Social and behavioral elements come into play in the family circle as the pain patient tries to play out the accepted role of sick person, exempt from normal responsibilities and passively waiting for a doctor to cure the disease. Weighing into the mix are financial problems accompanying the treatment of chronic pain—the frustrations of dealing with a public or private disability insurance system in which medical treatment is not always available, and in which approvals of doctor's visits and medical treatments may seem illogical or capricious.

Some people can cope quite well by themselves with continuing aches and pains, sometimes for many years. Other people with chronic pain have experienced medical false starts, including unnecessary and expensive treatments or medical procedures. As a result, many have become quite frustrated and cynical about the medical system, and irritable and depressed about their prospects of successfully coping with their pain. Given these facts, the differences between acute and chronic pain are quite important. Once these differences are understood, new treatment approaches can begin.

THE IMPORTANCE OF ACCURATE DIAGNOSIS

As Dr. Bonica has observed, it is important to receive a thorough medical examination that pinpoints the source of your pain as accurately as possible. This is the first step taken in most large pain treatment centers. If the type of pain is one for which further medical treatment is indicated, the best choice might be to go ahead with the treatment rather than try to manage the pain yourself. If you have received a thorough examination, however, and your doctors have told you there is nothing more they can really do, your best alternative may be the self-management model, which utilizes a medical doctor as an important resource, but ultimately depends on you.

Under the self-management approach, medical doctors, psychologists, physical therapists, and other experts may be more seen as teachers who help you build coping skills. That you understand the various factors contributing to chronic pain is important. This is because chronic pain itself is interactive—the chronic pain syndrome that creates additional pain and excessive disability spills over into every aspect of life. The chronic pain syndrome involves the mind, the emotions, and often even the way family members behave and communicate.

Even when the best doctors give the most sophisticated tests, a precise physical cause corresponding to the pain frequently cannot be identified. The sources of many types of chronic pain are maddeningly elusive. In 1968, a study of chronic pain patients found that 38 percent of patients

COMMONLY USED WORDS TO DESCRIBE PAIN

According to a study of 145 pain patients published in the *American Journal of Nursing,* the following words were used to describe pain, with the most commonly used words listed first.

treacherous	invading
mean	satanic, or
hateful	variation
detestable	nasty
sneaky	sharp
intense	cunning
dark	nervous
hidden	persistent
obnoxious	sly
faceless	strong
degrading	deceitful
cruel	dominating
inconsiderate	loud

reported real pain where no strictly physical cause was found. In back pain, this state of affairs is even more common. Melzack and Wall's medical textbook, *Textbook of Pain*, estimates that in approximately 80 percent of the cases of back pain, it is impossible to locate injured tissue that would account for the pain. This can be frustrating for patients and doctors, since government disability insurance systems require the doctor to identify a physical cause which accounts for the disability before many treatments can proceed.

GETTING A MEDICAL ASSESSMENT

A full and accurate assessment of your pain is likely to involve a thorough medical history, including a questionnaire, a review of medical records, and possibly consultations with previous physicians. A complete physical examination, including X rays or other appropriate medical tests, is part of most evaluations. During the physical examination, your doctor should ask many questions. The doctor should listen carefully to everything you are able to tell him or her about your pain in order to determine what kind of pain you experience, its location and frequency, and what makes it worse. A good evaluation includes the following:

1. *A health history*, including a pain chronology and questions about the pain's intensity and incapacitation.

2. *A physical examination,* including a general look at the body and examination of painful areas.

Taking a thorough health history, including a pain history, is particularly important in diagnosing chronic pain. Certain disorders, such as trigeminal neuralgia, classic migraine, and post-herpetic neuralgia, can be diagnosed simply from information in the health history. Questions about ongoing litigation or delayed compensation also should be raised during the taking of the health history, since either of these factors—or a history of unsuccessful treatments—can be a sign that emotional issues should be addressed as part of your treatment.

The health history should include a survey of drugs and medications you take regularly or frequently, including sleeping pills, aspirin, vitamins, laxatives, tranquilizers, oral contraceptives, and even coffee and alcohol. You'll be asked about allergies, particularly to drugs such as penicillin. Expect to answer questions about your general health, including history of major illness, surgery, injury, and hospitalization. You'll be asked about health problems of close relatives, about specific problems you have, and about your lifestyle, including your living situation, personal habits, and sex life. Answering these questions as frankly and honestly as you can helps a good doctor understand the precise dimensions of your pain.

Pain specialists may ask you to keep a *pain diary* for a period of time prior to a medical evaluation, perhaps two weeks. A pain diary is a detailed record of how much pain you experience, when you experience it, what medications you take and when, and what activity you were engaged in at the time you experienced pain. To be of good use, this record should be as complete as possible, perhaps updated at convenient times such as mealtimes. Keeping a pain diary frequently helps people find triggers or emotional links to the pain, including particular stresses that can intensify pain. Sometimes caregivers are asked to keep a pain diary for the family member in pain, and this, too, can be helpful in the assessment process.

During the physical examination, your doctor should look for obvious signs of anxiety or apathy, including tears. The doctor should observe your skin pallor, your nails, and your skin and hair for dryness or hair loss. The doctor also should test your vision, look at your pupils, test your hearing, and assess your bite, which is controlled by your trigeminal nerves.

The sensory part of the exam may be long, tedious, and somewhat uncomfortable. Your doctor may use a pin to test sensations at various points of your body. Examination of the painful area should include palpation of any affected area from several directions. A doctor may palpate or press the skin over the spine and nearby areas to try to find muscles that are in spasm, trigger points or tender points, and abnormal swelling or growth.

To understand its effects on your body, your doctor should check the effect of your pain on your range of muscle movement and other physical functions. A doctor may check your posture and stride, looking for poor postural habits that could affect or stress your muscles, or for structural defects such as scoliosis. Your mobility and muscle strength may be tested in various ways. For instance, the range of motion on flexible parts of the spine may be measured—your head should bend backward and forward freely, tilt to each side, and rotate up to 90 degrees in each direction. A doctor may check the strength of these movements, providing resistance against them with his or her hands. Strength and flexibility of muscle groups can be checked by various means, such as leg-raising tests that can help identify a disc disorder. After the examination, tests such as X rays, computerized tomography, or magnetic resonance imaging (MRI) scans may help verify the nature of a structural problem.

You should be checked for localized numbness or loss of reflexes, which can signal neurological abnormalities. A neurological examination should check deep tendon and superficial reflexes and motor symptoms to rule out the possibility of a nervous system lesion, or to locate it if one exists.

Jane Cowles, Ph.D., author of the book *Pain Relief,* suggests that the pain history accompany your medical records from doctor to doctor, or be an accessible part of your hospital chart. This document should include a list of all medications you take, how well they work, how much pain you have, where it is located and when it appears, how intense it is, and what you can do to control it and what makes it worse. Cowles says if your doctor has not taken a pain history, write one yourself and ask that it be included in your medical records.

YOUR ROLE IN THE PROCESS

If you have been shuffled around to several doctors, you may feel that no one is in control of your medical treatment. It may seem difficult to believe, but in theory you are the head of your own personal treatment team. As a practical matter, this is more true in the case of chronic pain than in acute pain, since by definition chronic pain cannot be eliminated by medical treatment.

With any doctor or treatment specialist, you are always the primary source of information. No objective test can accurately measure the intensity of your pain. You will always be the best judge of your pain's intensity and its changing nature, since you are the only person who really knows how much and where it hurts. You are the only one who can place your pain on a 1 to 10 scale at any point in time, or accurately describe its duration, intensity, and effects.

Although pain can't be measured with medical tests, the intensity and other qualities of the pain may be carefully

NUMERIC PAIN INTENSITY SCALE

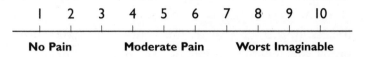

Patients are the best judges of how much pain they feel, which is why the Numeric Pain Intensity Scale is commonly used. The scale, shown above, usually about 4 inches or 10 centimeters long, is a subjective measure of pain. Medical professionals have the patient indicate, verbally or in writing, the point on the scale that corresponds to the intensity of the pain.

rated according to your reports. The doctor rates your pain by asking you questions and using standard diagnostic tools such as a 1 to 10 scale or a standard test form such as the McGill–Melzack pain questionnaire.

The 1 to 10 scale is a good subjective rating of pain intensity, which takes into account how the pain feels to you at that moment. It may be used to track changes in pain intensity over time. The McGill–Melzack questionnaire is a carefully designed series of questions that elicits specific, precise descriptions of your pain. The questionnaire contains twenty sets of adjectives that describe sensory, affective, evaluative, and other components of pain. It includes simple illustrations of the body on which the patient can draw the locations of particular pains. A short-form McGill questionnaire, which may be more suitable for some older patients, contains fifteen descriptors.

Your precise descriptions can help a doctor understand the particularities of your pain, since certain types of pain have certain characteristics. Nerve pain, for instance, is generally sharp, bright, and burning, and runs along a nerve pathway. Bone pain is often deep and very localized. Muscle pain is frequently diffused, aching, and poorly localized, and may be referred to other parts of the body. Among other data, this information helps a pain specialist establish a baseline against which the results of future treatments may be measured.

The medical system is structured so that one doctor has primary responsibility for your care. In a health maintenance organization (HMO), for instance, your primary care physician typically coordinates your visits to other medical specialists and shares relevant test results with other medical doctors. He likely will not try to tell other specialists how to treat you, but rather rely on their opinions. In the case of cancer pain, the medical oncologist who oversees cancer treatment often is in charge of pain management. For workers' compensation cases, such as those involving a back injury or chronic back pain, an orthopedist or neurosurgeon is often the hub of the treatment wheel. If you are seeing several physicians, find out which doctor is primarily responsible for your pain management.

As a consumer of medical services, the best attitude to take is that of a full partnership with your doctor. Doctors only recommend particular treatments to you; you must agree with their recommendations for treatment to proceed. As the American Academy of Pain Management points out in its Patient's Bill of Rights, you always have the *right* to know what may be done to you and why. If you don't receive a satisfactory explanation of a treatment your doctor is proposing, insist on an explanation in language you can understand. For any treatment to be truly useful to you, the benefits should outweigh the attendant risks.

DOCTOR-PATIENT COMMUNICATION

Good doctor-patient communication is an art involving both parties. As a patient, you have a responsibility to provide accurate information to the doctor, to be as honest and frank as you can, and to ask questions about issues that concern you. This can involve a change in attitude—learning how to communicate assertively, and to ask questions you want answered, rather than passively listening, and refusing to complain because you want to be considered a good patient.

If you have several questions for your doctor, it may help to write these down and mail or fax them to the doctor prior to your visit. Take a copy to the office with you. Go down the list and get your questions answered. Most doctors will let you tape-record their verbal instructions, which can help you remember exactly what they said. If you have a number of questions, ask the nurse for extra time with the doctor, but be careful not to waste their time with irrelevant questions. Sometimes it's useful to take your spouse or a friend into the doctor's office with you, to be your personal advocate. You may be able to get some of your questions answered over the phone by your doctor's nurse.

The usual paradigm, which works so beautifully for acute pain, doesn't work as well with chronic pain. Patients with chronic pain often are frustrating for doctors to deal with. Doctors want to cure people, and chronic pain can't be cured. Patients become discouraged because they are playing the role of "good patient" and aren't being rewarded.

COMMON MISCONCEPTIONS ABOUT PAIN

Misconceptions about the experience of pain are common, even in the medical profession. According to the textbook *Nursing Management of Patients in Pain,* by Margo McCaffery, here are eight common misconceptions:

1. *The health team are the experts on pain.*
   False—The patient knows more about the pain than any expert.

2. *A patient who uses his or her pain to get benefits doesn't really hurt, or may not hurt as much as he says.*
   False—Even manipulative patients may hurt as much as they say.

3. *Patients' pain can always be verified by behavioral or somatic expressions of pain.*
   False—Lack of pain expression doesn't mean lack of pain.

4. *"Real" pain has an identified physical cause.*
   False—Not all physical causes can be identified.

Looking at chronic pain as an interactive problem of which medical treatment is only one aspect is helpful. You also can help yourself.

You do have a right to leave medical treatment and pain treatment decisions to your doctor, if you wish. But you don't need a medical school degree to accept some responsibility for understanding which treatments and tests are recommended, and pursuing self-help methods which may be expected to help you. As the following story illustrates, medical treatment can be both part of the problem and part of the solution to learning to live with chronic pain.

5. *Psychogenic pain doesn't really hurt and is equivalent to malingering.*

   False—A localized sensation exists in psychogenic pain.

6. *Severity and duration can be predicted accurately on the basis of stimuli for pain.*

   False—No direct, unvarying relationship between any stimulation and pain perception exist.

7. *All patients can and should be encouraged to have a high pain tolerance.*

   False—Pain tolerance is unique, and varies from person to person.

8. *Health team members tend to make accurate inferences about the severity and existence of pain.*

   False—Studies show that they tend to underestimate pain.

NORM'S STORY

Three years ago, a man we shall call Norm was at the top of his profession. A hardworking, good-humored guy, Norm supervised the building of sets for movies, a job he had done for twenty years. Although he worked long hours, he had an enviable position in Hollywood, one that paid a handsome $100,000 a year. He knew his job was physically demanding and dangerous. Norm remembers seeing a co-worker fall 97 feet from a ladder to his death on a movie set, an image that still haunts his dreams.

As a hunter, fisherman, and former football player, Norm was quite physically fit. Because of the physical demands of his job, however, he had experienced acute back pain off and on for years. He returned home from work exhausted and sore many times. He frequently visited a chiropractor. Just before Christmas three years ago, in the middle of a long project, Norm recalls, "I woke up and heard someone screaming, and it was me."

He couldn't return to work. He went on private disability insurance provided by his union. He experienced sciatic pain that felt like exploding flashbulbs, or "someone running an ice pick down my back, which then went down either my left leg or right leg."

First, Norm went to an orthopedic surgeon who had an excellent reputation. This doctor recommended a series of four cortisone injections in his lower spine once a week for a month. This "knocked the edge off the pain," Norm says. A few weeks later, though, before he could return to work, he was mugged in his neighborhood, and his back went into spasm again.

Next, he went in for a microdiscectomy. Part of three bulging discs were shaved off in an attempt to relieve pressure against the nerve. His discs were found to be much worse than expected, and the doctor was not hopeful after the operation. The sciatic pain disappeared but was replaced by a radiating pain around his waist, which descended into his groin, a horror that "felt like I had an eight-ounce sinker attached to each testicle." At night, Norm was able to sleep only fifteen to twenty minutes at a time. The pain was worse at night. He had trouble sleeping. Walking was the only thing that gave him temporary relief.

"I remember going out for a walk and crying," he recalls. "There's nothing that will tear you down faster than that."

He tried fifteen sessions of physical therapy but felt it just made the pain worse, so he discontinued it. He tried TENS and acupuncture, but neither helped him much. The disability insurance company wouldn't pay for hypnosis or biofeedback treatments.

Norm's second back operation was a lumbar fusion, which involved the insertion of titanium rods on either side of his spine, attached by six screws held in place with bone grafts. "This was fairly successful. I got quite a lot of relief. It took six months from the date of the surgery to go into physical therapy, since the doctor didn't want me to disturb the bone grafts," he says. "The doctor told me to put my butt in a chair and stay there."

Physical therapy for this operation involved a special machine into which Norm was strapped for safe exercise. In the meantime, the private disability insurance ran out, so he went on workers' compensation. This meant longer waiting times to see a doctor, and a lower level of coverage and care.

Finally, Norm was able to go back to work for a month and a half. One day, though, while he was pushing something, he felt his Achilles tendon snap and immediately knew something was wrong.

He had another surgery to repair the tendon and spent several months on crutches with an altered gait. "I had physical therapy to rebuild my leg. I couldn't bend my toes without crying," he remembers. He went through intensive physical therapy, three times a week. Unfortunately, the exercise prescription given to him by his new doctor involved a step aerobics class. After forty-two minutes in one class, he suddenly experienced the return of horrible back pain and groin pain, which wouldn't go away.

His first doctor, the orthopedic surgeon, told him the surgeon was wrong to put him into a step aerobics class. But the doctor filed a report to workers' compensation categorizing him as "permanent and stationary," which is medical jargon for "as good as it's going to get." The previous back surgery had also made it impossible for Norm to have an MRI examination, since the implanted metal rods and screws would have made an accurate reading impossible.

Feeling more and more like a second-class workers' comp patient, Norm was referred to another doctor in the medical group, a woman who he felt was clearly in over her head with his case. This doctor took one look at Norm's X rays and said, "Everything looks Okay. Are you sure you're not imagining this?"

When he asked her for a refill of pain medication, "she accused me of being strung out on pain pills, even though I hadn't had any in four months." This particular doctor referred Norm back to his original doctor without giving him a prescription. She also wrote a letter to workers' comp, saying she believed Norm was addicted to pain medication and this letter went into his file.

"I've always taken the least amount of pain medication I possibly could," Norm explains, still baffled and hurt by this experience. "When I went in, I had been out of Vicodin for three days. At that point, I had to load myself up at night just to sleep for two hours. When I saw my original doctor, he said I didn't have a problem and wrote me a prescription for a hundred."

Fortunately, Norm and his wife had saved money when they were both working, but they were quickly running through it, which created financial stress. At one point, Norm was upset that workers' comp was refusing to pay for some of his medical treatments, and his lawyer wouldn't return his calls. Workers' comp enrolled him in vocational rehabilitation classes without notifying him in advance, which was ironic since he was unable either to sit or to lie down at that time. He was offered a $50,000 lifetime settlement by the workers' comp insurance company for all further medical expenses, which he refused.

Through these ordeals, Norm endured long bouts of depression and sometimes contemplated suicide. "When your lawyer doesn't return your phone calls, when your doctors won't give you any pain medication, you can go pretty far out there," he admits. "I remember walking down the street, crying, thinking I didn't want to do this anymore."

Frightened by his suicidal thoughts, Norm disassembled his guns and scattered their parts all over the house as a preventive measure when he was on antipsychotic drugs for a period of time. The depression intensified after he snapped his Achilles tendon and was unable to walk, which had been the only thing that relieved his pain.

"I certainly put my wife through the wringer," Norm says of his spouse, who is trained as a nurse. "She just kept poking me when I was down. She found a way to make me fight back some more."

He adds, "One thing I've learned is that if you're not your own advocate, nobody else will be either. If you're not a Type A person, they'll run right over you." Taking action to help himself was important for many reasons, Norm observes.

A few months before being interviewed for this book, Norm was referred to a pain specialist by a sympathetic and knowledgeable family doctor. After examining him, the pain specialist looked into the possibility of implanting a dorsal column stimulator, a device that releases mild electric shocks to disarm affected nerves. Tests were done with injections to locate the nerves and trigger areas. A temporary stimulator was tried out for several weeks to rule out any possibility of a placebo effect. Then a permanent stimulator was implanted, which has helped Norm control his pain.

"I run it for about an hour a night," says Norm, who can adjust the unit through a control box. "After using it, I can sleep for a couple of hours. As far as I'm concerned, I'm sold. If I'd done it three years ago, I could have skipped two of the four back operations. I'm going to give it another two months to see what it can do for me. Then I may go into vocational rehabilitation.

"I am on the road to recovery," he says, a bit of his optimism returning. "If this is as good as it gets, then I'll take it, because I'm better off now than I have been for a long time."

THE TREATMENT OF PAIN

It is generally agreed that the treatment of pain should begin by using the least invasive or more conservative types of therapy first. The most conservative options are not medical treatment, and they often take place at home or outside a doctor's office or hospital. These options always should be given a fair trial before considering others. Conservative treatment modalities are frequently part of the long-term solution to living with chronic pain.

If the mildest treatments provide satisfactory results, it's really not necessary to up the ante. Sometimes more drastic treatments do provide better results, or faster results, but they also can complicate the problem. The three major types of pain treatments you may receive are listed below, beginning with the mildest options:

- *Noninvasive treatments,* using physical or psychosocial treatment methods. These methods help control pain for many people with chronic pain. They include gentle treatments that do not harm the body, such as stress-reducing techniques, cognitive and social behavioral techniques, counseling, and most forms of physical therapy, including those that may be applied at home.

- *Pharmacological treatments,* using analgesic drugs that mitigate pain and other medications such as antidepressants. These are quite useful in providing short-term relief and also for cancer pain, but they are frequently overused in the treatment of chronic benign pain.

- *Other treatment modalities* such as minor or major surgery, palliative or ablative surgery, and radiation therapy. For the most part, major surgery to relieve pain is reserved for the most serious and intractable cases, such as those associated with terminal cancer. A few new surgical procedures, however, are quite effective for a few types of chronic pain.

Multidisciplinary Treatment

Some types of chronic pain may be handled quite successfully by the family doctor and good patient self- management. Many people can successfully control chronic pain for years using methods that work for them. A number of medical doctors specialize in pain treatment or in the treatment of particular types of pain, and these specialists do refer people to physical therapists, psychologists, and other specialists whose work they know.

If your pain has become difficult to control or causes you great discomfort, you may be treated at one of the many excellent multidisciplinary pain treatment centers in the United States. These centers often are associated with medical schools, teaching hospitals, or medical research institutions. Because chronic pain involves both body and mind, pain treatment centers and clinics have many types of specialists on staff, including doctors and psychologists. Even if you do not receive treatment at a comprehensive pain treatment center, understanding this approach to the treatment of chronic pain may help you manage your own pain, since any coping skills and techniques learned in a pain program ultimately must be continued at home.

Pain treatment clinics utilize specialists from several disciplines, including psychology, nutrition, physical therapy, and occupational therapy, in addition to medical doctors and nurses. Staff are trained in stress management, medication reduction, relaxation techniques, biofeedback, communications techniques, and physical and vocational therapy. Most programs include a chaplain or pastoral counselor who can be helpful in addressing the important spiritual dimension of pain.

The prototype for the modern pain clinic is the University of Washington's Multidisciplinary Pain Center in Seattle, which was founded about thirty years ago. Since then, more than a thousand pain treatment facilities have been established in the United States. The general thrust of the pain clinic movement has been to look at chronic pain as a syndrome that can be treated. Pain centers work on several fronts to help you understand and manage your pain and return to normal functioning as much as possible.

Comprehensive Treatment

According to *The Fight Against Pain* by Charles B. Stacy, M.D., and co-authors, the programs at most comprehensive pain clinics include the following:

- A full and accurate diagnosis identifying the source of pain and contributing factors

- A thorough personal evaluation examining the psychosocial factors of the pain, its impact on the patient's life, and patient expectations
- A systematic treatment plan, setting goals and specifying the types of treatment for the problem
- Comprehensive treatment involving several modalities, and including the participation of the patient and the family
- Restoration of as much normal function as possible
- An ongoing evaluation during and after treatment

Both diagnosis and evaluation are important, since not all people with pain benefit from comprehensive pain center treatment. Along with a complete medical examination, a standard psychological test such as the Minnesota Multiphasic Personality Inventory (MMPI) may be given prior to entering a program. Another standard test is the West Haven–Yale Multidimensional Pain Inventory (MPI), which surveys beliefs about pain and coping ability. Test results can be useful in distinguishing functional pain (whose cause can't be pinpointed) from organic pain. Tests can help predict the outcome of surgery or inpatient treatment programs for a particular patient. In addition, at a treatment center you may be interviewed by mental health professionals to gauge your attitude toward the pain itself, your feelings about treatment, and your future expectations.

Most insurance plans require that a referral to a pain clinic come from your primary care physician. Programs can be inpatient or outpatient and can last anywhere from a few weeks to six months. Inpatient treatment can cost $20,000 or more. A typical stay is about three weeks, during which you work with various experts, in groups and on an individual basis, on particular aspects of pain relief. Typically, family members and friends are urged to become involved, since part of the treatment includes the family's learning to encourage and practice healthy independent behavior, and to short-circuit unhealthy behaviors that lead to dependence and a feeling of invalidism. Physical conditioning and new

MEDICAL TREATMENT RIGHTS

According to the American Academy of Pain Management, patients who suffer chronic pain have a number of basic rights during medical treatment. The academy states that people who suffer chronic pain have the right to have all treatments "conducted with an overriding concern for the patient, and above all, the recognition of their dignity as a human being." Basic medical treatment rights, as enumerated in the Patient's Bill of Rights, include:

1. The right to considerate and respectful care.

2. The right to obtain from their certified provider, complete, current information concerning their diagnosis, treatment, and prognosis in terms the patient can reasonably be expected to understand. When it is not advisable to give such information to the patient, the information should be made available to an appropriate person in their behalf.

3. The right to receive from their certified provider, information to make informed consent prior to the start of any procedure and/or treatment. This shall include such information as medically significant risks

patterns of thinking about pain can help you control its worst effects.

With your input, goals are set at the beginning of a program. These can include an agreement to reduce your use of narcotic medications, and to learn and practice methods to reduce your pain levels. In your goals, you may wish to return to a higher level of occupational functioning by

---

involved with any procedure and probable duration of incapacitation. Where medically appropriate, alternatives for care or treatment should be explained to the patient.

4. The right to refuse any and all treatment, to the extent permitted by law, and to be informed of any of the medical consequences of their action.

5. The right to every consideration of privacy concerning their own medical care program, limited only to state statutes, rules, regulations, or imminent danger to the individual or others.

6. The right to be advised if the clinician, hospital, clinic, etc., proposes to engage in or performs human experimentation affecting their care or treatment. The patient has the right to refuse to participate in such research projects.

7. The privilege to examine and receive an explanation of the bill.

---

reducing your level of disability, or you may wish to achieve a greater level of strength, mobility, and overall physical fitness, including weight loss if necessary. Goals can include learning self-help techniques to help you reduce or cope with your pain.

You need to "buy into" the goals you help set for yourself. In some cases, you actually sign a contract agreeing to follow the program. Once goals are set, your participation is necessary for the program to succeed. After all, only you can

FINANCIAL ASPECTS

Financial problems commonly accompany chronic pain, since medical treatment is quite expensive and extends over a long period of time. Unemployment, pending lawsuits, billing mistakes, bureaucratic delays, and many other factors create financial stress.

Public disability insurance includes two systems administered by the federal Social Security Administration: two programs run by the Department of Veterans Affairs for military veterans, and workers' compensation insurance programs run by individual states. Medicare, the federal government's program for senior citizens, and private health and disability insurance companies also fund some treatments for chronic pain.

All health insurance programs have limits on the services they provide. In addition to the paperwork, wasted time, and grief involved in dealing with an insurance bureaucracy, many types of insurance limit the doctors you can see, the price they will pay for medical treatment, or the types of treatments or number of treatments you may take the medication (or not take the medication) as directed, perform therapeutic exercises regularly, utilize self–help relaxation techniques, learn coping strategies and skills, and adjust your own patterns of thinking to help you mitigate pain. These are all significant achievements. Some clinics issue diplomas on completion of a program, when a summary review takes place.

Many people emerge from pain treatment programs better able to cope with pain. Even people who do not meet all

---

receive. Even if you have good insurance, you may have to pay out of your own pocket for certain expenses.

Many older people utilize Medicare, which imposes restrictions on the care of chronic pain, including limits on payments to doctors. If you ask, many doctors will treat you in exchange for the Medicare assignment, which is the amount of money paid for a particular treatment by Medicare (usually about 40 percent of the going rate). State medical insurance programs such as Medicaid pay a great deal less, and many doctors will not accept a Medicaid assignment as their entire payment.

Workers' compensation pays doctors in the form of liens. This means that bills your doctor sends to the workers' comp insurance carrier are paid at the settlement of the case; this may be many months after you receive medical treatment. Private physicians usually accept liens, but many doctors feel they cannot accept too many because payment is deferred. Most hospitals do not accept liens.

the goals they set succeed in reducing the level of their disability, a genuine achievement. People often are able to return to work or productive activity, to better enjoy their family life or social life, and to better cope with their pain. If the treatment goals are not or are only partially met, it could be because the underlying disorder can't be completely alleviated, or because entrenched habits or behaviors are resistant to change.

"Pain programs can be very effective in eliminating the fear and helping people deal with pain," says a knowledgeable California man with osteoporosis who has been through two programs. "My chief complaint about them is that some of them tend to claim to be able to do too much. But I think they're good when their treatment is taken within the overall medical context, because there are a lot of common elements—no matter what the medical diagnosis—in dealing with chronic pain."

In general, comprehensive pain clinics have a better track record for treating chronic pain than do single forms of therapy, especially when pain has been present for a long period of time. They allow not only for different modalities of treatment, but also for an analysis of what works and to what extent, data that can be lost if specialists in different locations are consulted.

On the positive side, being treated as an inpatient at a comprehensive pain center gets you out of the home environment, automatically reducing the behaviors, distractions, and obligations present therein. Most pain centers allow you to be withdrawn from excess medications in a slow, orderly fashion, under a doctor's supervision if any problems are encountered. Multidisciplinary pain centers allow for structured, focused learning of pain control techniques and physical conditioning in an environment where questions can be answered and particular problems isolated and addressed. At pain centers, group dynamics allow for mutual emotional support and feedback between participants.

The primary drawback, however, is cost, which is not always covered by insurance. Other disadvantages include the environmental differences between the clinic and the actual living situation at home, where coping skills must be employed. Another disadvantage is that treatment centers can be hospital-like settings, with doctors and nurses present, and thereby can become an environment associated with illness rather than wellness. Parents may be unable to leave small children unattended, or to leave work undone. And no matter how many coping skills are learned in the controlled environment of a pain center, it is up to the patient to follow through and utilize those techniques at home.

The Chronic Pain Syndrome

According to the University of Washington, Seattle, here are some common problems encountered by people with chronic pain, which are characteristic of the chronic pain syndrome:

- Medications taken excessively or inappropriately
- Inappropriate patterns of accessing the medical system
- Physical inactivity and weakness
- Depression and other emotional problems
- Lack of coping skills to deal with pain and disability
- Family, work, and community problems associated with pain

All these factors can make the chronic pain experience worse, even uncontrollable, since they interact with each other in a highly negative way. They all can contribute to excessive pain and disability, but can be simultaneously addressed in treatment.

In treatment, the amount of medication you take often can be reduced or eliminated. This clears your mind considerably. You may be educated to understand the difference between the treatment of acute pain and chronic pain, and to learn what may be realistically expected of medical treatment. Because many people with chronic pain have gone through long bouts of physical inactivity, which often makes pain worse, physical stamina and fitness may gradually be increased to great benefit. Mood states such as depression and anxiety affect how much pain you feel; negative emotions often can be controlled or significantly reduced. Coping

PSYCHOLOGICAL TESTING

According to psychologist Richard Sternbach, four aims of psychological evaluations and training, as part of a comprehensive pain treatment strategy, are:

1. To determine how much of your pain and disability is due to mental factors, such as depression, financial difficulties, and family problems.

2. To sort out the factors in your personal environment that might be contributing to your pain and disability.

3. To determine whether you think about your pain in a way that makes the sensation and meaning of your pain worse.

4. To work with you and your loved ones to lessen pain and disability so that you may resume functioning.

strategies and skills can be learned by changing negative thought patterns, or by changing behavior that makes pain worse to behavior that reduces feelings of disability and pain. People may improve their communication skills to great benefit, learning how to be assertive in their interactions with others. Healthy communication skills can impact your family, work, and community life, as can healthy coping behaviors.

Taken together, physical improvements and healthy psychological coping skills may help you reduce your pain to a much more manageable level. Making even a little progress in any or all of these areas, and holding on to that progress, may well help bring you back from the edge of despair, and into the swirling stream of life.

Achieving Success in Treatment

Success in dealing with chronic pain does not involve completely eliminating it. Pain treatment centers aim to reduce pain and disability to more manageable levels, and to give you the tools to manage the remaining pain on your own. Many pain centers have respectable rates of success.

The University of Washington's pain center tracks patients prior to treatment, on completion of treatment, and twelve months after treatment. Patients have shown marked decreases in disability and depression compared to the baseline established when they entered the program. Those levels generally have been maintained after participating in the program. After treatment the intensity of pain experienced by the average patient drops about 1 point on a 10-point scale, a drop which is statistically significant but not profound, according to the program's head statistician, Mark Jensen, Ph.D. Patients who have completed the program generally report that the pain they experience bothers them much less than before, he reports.

At the Shealy Institute in Springfield, Missouri, neurosurgeon C. Norman Shealy, M.D., runs a twelve-day multidisciplinary outpatient program combining acupuncture, biofeedback, autogenic training (four hours a day), massage, ice, external electrical stimulation, exercise, diet therapy, behavioral therapy, and counseling. The goals of his program, as enumerated in his book, *The Pain Game,* are:

1. Getting the patient off drugs so that he can think straight.

2. Increasing the patient's physical activity to as near normal as possible.

3. Improving the patient's mood so that he feels happy and reasonably well-adjusted; then and only then

4. Getting him to return to work.

Dr. Shealy estimates that 80 percent of his chronic pain patients are capable of being rehabilitated in the first three categories. He goes on to say that a maximum of 30 percent of those who have been disabled two years or more actually could expect to return to work.

Long-term studies of patients who go through such programs are rare. One of these, published in 1998 in the magazine *Pain,* is a study of two-hundred and forty-nine patients done thirteen years after completion of a three-week program at the Mayo Clinic's Pain Management Center, in Rochester, Minnesota. The program's graduates described themselves as having better than normal mental health, but poorer than normal physical health. The study found that the former patients' mortality was about the same as that of the general population. About 47 percent were gainfully employed, but about a quarter reported that they had retired early. Body pain remained an issue.

The ultimate goal of multidisciplinary treatment programs is to interrupt the pain cycle that is creating unnecessary disability. Success can include removing the physical limitations on returning to a functioning life, including a return to work if that is possible, since the vast majority of patients seen at pain clinics are below retirement age. In the United States, one study of clinics found that only 7 to 10 percent of patients were over the age of sixty-five. In Canada, according to another study, 20 percent of patients were over the age of sixty-five. Physical therapy, exercise, and attitudinal changes often are fundamental in this process of creating change.

Medical Treatment

Medical treatment has an important place in the treatment of chronic pain, but it is not the entire solution. Trying to find a medical answer to a problem with no real medical solution is an exercise in frustration, as many doctors and patients will attest.

Second or even third opinions may be useful, particularly in the beginning if a medical diagnosis is indefinite, or if a radical treatment such as surgery has been recommended before conservative measures are given a fair chance to work. Doctors frequently refer patients whose problems they don't completely understand to specialists in particular areas, but sometimes these visits merely eliminate possibilities rather than finding a definitive solution or cure. The specialists may not be able to identify the source of the pain problem either, or may not be able to cure it.

Our results-oriented society puts great pressure on medical doctors to "do something," and to do it fast. There is a phenomenon called patient pressure, which are repeated demands by a chronic pain patient that the doctor give them something that will stop the pain. Many doctors try to comply. The quickest and easiest thing a doctor can do is to write a prescription, and patients often don't feel they've gotten their money's worth unless they receive one. As patients make the rounds of doctors, though, and as more and more doctors write more and more prescriptions, the overuse and ineffective use of drugs over long periods of time often becomes part of the problem rather than the solution. Even major surgeries sometimes make things worse. Our culture places great faith in technology and science, but medical doctors don't yet have a miraculous solution for every medical problem. This uncomfortable fact should be accepted.

Some people become frustrated trying to find a doctor who can make all their pain go away. Occasionally, these lengthy searches can lead to a very knowledgeable doctor or specialist, one willing to take the time to listen and examine you carefully, who intuitively arrives at a solution that can help you in the long run. In other cases, you may receive treatment that is only temporarily effective or even harmful. Pursuing a medical solution can become an end in itself, a dead-end obsessive behavior characteristic of the chronic pain syndrome, which can prevent you from accepting and dealing with your pain and moving on with your life.

There is more and more reason for hope. Billions of dollars are spent each year on medical research, and miraculous new medical discoveries continue to be made. Not giving up

UNPROVEN TREATMENTS

Arthritis is one example of chronic pain where unproven treatments are often sought—some $10 billion per year is spent on them, according to the Arthritis Foundation. Although many folk remedies and unproven treatments are harmless, a U.S. Department of Health and Human Services survey estimates that one in every ten people who try an unproven treatment experience harmful side effects. Even harmless treatments may be harmful if they cause good medical treatment programs to be abandoned.

Some potentially harmful unproven treatments:

- Dimethyl sulfoxide, or DMSO
- Large doses of vitamins
- Drugs with "hidden" ingredients such as steroids
- Snake venom

Some harmless unproven treatments:

- Copper bracelets
- Mineral springs
- Vinegar and honey
- Vibrators

---

can be seen both as a pain behavior and as an expression of hope and faith. If your pain has been diagnosed as a common problem such as osteoarthritis or tension headache, you probably would be best served by simply following your doctor's orders, working to reduce the pain as much as possible, and continuing to live your life as best you can. A healthy lifestyle, utilizing conservative self-management techniques, can make most pain manageable. On the other hand, looking for a miracle cure when none exists will most likely lower your spirits, deplete your finances, and irritate and frustrate you.

A note of caution: A few quacks work in the field of pain medicine, preying on unsuspecting patients by offering bogus cures or "quick fix" treatments for desperate people. If you have any doubt about the professional credentials held by your physician, consult reference books such as the *American Medical Dictionary* or the *Directory of Medical Specialists*. In addition, professional groups such as the American Board of Medical Specialties can be contacted through toll-free numbers and web sites such as those listed in the appendix at the back of this book.

Because chronic pain is different from acute pain, treatment cannot focus on the body alone. Many factors interact in the chronic pain syndrome. The treatment of chronic pain requires a good medical assessment and an understanding of the psychological, emotional, and social factors that often contribute to chronic pain. You may seek treatment at a multidisciplinary pain treatment center, from a pain specialist, or from your own medical doctor. Pain treatment involves specialists from many disciplines such as psychology, physical therapy, and stress relief who can teach you coping techniques. Ultimately, the best answer may be self-management. As chapter 3 explains, pain is first a physical experience, one registered in the nerves, but involving many parts of the body that can cause chronic pain.

CHAPTER THREE

Physical Pain

ᴄᴠ *How pain originates, and specific diagnoses of the causes of chronic pain.*

The experience of pain itself seems simple, but it is exquisitely complex. A painful stimulus experienced may be changed as it runs up the nervous system and is finally registered in parts of the brain. Your entire nervous system is affected by many natural pain-reducing substances produced in the body, as well as by natural substances that can intensify pain. Significantly, the "gate control" theory provides new insights into the mechanics of chronic non-malignant pain. This chapter looks at some of the biological influences that affect the onset, duration, and intensity of pain, including where pain originates in the human body.

This chapter is divided into two parts:

1. An explanation of the nervous system, which senses, transmits, transforms, and registers pain

2. A survey of the most common physical causes of chronic pain, such as back pain, headaches, and arthritis

THE NERVOUS SYSTEM

Although it seems instantaneous to us, the physical perception of pain comes at the end of a crackling process of sensation. This process begins when a stimulus electrifies the sensitive nerve endings of a neuron, or nerve cell. Impulses or sensations surge from one end of the nerve cell to the other, then up natural pathways of neurons and nerves. Impulses jump up the spinal cord to the brain, where the incoming message is perceived as pain.

Nervous impulses travel through each nerve cell as electrical energy, then leap over the tiny gaps between nerve endings with the aid of important chemical compounds called *neurotransmitters.* This makes pain an amazingly quick and complex electrochemical process.

The human nervous system is more complex than any electrical or telephone system within a large city such as New York or Chicago. The human body contains millions of tiny pain-sensing, or *sensory,* nerve cells scattered throughout the skin, muscles, and most other parts of the body. The skin of an adult male, for instance, contains approximately five million sensory nerve cells, which are most abundant in sensitive areas such as the fingertips. These pain-sensing cells constantly pick up and relay information to the brain via busy pain *pathways,* rivers of nerve fibers that teem with traveling electrochemical nervous impulses.

More than a half million sensory fibers from the skin enter the spinal cord at the *dorsal horn,* located in a lower portion of the spine. The dorsal horn is one point at which pain impulses are believed to be modulated, a sort of natural "gate" that can decrease or regulate incoming pain impulses.

THE NERVOUS SYSTEM

The **somatic nervous system** comes from the Greek word *soma*, which means "body," and its nerves carry messages to and from the body and the brain. *Afferent* nerves carry sensations from the skin, muscles, and other parts of the body to the brain. *Efferent* nerves carry messages from the brain back to muscles and glands to initiate a response.

The somatic nervous system is divided into two parts: the *central nervous system*, which includes the brain and spinal cord; and the *peripheral nervous system*, which links the central nervous system with the rest of the body, carrying impulses and pain sensations back and forth.

The **autonomic, or "self-ruling," nervous system** is a part of the peripheral nervous system and controls bodily functions of which you are not normally conscious. It's believed to be a one-way street, relaying messages only from the brain to the body, rather than back and forth. The autonomic nervous system works automatically, controlling things you don't consciously think about such as blood pressure, heart rate, and perspiration.

The autonomic system includes the *sympathetic* nervous system, which is mostly below the neck and controls such functions as breathing, sweating, and blood pressure. The *parasympathetic* nervous system is mostly above the neck and controls similar functions such as dilation of the pupils in response to light.

Sensory nerve fibers run up both sides of the spinal cord to the brain, which together are known as the *central nervous system.*

The central nervous system registers and reacts to pain that usually begins in other parts of the body served by the *peripheral nervous system.* The brain and the spine are composed of neurons, or nerve cells. Neurons are most compact in the brain, less compact in the spinal cord, and most extended in the parts of the body farthest away from the brain such as the hands and feet, where outstretched nerve endings gather sensory information. The nervous system thus may be seen as an extension of the brain, or the brain with its approximately 100 billion cells as the most highly developed part of the nervous system. Sensations such as pain may be seen as a primitive form of thought.

The brain must filter the messages it receives. It must process a constant tide of sensory impulses, the equivalent of background noise. The constant and intense stimulation of continuous modern life has a predictable effect on the nervous system whose task is partially to sort out important information from trivial information. In civilized societies, many people have nervous systems that are often in a state of overstimulation, which can intensify stress and pain. For this reason, turning down the volume of stimulation by practicing relaxation exercises and other stress-reducing techniques often helps take the edge off pain.

Pain-Modulating Substances

Certain substances produced in the body modulate the experience of pain, mitigating or intensifying it. Many of these chemicals have been discovered only in the past few decades, and some of this knowledge has been incorporated into pain treatment.

Every person's built-in, or *endogenous,* pain controls involve certain neurotransmitters released by the nerves as they transmit messages, or substances produced elsewhere in the body, such as the adrenal glands or the brain. The presence of these neurotransmitters can suppress or stimulate the firing of other neurons, thereby either increasing or decreasing the sensation of pain.

The *endorphins, enkephalins,* and *dynorphins* are neurotransmitters believed to chemically "close the gates" of pain sensation at points along the spinal column or the brain. Narcotic drugs mimic the action of these natural pain relievers on the body, but since the opiate drugs were discovered first, these substances are called *endogenous opioids.* Quantities of endogenous opioids can be increased by aerobic exercise, stress reduction, certain medical treatments such as transcutaneous electrical nerve stimulation (TENS) and acupuncture, and even suggestion and laughter. The endorphins and other natural pain relievers affect emotions and changes in mood by chemically binding themselves to receptors of pain-sensing neurons, making them less sensitive. For this reason, endogenous opioids have an important effect on anxiety and depression.

Other important substances, produced by nerve cells in the brain, send messages back down the spinal pathway to stimulate the release of endogenous opioids. One of the most important of these is believed to be *serotonin,* a chemical that can mitigate pain without completely blocking pain signals. Low levels of serotonin produce insomnia and depression, and decrease pain tolerance by decreasing blood flow to the site of pain. The substance is believed to be broken down in the body during a migraine headache attack and excreted. Serotonin levels often are altered in patients with fibromyalgia and depression. Chronic pain sufferers generally have lower levels of endorphins and serotonin in their spinal fluid than normal, according to the medical textbook *Pain Medicine* by P. Prithui Raj, M.D.

Other chemical substances produced within the body are irritants to nerve cells and thus can intensify the sensation of pain. These include *lactic acid, bradykinin, serotonin, potassium ions,* and the recently discovered *Substance P.* Substance P is a pain-producing chemical often concentrated in the fingers and toes that acts as a transmitter in sensory nerve fibers that have a role in mediating inflammation. As a result of negative stress, the release of neurotransmitters such as *noradrenaline* or *norepinephrine* from the adrenal glands and sympathetic nerves intensifies the sensation of pain by making other neurons more receptive to pain impulses.

Stemming the Tide of Impulses

The process by which a painful sensation is detected by distant nerve endings and transmitted up the nervous system to the brain is called *nociception.* Nociceptors, or transmitting nerves, relay painful sensations from muscles, joints, or other parts of the body. Nociceptors transmit sensations of pain produced by chemical irritants, inflammation, reduced oxygen to the tissues, or other trauma. The transmitting nerves are resilient; unfortunately, they don't become less responsive even when pain transmission is sustained.

In treating acute pain, the assumption is that pain impulses begin in the peripheral nervous system and are accurately transmitted to the brain. This isn't the case with chronic pain. Researchers believe that chronic pain sets up pathways or "loops" between the spinal cord and the brain, where the pain resonates or reverberates back and forth, more or less feeding on itself, as in phantom limb pain. It is also known that the *afferent* nerve fibers that transmit pain signals can discharge without stimulation—in other words, under certain conditions nerve cells can "cross talk," with spontaneous discharges between adjacent neurons even when no actual painful stimulus is received.

Nerve cells and the nerves themselves can be damaged, producing pain. In addition, nerve cells can completely or partially regenerate. Damage to any part of the peripheral nervous system can be followed by the so-called sprouting from a damaged nerve. As this nerve cell sprouts new nerve endings, it can become quite sensitive and produce pain.

Huge numbers of stimuli interact in the nervous system. These impulses move through a system of gates or controls, which can affect the progress of any stimulus and even determine whether it is received by the brain or not. Gates and controls can either block pain transmission or intensify the signal of pain.

Gate Control Theory

The gate control theory of pain, proposed by Ronald Melzack and Patrick Wall in 1965, was an enormous breakthrough in the way scientists conceptualize pain. At one time, many doctors thought of the nervous system more or less as a series of wires that merely carried impulses to and from the brain. Melzack and Wall proposed a more complicated neurological model. They postulated a series of built-in "gates" or "controls" within the nervous system that can either increase or inhibit the sensation of pain. Their theory suggests

THE DIMENSIONS OF PAIN

Pain is more than a simple impulse sent from the site of pain to the brain. The experience of pain may be subdivided into what the gate control theory calls three *dimensions*: the sensory-discriminative, the motivational-affective, and the cognitive-evaluative. These involve the peripheral nervous system as well as many parts of the brain. These three dimensions are important because the brain may send signals back down the nervous system that can either intensify or dampen the perception of pain.

Sensory elements include the sense of pain's physical location, its intensity, its quality, and its duration.

Discriminative elements refer to the brain's ability to sort out or discriminate between the sensory elements and register what kind of pain it is.

Motivational elements refer to tendencies toward action that our emotions stimulate us to take in response to pain, including isolating ourselves, taking positive action, and so forth.

Affective elements are emotions accompanying the actual pain, such as anger, depression, fear, guilt, despair, and irritability.

Cognitive elements are rational or mental aspects that include attitudes toward yourself, thoughts that accompany your emotions, expectations about your ability to cope with pain, your mental awareness of pain, your focus of attention, your memories, and your perception of life events.

Evaluative elements are how you look at or evaluate the experience of pain.

that synapses along the nerve pathways inhibit or balance the flow of powerful streams of nerve impulses, like small dams along a creek that can be lowered or raised as needed. These "gates" are believed to exist so that the brain is not overwhelmed by billions of messages constantly flowing up the nerve pathways toward the brain from all parts of the body.

According to Melzack and Wall, the sensation of pain includes several different dimensions. These include the sensory-discriminative dimension, the motivational-affective dimension, and the cognitive-evaluative dimension that originate in or are greatly influenced by the mind. Therefore, pain is not just a clear sensation transmitted as is from the site of an injury by the *afferent* nerves to the brain; it may be modulated along the way in the spinal cord or even in parts of the brain. *Efferent* brain fibers carrying messages from the brain to the body are even believed to be involved in the perception of pain. "It is possible for brain activities subserving attention, emotion, and memories of prior experience to exert control over the sensory input," Melzack and Wall wrote in 1982.

Pain produces different types of psychological content and meaning in the brain. One is *discriminatory* content; this includes a mental sense of where the pain originates and what it feels like—stabbing, aching, throbbing, and so forth. Another is *motivational* content, which includes the sense of how unpleasant a particular pain is, creating a motivation to escape from it or to end it. Another is *cognitive* content; this intellectually compares information already embedded in the memory, producing an evaluation of the current pain by the mind. All these combine in the sensation we recognize as pain.

The gate control theory helps explain how some types of treatment that are not strictly medical may affect the intensity of pain by stimulating the body's natural self-regulatory mechanisms.

From a physical point of view, this theory holds that different types of nerve fibers, including so-called C fibers and A fibers, act in concert to convey or inhibit the transmission of pain impulses up the spinal cord to the human brain.

The A fibers are always working, sending continuous sensual messages to the spinal cord, then up to the brain, basically holding open the "gate" through the dorsal horn of the spinal cord. Certain A fibers, called *A-delta fibers,* carry impulses most rapidly. Messages sent and received along A-delta fibers allow your body to react quickly to a stimulus, such as a stubbed toe. Messages moving up A-delta fibers are associated with acute pain, including many forms of cancer pain. When stimulated, A-delta fibers send sharp, acute pain warnings at approximately forty miles per hour. Meanwhile, *A-beta* fibers fire off painless touch and pressure sensations at speeds of up to two-hundred miles per hour.

Much of the time, large-diameter *C fibers* are not active. When a tactile, thermal, or chemical stimulus is applied, however, the C fibers become active. They slowly fire electrochemical messages up the nervous system at a speed of less than three miles per hour, producing the sensation of pain. The job of the C fibers is to warn you that your body may have suffered some harm; this signal is valuable after an insult or injury has occurred because the lingering pain sensations tell the body to "take it easy." For instance, messages from C fibers would naturally cause you to limp until the fracture or damage to an injured ankle has healed. The C fibers frequently are the carriers of the type of slow, burning, aching pain signals associated with chronic nonmalignant pain.

TYPES OF PAIN

Three major types of pain arise from tissue damage and are carried by either the smaller A-delta fibers or the larger and slower C fibers:

1. *Prickling pain,* coming up the A-delta fibers, usually results when you break or irritate the skin.

2. *Burning pain,* which is associated with slower C fibers, is also associated with impulses received via the skin.

3. *Aching pain,* also coming up the C fibers, usually comes from deeper inside the body.

Different nerve fibers can counteract the positive and negative effects of each other. For example, if you hit your elbow against a hard object, your body produces howling acute pain signals carried to your brain by the A-delta fibers. You might instinctively rub your elbow, however, sending a flood of contradictory unpainful impulses up the A-beta fibers and blocking the pain signals when the flood of nerve impulses meet at the gate. This process is called *counterirritation,* the way certain forms of temporary pain control such as massage and TENS are believed to help control pain.

In addition, a great number of cognitive and emotional factors can affect the opening and closing of chronic pain "gates." These mental factors, addressed in various ways in treatment, often can reduce the experience of pain.

You can do many things to diminish the sensation of pain or make it more manageable. According to Richard Hanson and Kenneth Gerber in their book, *Coping with Chronic Pain*, individuals can take steps to help themselves in physical, emotional, and mental ways as well as lifestyle actions.

I. Physical self-management
- Application of heat or cold
- Massage
- TENS
- Exercise, including stretching or range-of-motion exercises

II. Emotional self-management
- Keeping emotionally stable by avoiding excessive or inappropriate anger, depression, fear, or anxiety
- Managing tension you feel through rest breaks and time-out relaxation exercises
- Experiencing positive emotions such as laughter, love, joy, compassion, optimism

CAUSES OF PAIN

What follows is an explanation of some of the physical conditions that can result in chronic pain, including muscle pain, back and neck pain, headache, arthritis, and other disorders.

It should be noted that most people with chronic pain become physically unfit. As a result, chronic pain ultimately involves the muscles, joints, and entire body regardless of the actual source of the pain. Fortunately, working to increase physical fitness can be helpful in combating chronic pain, as explained in chapter 5.

III. Mental self-management
- Distracting your attention away from the pain to other thoughts or other physical activities
- Increasing your involvement in life activities and your interest in them, including social activities
- Having positive attitudes toward yourself, others, and the future

IV. Actions
- Maintaining an appropriate level of physical activity
- Striking a good balance between work, recreational, and social activity
- Maintaining good physical health through appropriate and regular exercise, good eating, and avoiding unhealthy lifestyle habits such as smoking and drinking

MAJOR CATEGORIES OF PAIN DISORDERS

The six major categories of pain disorders discussed in this chapter include:

1. Back pain, neck pain, and other spinal pain
2. Joint disorders, including temporomandibular disorders
3. Headache
4. Muscle pain
5. Visceral pain
6. Neuropathy and neuralgia

PAINS NOT WELL TREATED

In their medical textbook, *Textbook of Pain*, Ronald Melzack and Patrick Wall list three classes of chronic pain that are not well treated at the moment:

- *Pains whose cause is apparent but where medical treatment is inadequate,* such as deep-tissue disorders, osteoarthritis, rheumatoid arthritis, post-traumatic pains, inadequate blood supply (angina, claudication, Raynaud's disease), peripheral nerve disorders, cancer infiltration, amputation, neuropathies (diabetes, alcohol, viral), root and cord disorders, postherpetic neuralgia, spinal injuries

- *Pains whose cause is unknown but where treatment is adequate,* such as trigeminal neuralgias, tension headaches

- *Pains where cause is unknown and treatment is inadequate,* such as back pain, fibromyalgia, idiopathic cystitis, idiopathic pelvic and abdominal pain, migraine

Back and Neck Pain

Spinal pain, including back pain and neck pain, is a leading cause of long-term disability. One well-known medical doctor estimates that 10 percent of American adults between the ages of thirty and forty have a significant episode of back pain, and that about a fourth of those will have recurring low back problems. In the course of a lifetime, about 75 percent of all adults will experience significant low back pain; 5 percent of them will require hospitalization, and 1 to 2 percent of them will have surgery. Why most back pain heals and other cases become chronic is unknown.

Spinal damage occurs most frequently in the two parts of the spine that move the most: the neck and the lower back. Either a major injury or a very small microinjury can trigger a so-called *functional* problem whose physical cause can't be found.

Spinal injuries can begin with an accidental fall, whiplash, or heavy lifting and turning by a person who is out of shape. This trauma can strain muscles, tear ligaments or tendons, or suddenly compress discs. Chronic back pain is strongly associated with heavy work in general, static work postures, frequent bending and twisting, lifting and forceful movements, repetitive work, and vibrations. These can put physical stress on the spine as well as on the muscles and tendons that support it. Various types of emotional stress, including unresolved psychological issues, are other causes of continuing back pain involving the muscles, since unconscious tightening of muscles creates muscle tension and ultimately pain.

The causes of some chronic spinal pains are not well understood. According to William Harsha, M.D., of Orthopedic and Rehabilitation Medicine in Oklahoma City, only about 30 percent of back problems can be explained by the results of even the most sophisticated diagnostic tests. Lower back problems are believed to spring mainly from irritation of the peripheral nerves within or near the exit to the spinal canal, or from problems in muscle or soft tissues connecting segments. These two diagnostic categories often overlap, Dr. Harsha observes.

Muscle pain is a tight, squeezed feeling, more like a slow, deep ache than a throbbing, stabbing pain. Muscles are densely packed fibrous strips that expand and contract. Connected to the skeleton and other parts of the body, they support our upright posture and allow us to move in space. Overworked muscles become inflamed. Even small, simple, continually irritating movements create *microtrauma,* which leads to muscular pain. Microtrauma can result from poor posture; habitual repeated movements; grinding the teeth; sitting in uncomfortable, poorly designed chairs; performing work that requires bending at the waist; or even tensing certain muscles as a response to psychological stress. As muscles become inflamed, irritating chemical waste products build up in the muscle.

Muscle guarding causes muscles to contract near an injured area, shutting off blood flow in and out of the site. For example, this causes us to limp and favor one leg when the other leg has been injured. Muscle fibers also can cramp or go into *spasms,* long, involuntary contractions that constrict blood vessels. These protective responses "seal off" inflamed sites, basically to allow healing, but also contribute to pain.

A slowdown in blood flow to the muscles creates pain because blood carries nourishing oxygen and food into muscle tissues and carries out irritating waste products such as lactic acid. Nerves also are sensitive to reduced blood flow, more so than muscles. The shutdown of blood flow comes through constrictions in the body's smallest blood vessels, called capillaries. Like small water valves, the capillaries usually are opened further when increased oxygen is needed at the affected site, or to carry away carbon dioxide and other waste products.

The human spine is designed to carry the weight of your body for a lifetime. It is the principal weight-bearing axis of the human body and is strong and flexible. The adult spine is about 18 inches long; it contains twenty-four individual mobile bones, or vertebrae, mounted one over the other more or less like odd-shaped building blocks. The vertebrae, separated and cushioned by discs—pads of fibrous tissue around a soft core—rise above the sacrum, which is connected on either side at the sacroiliac joints to other bones in the pelvis. This design basically transfers the weight of the upper body to the legs, a balancing act assisted by the appropriate muscles, ligaments, and tendons, which allows us to stand proudly upright. The parts of the spine are held together with muscles and other connective tissue, which can be strained or torn.

The vertebrae are interlocked, flexible bones and are worn down by use over time. Running up through the vertebrae is a delicate rope of nerves called the spinal cord; bundles of nerves exit and enter the spine at various points to connect the brain with all the nerves of the body.

Back or neck pain may spread as nearby muscles go into a spasm or contraction due to a muscle-guarding reaction. Pain may be referred or shifted elsewhere in the body. There is no medical consensus about why back or neck pain can become chronic. Some speculate that sensory nerves that sustain various forms of damage become very sensitive, or that pain reinforces a psychological pattern, creating an ongoing cycle.

Back pain is treated in many ways. A 1983 study published in *Spine* magazine showed that ten years after treatment, patients with spinal problems who were treated conservatively with physical therapy fared about as well as patients who underwent surgery. In addition to physical therapy, drugs, and surgery, stress-relieving and educational strategies such as those employed by John Sarno, M.D., explained a bit more in chapter 8, are used to treat certain back problems.

Functional disorders. Many types of spinal pain are classified as *functional disorders.* Functional disorders are those for which a physical cause cannot be identified. Some functional disorders apparently originate in the muscles and tissues that control the movement of the spine. Back pain also can arise from an unstable joint system, particularly an unstable facet joint system, since this holds the vertebrae together and keeps them properly aligned. Leg pain can be referred from the spine as the result of nerve-root irritation, which can spring from a protruding invertebrate disc, compromised circulation to the nerve root, or inflammation in the space between joints or between disc and joint. Diagnostic tests such as magnetic resonance imaging (MRI) and computerized tomography (CT) scans of the disc protrusion and the relationship of that to the nerve root are essential to confirm these possibilities. Back surgery should be a last resort.

Structural defects in the discs separating the vertebrae, and other elements of the joints that connect them, often are determined to be a cause of back or neck pain. Discs are natural shock-absorbing pads that protect the bones and delicate nerves of the spinal cord during movement. The discs dry up slightly and shrink a bit as we age. As the body gradually shuts off their blood supply, discs flatten out and become less resilient, losing their ability to act as shock absorbers. As a disc ages, nearby ligaments may thicken and fold. Bone spurs may grow from the outer edges of the vertebrae, producing pressure and irritating nerves.

There is no such thing as a "slipped" disc, since discs are securely held between the vertebrae and can't actually slip anywhere. Under continuous pressure, however, a disc can "bulge" outward. Pressure can force out some of the disc's soft inner core, sometimes in the direction of the nerve roots; this is called a *herniated disc.* Some disc herniation is normal as we age. If the extruded material traps a nerve root against a section of bone, this "pinched nerve" may cause irritation and pain near the disc itself. If the herniated disc stresses the ligaments that hold the joint together, it can help create "trigger points" that refer pain to nearby muscles. Damage to a disc in the upper spine may refer pain to an arm or shoulder. Damage to a lower disc may produce hip pain or send pain radiating or shooting down a leg. A condition called *sciatica* is believed to be the result of damage to a lumbar nerve root, which sends pain shooting down the sciatic nerve, the primary nerve in the leg.

Other spinal problems. Defects in several discs in the lower back or neck are known as *spondylosis*, or vertebra disease, which is considered to be a form of osteoarthritis. *Spondylolisthesis* is the slipping forward of a portion of one vertebra onto another. It can result from stress fractures or defects in a vertebra or disc that allow the bone to slide, creating back pain or sciatica if the vertebra presses on a nerve.

Ankylosing spondylitis, or Marie-Strumpell disease, is believed to be an autoimmune disorder involving a hereditary predisposition. It is an inflammation that begins at the base of the spine and gradually proceeds up the spine. Hip joints and shoulder joints also may be involved, and it is sometimes mistaken for a disc disorder. The spinal inflammation creates pain, followed by excessive bone growth that impedes mobility. People who suffer from this condition sometimes have an exaggerated, bent-over posture, sometimes called dowager's hump. Attacks come and go, often with long periods of remission in between.

Another condition, *spinal stenosis,* or narrowing disease, is a condition in which the spinal canal has become too small for the nerves and spinal cord inside. Spinal stenosis is believed to come from spondylosis, which narrows the canal enough to create pain; it results in weakness and pain in the buttocks and in both legs. This pain is frequently made worse by standing, and is relieved by sitting down.

Scoliosis, a lateral curvature of the spine, is one of the most common structural abnormalities of the skeleton. Scoliosis can be congenital or appear during early childhood growth. Treatment should begin when the curvature becomes noticeable, since children's bones are easier to adjust than those of adults.

Osteoporosis often has spinal pain as a symptom. The inner structures of bones can weaken and become brittle because of loss of calcium. Weakened bones of the spine are susceptible to fractures that can compress the vertebrae, trap nerve roots between bones, or stress the muscles of the neck and back.

Arthritis

Arthritis is the most common chronic disease in men and a leading cause of disability in later years. Because the degeneration it creates is not reversible by any known means, arthritis cannot be cured. It affects sixty-six million people in the United States, about one-third of whom curtail their daily activities because of pain, according to the American Society of Anesthesiologists. Almost every person over the age of sixty will exhibit some degree of arthritis on an X ray, even if no pain or discomfort is experienced.

All of the more than one hundred identified forms of arthritis are diseases of the joints, affecting the body where the bones of the skeleton meet to permit movement. Normal flexibility and movement become limited both by pain and by structural deformities that occur in and around the joints. Joints are naturally smooth and well fitting, covered with a dense protective layer of cartilage. But after the onset of arthritis, they can become as difficult to move as an old door whose hinges need oiling. Every joint is encased in a capsule of connective tissue; a thin inner lining called the *synovium* produces and releases *synovial fluid,* which lubricates the joint. Ligaments of gristle bind each joint to the body, holding it in place, protecting it, and limiting its range of motion.

Generally speaking, pain and restricted *range of movement* at one or more joints suggest some form of arthritis. The joints of the hands, spine, hips, and knees are most frequently affected. Arthritis makes certain movements difficult or painful, and it is typically relieved by rest. The pain is often described as a deep, dull ache in the affected joint. Pain can be referred to other locations. Arthritis is a diagnosis in itself, but it also can be triggered by lupus, inflammatory bowel disease, rheumatic fever, tuberculosis, Lyme disease, gonorrhea, and other systemic disorders.

In some cases arthritis can be stabilized, but in most cases degeneration continues. The most common forms are osteoarthritis and rheumatoid arthritis.

Osteoarthritis. *Osteoarthritis* is a degenerative joint disease that comes on gradually, with episodes of discomfort becoming more frequent and more severe. Its severity ranges from mild to annoying to disabling. Normally most noticeable in the morning, it is typically made worse by repetitive movement or stress on weight-bearing joints, and relieved by rest.

The disease usually affects the weight-bearing joints as well as the joints of the fingers. These are the joints most stressed during work and other normal activities. These joints very slowly stop their normal process of renewal, then begin to degenerate.

Osteoarthritis is believed to begin with small cracks or breaks in the bone's covering layer of smooth, resilient cartilage. As cartilage wears down, it gradually flakes off, leaving small portions of bone unprotected. Hollows or cysts form in these areas, causing bone surface to become pitted or rough. Rough or bare bones rubbing together produce the grinding or "popping" sensation called *crepitus.*

As osteoarthritis progresses, the affected joint or joints become tender, swollen, and inflamed. Inflammation can trigger the growth of *bone spurs,* or *osteophytes,* which restrict joint mobility, causing further swelling and stiffness. Muscles adjacent to the joint may suffer muscle spasm, fatigue, or referred pain. The pain of osteoarthritis is more or less continual until joints "burn out," bringing cessation of inflammation and pain.

Rheumatoid arthritis. Rheumatoid arthritis is similar to osteoarthritis, but it is an autoimmune disease, often hereditary, that typically strikes people between twenty and forty years of age. Its presence is frequently confirmed by an antibody called *rheumatoid factor* in the blood, or by the presence of anemia.

Rheumatoid arthritis affects the joints in the hands and feet. Inflammation begins in the lining of the joint capsule. The lining thickens and releases irritating chemicals that help the inflammation spread into other parts of the joint capsule, including nearby ligaments and tendons. This creates heat, swelling, and pain. Destructive chemical enzymes erode cartilage, bone, and soft tissues around each affected joint, reducing mobility and weakening supporting ligaments and tendons, which over time may cause the joint to become deformed or even dislocated. Joint pain may lead to muscle guarding and muscle pain. Rheumatoid arthritis may produce tiny, firm growths called *rheumatoid nodules* under the skin of the hands, arms, or legs.

Other joint disorders include *juvenile rheumatoid arthritis,* which appears between the ages of two and five and subsides around the time of puberty. *Psoriatic arthritis,* a skin disease, sometimes is accompanied by an inflammation of the joints and resembles rheumatoid arthritis. *Infectious arthritis* can spring from a viral, bacterial, or fungal infection of the joints.

Lyme disease is a bacterial infection carried by ticks. It often first appears as a form of the flu, with a rash near the bitten area, but can include arthritic symptoms weeks or months after the initial infection. *Reiter's syndrome,* caused by an infection, occasionally can cause a reactive arthritis that persists and is treated like rheumatoid arthritis.

Gouty arthritis is brought on by excessive uric acid in the bloodstream, the underlying cause of gout, a painful inflammation of the joints, particularly in the hands and feet. This acid accumulates in the tissues and can form crystals in the lubricating fluid of joints, particularly the knees, elbows, hands, and feet. *Pseudogout* releases calcium crystals into the synovial fluid, where they provoke inflammation and pain, and is treated in a similar manner to that of gout.

Bursitis normally comes and goes but can become chronic and create chronic pain. It's caused by inflammation of the *bursae*, small sacs filled with synovial fluid that cushion tissues that rub against each other during movement, such as those in the shoulders, elbows, and knees. The bursae sometimes acquire calcium deposits, which can be removed by aspirating calcium with excessive fluid from the sac. As in many joint disorders, immobilizing the nearby joint can be helpful but needs to be followed by appropriate exercise to restore mobility.

TMJ disorders. *Temporomandibular joint disorders,* called either TMJ or TMD disorders, can be quite painful. These joints are located where the jawbone pivots against the skull, the only joints in the body that work together as a unit. Muscles open and close the jaw pivoting on this joint, with the teeth limiting the lower jaw's upward motion. Temporomandibular joints are more complex than other joints, since the back ends of the lower jaw rotate and slide forward along an articular disc made of cartilage. If you can open your jaw and put in three fingers stacked on top of each other, or turn your head left and right and eat without experiencing pain, you probably don't have TMJ disorder.

TMJ disorders can create persistent, severe pain in the form of headaches, neckaches, shoulder aches, toothaches, pain in the joints while chewing, tenderness, ringing or rushing noises in the ears, an inability to open the mouth easily, and clicking, grating, or popping noises when the jaw opens and closes. Habitual clenching or grinding of the teeth (often a response to stress) causes microtrauma. Malocclusions, poor postural habits, and trauma such as whiplash injury in an automobile accident are other possible causes. Excessively clenching the chewing muscles can cause fatigue, resulting in muscle guarding that may refer pain to other areas.

There are three general types of TMJ disorders—those associated with myofascial pain, joint inflammation, or displacement of the articular disc. Myofascial pain may be concentrated in the chewing muscles or express itself as pain in nearby muscles in the neck, head, or shoulders. Inflammation of the synovial lining, called *retrodiscitis,* involves the tissue that connects the disc to the temporal bone. Displacement of the articular disc produces the symptom of clicking when the mouth is opened, caused by the jaw moving out of its customary position.

Dentists frequently treat this particular disorder, in tandem with other specialists such as oral surgeons, orthodontists, neurologists, physical therapists, and psychologists. Like many other forms of chronic pain, TMJ disorders normally are treated first with noninvasive techniques such as physical therapy, heat, cold, TENS, and exercise. Other treatments limit the movement of the lower jaw or involve a switch to a soft-food diet. Education helps develop a basic healthy resting position: jaws open slightly, tongue resting against the roof of mouth, lips together, and breathing through the nose, taking care to bring the teeth together only when eating.

TMJ disorders frequently are treated with a device called an *occlusal splint,* a U-shaped piece of plastic that fits over the teeth to keep the jaws from completely closing, thereby reducing stress on the joints. The best splints are probably hard plastic and made from a cast of the teeth, although a few practitioners use soft rubber splints. Splint therapy can last from three to six months. A *repositioning splint* is more complex and repositions the lower jaw to take pressure off the joint. Repositioning splints change the bite during use and may be permanent or temporary. More severe treatments include grinding and smoothing the surfaces of individual teeth to change the jaw relationship; braces to change the position of the teeth; and restorative dentistry to improve the bite. As with most chronic pain, surgery should be a last resort, undertaken only after conservative measures have been given a fair trial.

Headaches

The headache is one of the most common complaints heard by medical doctors. Headaches can be symptoms of other injuries or diseases, such as concussion, flu, TMJ problems, or cancer. They also are painful disorders in their own right and are treated as complaints rather than symptoms. According to the National Headache Foundation, at least twenty-one different types of headache exist, although most fall into two or three major categories.

One of the primary triggers of headache pain is constriction of the blood vessels, which causes a mild oxygen starvation resulting in great pain. In the case of migraine headaches, a pattern of blood vessel constriction and then dilation is believed to develop around the brain, triggering the release of chemical substances that increase swelling and inflammation, although vacillating hormone levels, stress, genetics and other factors are thought to be the actual cause.

Many headaches respond to drug treatment, or simply disappear on their own. The most common headaches that cause chronic pain are classified as *tension* headaches or *vascular* headaches.

Tension headaches. Tension headaches are the most common form of headache. They are believed to result from prolonged muscle contraction. Some tension headaches occur at one precise location, whereas others are experienced from the forehead down to the neck. Grinding or clenching the teeth may be the cause, as the chewing muscles produce trigger points that refer pain to the head.

The current thinking is that constant muscle contraction brings on muscle fatigue and oxygen debt, allowing the accumulation of histamine, bradykinin, and other chemicals that increase pain sensitivity and amplify the experience of pain. Emotional stress, too, can cause the muscles to contract in the head or neck, triggering the headache, which in itself can cause more stress, anxiety, and worry. Tension headaches occurring after trauma are called *post-traumatic headaches* and may result from muscle guarding.

Vascular headaches. Vascular headaches originate within the large and small blood vessels, including the arteries that carry blood to the head. These particular arteries sometimes suddenly dilate too much, stimulating pain-sensing receptors on artery walls. Vascular headaches usually are experienced as a throbbing pain on one side of the head. Emotional stress can trigger vascular headaches, as can surges of powerful emotions such as anger. They also can be a result of high blood pressure, chronic kidney failure, or other diseases such as the flu, mononucleosis, or Lyme disease.

Vascular headaches that recur with particular symptoms are called *migraine* headaches. Sometimes migraine and tension headaches can be experienced simultaneously. *Migraine* comes from a Greek word meaning "half the head," since the pain is experienced on one side of the head. Many people with migraines describe the pain as a feeling that their skull is going to pop off. Migraines usually are accompanied by stomach upset, with nausea strong enough to cause vomiting and subsequent dehydration. Many people experience a visual aura before the onset of the headache, consisting of bright spots before the eyes, a partial blindness, or a bright spot gradually growing larger. This is thought to be caused by tightening of the brain arteries.

Sleep disruptions, bright lights, loud noises, pungent smells, or other strong stimulation can make the migraine headache worse, as can physical or mental activity. It's not uncommon for migraine sufferers to retreat to a dark room and wait for the headache to pass. A migraine attack often is preceded by a heaviness first in the limbs and then in the face, and is sometimes followed by a prickling "pins and needles" feeling on the skin.

Migraine headaches often run in families. Distinctive features include their recurring quality, averaging one to three per month; and their similarity in form, since one feels like the next. Women experience migraines more frequently than do men. Some women experience migraines around the time of menstruation; some report relief when they become pregnant.

Like migraine headaches, *cluster headaches* tend to be experienced only on one side of the head, with pain concentrated behind the eyes. They tend to occur once or more than once a day for months, with months or even years of remission in between. Typically, cluster headaches come on suddenly at night, lasting from a half hour to two hours. Men are afflicted more frequently than women. A similar condition called *chronic paroxysmal hemicrania* often affects women; these painful attacks resemble cluster headaches, except they are shorter and much more frequent, sometimes occurring more than a dozen times a day.

Another type of vascular headache called *temporal arteritis* is believed to be an autoimmune disease affecting the carotid arteries, most specifically the branch near the temples of the head. Temporal arteritis can be dangerous, leading to stroke or blindness if not treated. It is associated with *polymyalgia rheumatica,* a condition that produces joint or muscle pain.

Activities involving heavy exertion, such as weight lifting or marathon running, can create what are called *effort headaches.* Certain foods or food additives, particularly nitrates or nitrites found in some packaged lunch meats, can trigger so-called *hot dog headaches.* A few people have *orgasmic headaches* during or prior to having sex.

Muscle Disorders

Some of the most painful muscle disorders produce little hard, measurable evidence of their existence. Whatever damage exists doesn't show up on X rays or other tests. These *functional* muscle disorders are mainly diagnosed by their adverse effect on bodily function, rather than by results of diagnostic tests. Even though the precise cause of many functional muscle disorders is not known, the pain they produce is quite real.

The two primary functional muscle disorders are *fibromyalgia* and *myofascial pain syndrome* (MPS). *Fibromyalgia* (also known as fibrositis, chronic rheumatism, myalgia, pressure point syndrome, and psychogenic arthritis) literally means "pain of the fibrous muscles," and it is believed to be a significant cause of disability even though it was not formally recognized as a distinct illness until 1987. Estimates say as much as one-fifth of the U.S. population may suffer from fibromyalgia on any given day. Myofascial pain syndrome involves the muscles and connective tissues, called fascia, that both bind muscle fibers together and form ligaments and tendons connecting to the bones and other parts of the body. Generally speaking, fibromyalgia is widespread throughout the body, whereas myofascial pain is localized.

The causes of these two functional muscle disorders are not known. One primary cause may be trauma, such as a whiplash injury, which can cause bleeding within muscle tissue and produce scar tissue called adhesions that can interfere with smooth muscle function. In other cases, no obvious physical trauma is involved.

Pain from fibromyalgia can occur simultaneously in several areas of the body, and it is sometimes considered a rheumatoid disorder because so many features are the same. More than 90 percent of people diagnosed with fibromyalgia complain of widespread discomfort and of "aching all over." Symptoms include sleeping problems, morning stiffness, fatigue, numbness and tingling sensations, headache, irritable bowel syndrome, depression, and anxiety. Fibromyalgia is characterized by so-called tender points, or small areas of the body that become quite painful when pressed, making the patient jump or recoil, which physicians call a "jump sign." A diagnosis of fibromyalgia is typically confirmed by chronic pain present for longer than six months, and tenderness in at least five of forty well-defined points. Many patients complain of having a disordered memory. According to Paul Rosch, M.D., president of the

American Institute of Stress in Yonkers, New York, about half the patients who suffer fibromyalgia link the onset of their symptoms to a stressful event. Symptoms such as greater sensitivity to pain, sleep disturbance, and headache often increase with emotional stress.

Although its cause also is unknown, *chronic fatigue syndrome* may have a link to fibromyalgia. It's estimated that 70 percent of chronic fatigue sufferers also experience fibromyalgia. Chronic fatigue syndrome is a functional disorder defined by its symptoms, which include unexplained physical weakness and fatigue lasting more than six months. Reduced work, social, and personal activities are common, as are sleep disorders.

Myofascial pain normally is concentrated in a few areas, although it can spread to other parts of the body. It is sometimes confused with arthritis because the pain patterns are similar. The major characteristic of myofascial pain is its trigger points, small points on the skin that are quite sensitive. Pressing these trigger points can cause or "refer" pain to other parts of the body, usually along established pathways. For instance, trigger points in the muscles at the top of the back can produce painful headaches at the base of the skull or in the temples. Trigger points in the chewing muscles of the jaw can trigger earaches or toothaches. Taut bands of muscle that can be felt below the skin are also associated with trigger points. It is not completely understood how trigger points refer pain, but apparently connections are crossed somewhere in the nervous system.

Other less common muscle disorders include *polymyalgia rheumatica,* believed to be caused when the immune system attacks the body itself, particularly the connective tissues. It creates a deep aching pain that is concentrated in the muscles of the neck, shoulders, or pelvis and is usually worse in the morning. Other symptoms include muscle weakness, lassitude, loss of weight, loss of appetite, and low-grade fever.

Polymyositis literally means "an inflammation of many muscles," and it also is believed to be an autoimmune disorder. A form of polymyositis affects the skin and is called *dermatomyositis.*

Nerve Disorders (Neuropathies)

Damage to the nerves themselves may cause a number of painful disorders collectively known as *neuropathies.* These are among the most difficult types of chronic pain to treat successfully. Traditionally called *neuralgias* or nerve pains, disorders classified as neuropathies include causalgia, reflex sympathetic dystrophy, stump pain, phantom limb pain, shingles or postherpetic neuralgia, tic douloureux, and peripheral neuropathies.

Causalgia and reflex sympathetic dystrophy. *Causalgia* begins with a severe injury that creates a partial destruction of a major nerve, such as a battle wound or traffic accident injury. *Reflex sympathetic dystrophy* (also known as major causalgia, minor causalgia, shoulder-hand syndrome, post-traumatic pain syndrome, post-traumatic vasomotor disorder, post-traumatic spreading neuralgia, or post-traumatic painful osteoporosis) can spring from a lesser injury, such as a cut or fracture, surgical procedures, or certain diseases or infections.

A deep burning pain signals the onset of both causalgia and reflex sympathetic dystrophy, accompanied by tenderness and aggravated by movement or mental stress. The pain can spread, causing loss of mobility and stiffness, and sometimes moves from one extremity of the body to another.

Worsening pain can cause an extremely heightened sensitivity to pain called *allodynia,* in which intense, severe pain is caused by even trivial stimuli. Muscle wasting and weakness can follow the onset of these conditions, along with joint swelling. Early diagnosis is difficult but presents the best chance for reversing the symptoms permanently.

Both causalgia and reflex sympathetic dystrophy are believed to involve malfunctions of the sympathetic nerves within the autonomic nervous system. These nerves regulate involuntary bodily functions such as heartbeat and breathing. In both conditions, sympathetic neurons release the neurotransmitter noradrenaline, making the damaged sensory nerves unusually sensitive to pain.

Stump and phantom limb pain. Pain following the amputation of an arm or leg takes the form of *stump pain,* in which pain is felt where the amputation occurred, and *phantom limb pain,* which is pain perceived to occur in the amputated hand, foot, or limb. Some people experience both stump and phantom limb pain. Phantom tooth pain sometimes follows a tooth extraction.

Stump and phantom limb pain may be periodic or constant and have a burning quality. Phantom limb pain may involve a "pins and needles" type of pain or other unusual sensations, and it can be quite a frightening experience; some sufferers fear they are going insane.

The shock of amputation also can bring about stump or phantom limb pain. Both types of pain apparently involve changes in the nervous system. The conditions frequently vanish over time, although both are difficult to treat effectively in chronic form. An estimated 3 to 7 percent of amputees experience phantom limb pain that persists for a year or more.

Stump pain can involve the appearance of *neuromas,* tiny, hypersensitive knots of former sensory nerves that have imperfectly repaired themselves at the site of the amputation. Attempts to remove these through surgery usually just create more.

Tic douloureux. *Tic douloureux,* which literally means "painful twitch," also is known as *trigeminal neuralgia.* This very painful condition originates in the three-branched trigeminal nerves, the primary sensory nerves of the face, which connect directly to the brain. It can trigger a facial twitch, or tic, responsible for the descriptive French name.

The pain of tic douloureux is a horrible, shocking, stabbing, severe sensation, hitting one side of the face and often radiating down the jaw but lasting for a fairly short time. It is followed by a lingering sting and sensitiveness that can last several more minutes. When it occurs, the intense pain is completely disabling.

Ferocious attacks of tic douloureux can be set off by seemingly innocuous pressure or changes in temperature. Attacks can occur in flurries, with fairly long periods of remission, but can become more frequent. Weight loss is common. The current thinking is that the trigeminal nerve is compromised when a blood vessel presses against a nerve root at a location fairly near the brain, which causes the nervous system to misfire. *Glossopharyngeal neuralgia* causes pain in the mouth and throat, involving irritation to another cranial nerve, and is treated in a manner similar to that of tic douloureux.

Postherpetic neuralgia involves the chicken pox virus carried from childhood and triggered by a mild local irritation such as minor surgery. When one nerve is affected, this disorder is called shingles, characterized by its itching rash.

Postherpetic neuralgia usually goes away a few weeks after treatment, but occasionally it lingers, especially among older people, creating continuing pain as a result of nerve damage. Most treatments of shingles are aimed at helping the patient bear the pain until the immune system builds up the strength to attack the virus and send it back to its hiding place.

Peripheral neuropathies. *Peripheral neuropathies* are pains that affect the nerves at the periphery of the nervous system, often the arms, legs, feet, and hands, or sometimes in the skeletal muscles, locations where nerve cells are longest. Peripheral neuropathies can create a tingling "pins and needles" type of pain but more commonly create numbness, coldness, or a burning feeling. Other symptoms are a degree of muscle weakness and loss of reflexes and motor control.

Peripheral neuropathies can accompany long bouts of diabetes or alcoholism. Excessive alcohol consumption robs the body of B vitamins. Poisons, cancer treatments such as chemotherapy or radiation, or even other diseases also can create peripheral neuropathies.

It is not fully understood how nerves are damaged or affected in peripheral neuropathy. In the case of diabetes, for instance, researchers theorize that excess glucose in the bloodstream may cause the outer layer of cells on neurons to swell up and choke off more functional inner nerve cells.

Visceral Pain

Pain in the internal organs, or *viscera,* usually is experienced as pain in the chest, abdomen, or pelvis. Visceral pain often is referred to other parts of the body where nerve endings are more profuse, and may be a considerable distance from the source of pain. Sensory nerves are spaced far apart in the viscera; since nerve receptor ends frequently overlap, several nerves can pick up a pain sensation. This makes visceral pain more diffuse, general, and less precisely located than other forms of pain. For example, the pain of *angina pectoris,* which emanates from the chest or heart, often is experienced in the left shoulder or left arm.

Spasms in the muscles that support the skeleton as a result of muscle guarding are common in visceral pain, and tenderness may spread as a result. In general, the tissues of the internal organs also are quite sensitive to oxygen deprivation, blockages, and blood vessel dilation. Sweating, fluctuating heartbeat, nausea, or changes in blood pressure are symptoms that may result from increased activity in the autonomic nervous system and often accompany visceral pain.

Major types of visceral pain include angina pectoris, reflux esophagitis, peptic ulcers, irritable bowel syndrome, diverticulosis and diverticulitis, dysmenorrhea, pelvic inflammatory disease, and endometriosis.

Angina. *Angina pectoris,* or angina, which literally means "strangling," is a symptom of coronary heart disease. The pain can be experienced as a viselike tightening in the chest or throat, or as pain in the center of the chest that radiates out to the shoulder and arm, often on the left side. Other symptoms include anxiety, sweating, fear of dying, and rapid pulse caused by a rise in blood pressure. Angina can be triggered by psychological stress as well as various forms of physical stress, such as exertion, overeating, or even sudden changes in temperature. Angina begins when fats accumulate along artery walls, forming hard plaque that narrows arteries. This buildup decreases normal blood flow to the heart muscle, at times causing an oxygen shortage and a buildup of metabolic products in the heart muscle, resulting in pain. Attacks usually subside in five to fifteen minutes but can last longer.

Although drugs and surgical procedures frequently are employed to treat it, angina and other forms of heart and coronary disease can be successfully controlled through multidisciplinary programs, such as the well-publicized program begun by Dean Ornish, M.D., at the medical center of the University of California at San Francisco. Dr. Ornish has demonstrated how to control heart disease with a low-fat, basically vegetarian diet combined with exercise, yoga, meditation, and group support, stress reduction, and improved communication skills. Ornish's regimen can work but is not for everybody. Simply learning to relax and reduce stress can help ward off attacks of angina and many other ailments.

Reflux esophagitis. Reflux esophagitis creates referred pain, commonly called heartburn, that resembles the pain of angina. It is caused when powerful stomach acids, helpful in digesting food, escape past the esophageal muscle, a natural barrier between the stomach and esophagus. Overweight people, older people, and pregnant women often experience this condition. If it continues for a long time, it may cause ulcers, scarring or blockages. Lifestyle changes such as losing weight; avoiding stimulants such as tobacco, alcohol, and coffee; avoiding bedtime snacks; and keeping the head elevated 4 to 6 inches while sleeping can be preventative measures, since lying down flat stimulates the flow of acid out of the stomach.

Peptic ulcers. *Peptic ulcers* are small sores in the stomach or small intestine that create a burning, gnawing pain in the gut that comes and goes. They are quite common, affecting one in every five American men, and one in every ten American women at some time during their lives. Ulcer sores begin when the thick coat of mucus normally lining the stomach erodes, or when excess stomach acid is released into the small intestine. Acid penetrating the mucus produces an inflammation in intestinal tissue, which produces pain. Ulcer attacks are periodic, sometimes occurring as frequently as one or more times a day, with periods of attacks relieved by periods of relative remission. Peptic ulcers are called *gastric ulcers* in the stomach, and *duodenal ulcers* in the small intestine. Excessive alcohol, caffeine, tobacco, stress, and hurried or irregular meals can trigger ulcer attacks. Lifestyle changes including stopping smoking and reducing or eliminating alcohol and caffeine intake are helpful in controlling them.

Irritable bowel syndrome. *Irritable bowel syndrome,* sometimes called spastic colon or irritable colon, is a functional disorder. Pain is similar to ulcer pain and is experienced as cramps in the abdomen. Digested food moves too quickly or too slowly through the colon, causing diarrhea or constipation, and creating painful bloating from internal gas. Pain caused by muscle cramps or spasms can result. A high-fiber diet can be helpful, as can avoiding particular foods such as beans and cabbage. Stress-relieving techniques are frequently useful, as is psychological therapy.

Diverticulitis. In the lower or sigmoid colon, *diverticulitis* is caused by an infection of tiny sacs called diverticula, which push outward through the colon walls. Pain and fever can spring from the inflamed sacs, which in serious cases may perforate the wall of the intestine, causing a dangerous abdominal infection. *Diverticulosis* is a more common and more mild disorder accompanied by diarrhea or constipation and occasional bleeding. The best treatment for both is now believed to be a high-fiber diet of whole grains, fruits, and vegetables, although other treatments are sometimes employed.

Crohn's disease. *Crohn's disease* and *ulcerative colitis* are diseases of the intestinal lining that produce inflammation and pain. Believed to be autoimmune diseases, both produce abdominal pain and diarrhea; both recur and sometimes increase in severity. Crohn's disease may refer pain to the lower right abdomen, where it can be mistaken for appendicitis. Ulcerative colitis more often refers pain to the lower left side, over the colon. In Crohn's disease, inflammation is in either the small intestine or the colon; in ulcerative colitis, inflammation and sores are limited to the colon, usually in the rectal area. Either can lead to dangerous bleeding or, in severe cases, to infection. Neither can be cured, but remission can be achieved.

Chronic pelvic pain. Two painful conditions that cause chronic pelvic pain in women are pelvic inflammatory disease and endometriosis.

Pelvic inflammatory disease involves an infection of the reproductive organs by bacteria or other microorganisms. Many microorganisms are sexually transmitted. Inflammation may spread, creating tissue damage and adhesions. Pain, fever, fatigue, and abnormal vaginal discharges are symptoms, as is a recurring ache in the lower abdomen and sometimes backache. Other symptoms include menstrual pain and pain during intercourse. Most pelvic inflammatory disease is acute, but occasionally it becomes chronic if healing is incomplete.

Endometriosis can cause severe, steadily aching menstrual pain, or pain during or after intercourse. It begins in the inner lining of the uterus, called the *endometrium,* which normally thickens and is sloughed off during menstruation. Sometimes the endometrium doesn't completely dissolve, leading to the formation of scars or tiny, blisterlike cysts outside the uterus. Clear diagnosis is necessary before treatment begins, since hormone treatment and surgeries ranging from conservative surgery to remove abnormal growth, to the more radical hysterectomy, are used to treat it. If chronic pelvic pain is without an obvious pathology, pain will continue after a hysterectomy is performed in a significant percentage of cases.

Pain is a complex sensation ultimately involving the entire nervous system, including the spine and the brain. It can originate in disorders of the spine, joints, muscles, viscera, and organs, and from disorders or malfunctions within the nervous system itself. All forms of chronic pain involve the body, and they all also involve the mind. The emotional, social, and psychological dimensions of pain, examined in the next chapter, are important in dealing with chronic pain, since the mind can greatly intensify or diminish pain's ultimate effects.

The Mind

Chronic pain has emotional, behavioral, and mental aspects that can be addressed in many ways.

The mind is a crucial element in the experience of chronic pain. Your mental outlook and your emotions can either amplify or inhibit the debilitating pain cycle. The fact that pain has emotional, behavioral, and mental components doesn't mean that the pain isn't real. These components are addressed in multidisciplinary programs because learning good coping skills makes pain more manageable. Working to understand and apply these to yourself can help you manage chronic pain and possibly improve your sexual functioning and many other aspects of your life.

Mind and body are so obviously intertwined in the experience of pain that the Greek philosopher Aristotle classified pain as an emotion—that is, a feeling that is the opposite of pleasure. The Roman emperor and Stoic philosopher Marcus Aurelius regarded pain entirely as a phenomenon of the body that could be overridden by the mind. "If it lasts, it can be borne," he wrote. The Greek philosopher Epictetus stated, "People are not disturbed by events themselves, but rather by the views they take of them."

"Pain is always subjective," wrote the authors of a comprehensive definition of *pain* by the International Association for the Study of Pain. "Each individual learns the application of the word through experiences related to bodily injury in early life. It is unquestionably a sensation in a part of the body but it is also always unpleasant and therefore is also an emotional experience." The authors added that pain is "always a psychological state."

The mental aspects of the pain experience, according to Ronald Melzack and Patrick Wall's gate control theory (see

---

MENTAL FACTORS INVOLVED IN PAIN

According to *Coping with Chronic Pain* by Richard Hanson and Kenneth Gerber, mental factors are involved in the actual experience of pain in five ways.

1. *Consciousness* is a mental factor, since it's impossible to feel pain while you're asleep or unconscious.

2. *Focus of attention* is important, since pain is worse when you mentally focus on it, and recedes when you can focus your attention elsewhere.

3. *Memories* of past pain can color the way you view pain and events related to it, particularly if you believe a specific event or medical procedure "caused" your pain problem.

4. *Expectations* regarding pain are entirely mental, and have implications for your general well-being.

5. *Your mental attitudes and beliefs* regarding yourself and other people affect how you experience pain.

---

chapter 3), include motivational tendencies that move or don't move you toward escape or attack. They involve cognitive information also processed in the brain such as your own thoughts about pain, your past experiences, and the expected outcomes of overt responses that characterize pain, as Melzack writes in his book, *The Puzzle of Pain*. The placebo effect, which colors every scientific experiment involving human beings, is an endlessly demonstrated example of the mind's influence over the body, as is the simple act of blushing.

Mental strategies can be quite helpful in mitigating chronic pain, whether it is of organic or functional origin. Without question, pain that is not relieved causes physical, emotional, and social havoc. Negative reactions and responses feed into a pain cycle in which one thing leads to another. This can slowly transform you into a passive and dependent invalid unless the cycle is broken. Substituting positive coping actions for negative reactions will help you diminish the intensity of pain.

Choosing to fight back, or actively and methodically working to live and manage your life rather than passively enduring the slings and arrows of chronic pain, can be extremely empowering and therapeutic. A study of rheumatoid arthritis patients published in 1987 showed that people who coped actively with their disease reported less pain, less depression, less functional impairment, and a higher sense of self-efficacy than did people who coped with it passively. An earlier study in 1981 concluded that the success or failure of any rehabilitation program was directly related to the ability of the patient to practice positive thinking related to living a useful life despite the presence of pain.

JULIA'S STORY

ॐ A bright, friendly woman we shall call Julia grew up on Long Island, New York. At the age of forty-two she returned to school and got her nursing degree, fulfilling a lifelong dream that began when she read stories of Sue Barton, nurse, as a young girl. Happily married with four grown children, Julia worked in an intensive care unit at a major hospital until about eight years ago, when she began to experience puzzling bouts of pain. Although she thought of herself as a healthy, vigorous person, Julia felt her strength unexplainably decreasing. At work, she began to have a difficult time turning patients over in bed, something that never gave her any trouble before. "I couldn't understand why I was slowing down," she recalls.

Over time, Julia saw six doctors. She was given many tests and several prescriptions, but never a clear diagnosis. As a nurse, it frustrated her that the doctors couldn't tell her what was wrong. "Some of the doctors I saw acted like I was crazy and didn't believe me," she remembers. Finally she saw an article in *Family Circle* magazine that led her to suspect she had a relatively new health condition now called fibromyalgia. The family practitioner Julia worked for part-time confirmed her suspicion.

"She recognized it. She didn't think I was crazy or imagining it," Julia says. "You have all these muscles in your body, and they hurt all the time. If you don't sleep, it aggravates it. If they can give you something to help you sleep, the pain won't be so bad the next day. The thing is, there's no cure for it. You hurt all over. And depression makes the pain worse.

"The problem with chronic pain is that you really don't look sick," she says. "If you went to the support group I attend, you'd look around at the people who are there and they'd all look like normal people to you. People don't see me in the morning when I break out into tears because I can just slightly move. They don't see me moaning and groaning to get this and that. I try to keep to myself and I try not to complain," she says. "Chronic pain is the silent disease."

Julia's husband died of cancer about five years after she was diagnosed with fibromyalgia. This was a very stressful and depressing time in her life. Her children had moved away and weren't supportive. Her pain didn't improve, and sometimes it got much worse.

"How do you cope? I guess it's the will to live," she says. "Sometimes you don't want to, to tell you the truth."

After her husband died, Julia went through a period of deep inner reflection. Along the way, she tried acupuncture and magnet therapy, but neither relieved her pain. At different times, she was prescribed more than a dozen different medications, including muscle relaxants, antidepressants, sedatives, NSAIDs, oral cortisone, and even a mild narcotic that didn't work.

Because she understands medicine, the former nurse has avoided some of the unconventional treatments offered by some doctors who prey on people who will try anything to get well. "Some doctors will take advantage of you," she says. "Some of them put you through a lot of tests you might not need."

Julia finally found a very good physician, a rheumatologist with an office a few miles away who is one of the best in his field. He keeps up on recent developments in rheumatology, and she trusts his judgment. So far, muscle relaxants are about the only drugs that help—they allow her to sleep, and she wakes up with muscles that are relatively relaxed and not tense.

Julia continues to work part-time in a family practitioner's office, which helps her in many ways. It gets her mind off the pain and gives her personal satisfaction—patients happily report to her boss that they can't feel it when she gives them a shot. And Julia regularly attends a support group for people with chronic pain, where she has met many friends who call her on the phone to check in, chat, or to ask her advice.

"They say you have to accept chronic pain, but I will *never* accept it. I will acknowledge it, but that's the best I can do," Julia admits. "I'm very angry about the whole thing. My pain threshold is so low, I have my dentist give me gas to put me to sleep when I get my teeth cleaned. I *hate* pain. The days when it's bad I get very angry, and I'm grateful for the days it's not too bad."

Julia has begun a program of exercise, walking two miles a day as often as she can. She walks her two spaniels, who have given her a lot of love and comfort through her good days and bad days.

"I can't let the pain take over my whole day—I have to take care of my dogs," she says. "I think anyone who has chronic pain should get a dog. They don't want anything from you, and they give you unconditional love."

Julia adds, "You put up with the pain because you have no choice. There's no way of really dealing with it, but everybody finds their own way—some try to ignore it, some feel sorry for themselves, some try to live on medication. As for me, the honest truth is that I wouldn't have gotten through it without my dogs. They're special animals, and they pulled me through it. You have to feel that you're on the earth for something, and that you're wanted. You have to have something to love, and something to love you in return."

POWER OF THE MIND

The perception of physical pain can be created, amplified, or diminished in the mind. A study of people with back disorders showed that muscle tension in their backs measurably increased when they merely *described* the pain and stress they experienced in the past. Phantom limb pain (see chapter 3) is pain experienced and felt in a limb that has been amputated; this pain must be experienced in the mind, since the amputated limb no longer exists. More heroic examples of the power of the mind can be seen in people under certain types of great physical and emotional stress. In the thick of battle, soldiers often heroically continue to fight—without feeling pain—in spite of what should be completely painful and debilitating physical wounds. In competitive sporting events, athletes often continue to participate even with debilitating injuries, since their attention is focused on the competitive event and not on their pain.

Normal emotional responses to chronic pain include denial, anger, and depression. Denial is a first-phase response that gives the individual time to adjust to reality. Anger is another normal response, but many cultures are taught to suppress it. William Harsha, M.D., notes that anger produces more energy than any other emotion, and it sometimes can be channeled into productive activity. The energy that anger produces builds up if it is suppressed, leading to depression and muscle tension, which contribute to the chronic pain syndrome. Among other things, depression lowers individual pain tolerance and contributes to physical inactivity and feelings of hopelessness and helplessness. Muscle tension creates more pain.

Emotions are not harmful in themselves, but negative emotions feed into the pain cycle. Obsessively focusing on the pain intensifies it in your mind and also can lead to other behaviors such as seeking more and more medical treament, using additional narcotic drugs, and engaging in unnecessary conflicts with family and caregivers. There are no wrong emotions, as many have observed, only wrong actions. Even the perceived uncontrollability and unpredictability of negative emotions and pain may be harmful, because this may lead to your focusing more and more of your attention on the pain.

Psychologists look at emotions as action tendencies. Our feelings can compel us to take certain actions. Anger, for instance, might compel us to shout, wave our arms in the air, or take physical action. Fear might lead to physical withdrawal, excessive bed rest, and immobility—valuable in

MYTHS ABOUT CHRONIC PAIN

Here are four myths about chronic pain, according to clinical psychologist Laura S. Hitchcock:

1. *Chronic pain for which no physical cause can be found is psychogenic, or "in the head."*

   FALSE: Even the sophisticated medical tests and measuring devices available to doctors can't find everything that can go wrong in the human body. In addition, some patients are not correctly diagnosed.

2. *Chronic pain often or usually is a "masked depression equivalent."*

   FALSE: Recent studies don't support this psychological cliché. Depression is normal at times for any person coping with chronic pain or any other chronic illness. Stigmatizing behavior of health professionals who imply "it's all in your head" can contribute to depression.

3. *Patients involved in lawsuits or receiving disability payments exaggerate pain for financial gain and won't improve until payments stop.*

   FALSE: Although malingerers do exist, they are relatively rare. A study done by Nelson Hendler, M.D., published in healing acute pain, but ultimately self-defeating in healing chronic pain. Anxiety or fear of creating some additional future pain may lead to the avoidance of certain physical motions or activities, which creates excessive physical disability.

Anxiety is a fear of something that hasn't occurred, a stress created in the mind that heightens bodily awareness, constricts blood vessels, and causes the release of pain-pro-

---

a 1989 issue of *Pain Management* showed that the average worker receiving workers' compensation actually *lost* $34,000 over 4.5 years in benefits, overtime, and so forth. Hendler concluded that "financial gain is never an issue in workers compensation cases," an idea he called "a medical school myth."

4. *Narcotic drugs are never appropriate for the treatment of chronic pain.*

FALSE: By reducing pain and increasing function, opioids can play a key role in pain management for patients in whom other medicines or treatment modalities have failed. However, patients must have no history of drug or alcohol abuse, and doses must be carefully monitored to provide maximum relief and minimum side effects. Pain authority Ronald Melzack argued in a 1990 issue of *Scientific American* that narcotics taken for pain relief are not addictive.

---

ducing substances such as bradykinin and Substance P. By lowering the pain threshold, anxiety and fear intensify pain. Studies have shown that high anxiety levels correlate with higher ratings of pain. In fact, some doctors think morphine works as a painkiller simply by reducing levels of anxiety and fear.

In any chronic illness, powerful negative feelings such as fear, anxiety, and anger are normal. Other common negative feelings include frustration, resentment, isolation, loneliness, guilt, irritability, and a feeling your life is out of control. Depression and despair often accompany chronic pain. Family, social, and work relationships are usually disturbed, and roles often change. People suffering terminal illness sometimes "give up," and often this is because they simply feel there's nothing they can do to control or improve their situation. Several studies have shown that simply giving the patient a *feeling* of control over the pain helps relieve it.

Among older people who experience chronic pain, the normal traumas and disappointments of life, such as losing friends and loved ones and experiencing the limits of one's dreams and hopes, also may contribute to feelings of despair and depression. These feelings affect pain threshold and tolerance and can create a cycle in which psychological effects mask physical effects and vice versa. The Medicare program long ago recognized the psychological aspects of pain, and requires that all chronic pain patients visit a psychiatrist or psychologist.

An important factor in mental health is what psychologists call self-efficacy, a belief that you can do what's necessary to survive. This is similar to what is sometimes called the will to live. In coping with any illness, particularly chronic illness, your own belief that you can handle a situation are important. Positively reinforcing your successes in learning to control or manage pain can help you feel powerful enough to meet the challenge of living with pain.

Also of interest is a concept called self-reinforcement. Self-reinforcement can help you reestablish a feeling of self-control. Basically, self-reinforcement involves rewarding yourself when you achieve a goal. Many people with chronic pain, however, become dependent on external rather than self-generated rewards, including the rewards of so-called pain behaviors which may come from caregivers and other people. If this is the case, you may have trouble setting appropriate goals for yourself and reinforcing your own good behavior. Another concern is that people who are depressed often devalue their own performances and find it difficult to reward or recognize their own achievements, even when they make a significant breakthrough.

BREAKING THE PAIN CYCLE

The chronic pain syndrome involves not only the physical experience of pain, but also poor patterns of thinking, behavior, and communication that reinforce physical and mental disability. In pain treatment programs, psychologists, social workers, dietitians, physical therapists, and occupational therapists can assist you in the process of mentally and physically strengthening yourself. They can give you useful tools to help self-manage pain.

Although the experience is different for every person, chronic pain often has an emotional cycle, which can begin and end in hope. According to Nelson Hendler, M.D., an assistant professor of neurosurgery at Johns Hopkins University, Baltimore, Maryland, this cycle begins with chronic pain. In the beginning, people are frequently optimistic, able to bear their pain even if it is quite severe. After a couple of months, though, emotions such as fear, anxiety, apprehension, and dread may set in. If six months pass with no medical relief, depression often sets in. When this occurs, it's important to understand that depression is treatable. Emotional problems can be dealt with even if the actual level of pain doesn't subside. Acceptance is the fourth stage for many chronic pain patients, Hendler says, at which you accept the fact that you may have just some ongoing pain. At this point, you can actively begin to work or even to fight to regain some control over your life and your environment. In some cases, Hendler adds, the decision to fight back can be both medically and psychologically therapeutic.

DEPRESSION

Many chronic pain patients are depressed. In fact, some doctors believe that chronic pain and depression are basically identical, and that much chronic pain actually should be considered a type of mood disorder. Pain and depression have biological responses in common—both alter levels of certain neurotransmitters that modulate pain. A lack of physical fitness, excessive drug use, stress, and isolation from other people all can contribute to feelings of depression. Depression can intensify the perception of physical pain and the feelings of hopelessness that become part of the pain cycle.

People who suffer from clinical depression typically use more physical and mental health services than other people, although that treatment is likely to be inadequate. Few receive treatment directed at their depression. Suicide rates are high among people with severe depression, another reason why it's important to seek help.

According to research published in 1987, between 30

and 100 percent of chronic pain patients are affected by depression—much higher percentages than may be found among the general population, of which between 9 and 14 percent are depressed. Depression may range from mild to severe, from a mild case of the blues to the most severe form, called clinical depression. Symptoms can include sleep disruption, appetite disturbance, sexual dysfunction or loss of libido, bowel changes, hypochondria, chronic irritability, social withdrawal, inactivity, a lack of interest in normal activities, a depressed mood state, and a feeling that one's life is out of control. If these symptoms continue over a period

WHAT IS DEPRESSION?

While the word *depression* is popularly used to signify a general feeling of the blues, a serious clinical depression (which may be treated by a psychiatrist) has specific diagnostic criteria that include the occurrence of at least four of the following every day for at least two weeks:

- Poor appetite or significant weight loss or weight gain
- Insomnia or hypersomnia
- Psychomotor agitation or retardation
- Loss of interest of pleasure in usual activities, or decreased sex drive
- Loss of energy or fatigue
- Feelings of worthlessness, self-reproach, or excessive or inappropriate guilt
- Complaints or evidence of diminished ability to think or concentrate
- Recurrent thoughts of death

of time, they are signs that a mental health professional should be consulted. From the outside, it can be difficult to identify depression. This is because some people steadfastly deny that they are depressed, preferring to maintain the "stiff upper lip" so prized by our individualistic society. But depression is treatable. If your insurance does not cover visits to a mental health professional such as a psychiatrist, many communities have mental health clinics where services are billed on a sliding scale. Talking with a minister, priest, or religious counselor also may be useful.

You can take action to control indirectly the effects of depression. According to the *American Medical Association Essential Guide to Depression,* lifestyle changes such as being kind to yourself, sticking to a routine that suits you, avoiding recreational drugs and alcohol, educating yourself about depression, giving yourself time to recover and reaching out to others may hasten a recovery during treatment. Counseling, stress-relieving techniques, lifestyle changes, short-term use of antidepressant medications, and even aerobic exercise can help. A 1981 study of depression by the National Institute of Mental Health compared short-term psychotherapeutic treatment, antidepressant medications, and cognitive therapy treatment on people who were depressed and found that all three were more effective than no treatment at all.

Most people are better able to control their actions than their moods. You cannot snap your fingers and make depression go away, but you can act to stop the downward emotional spiral. For instance, doing something you know you usually enjoy, even if you don't feel like it, can be helpful. If your pain awakens you from sleep, you could get up and work on some simple manual task, or read a book until you feel tired, rather than lying in bed and becoming more and more depressed and disheartened about the pain. Doing physical conditioning exercises or relaxation exercises, telephoning a friend, or just taking a walk around the block can help get your mind off your problems when you feel overwhelmed. The slogan "Move Your Muscles, Change Your Thoughts," used by a self-help group of former mental patients called Recovery, Inc., is useful to remember if you are having a bad time, according to psychologist Richard Sternbach.

HOW THERAPY HELPS

Many people who experience chronic pain have intense emotional and psychological reactions to their suffering, bound up with its physical pain and their ideas and perceptions about it.

The experience of chronic pain can be an emotional steamroller—overwhelming and overpowering, seizing the attention so completely that it is difficult to think of anything else. Pain signals a threat to the self, although with chronic pain that signal is often a false alarm. Uncontrolled pain can signal a complete loss of control and independence, perceptions that contribute to depression and even to suicide.

Your personal style of evaluating and reacting to pain also can increase its intensity. If you have a "catastrophic" style of appraising pain—that is, seeing the pain as a series of catastrophic train wrecks—this results in your perceiving excessive threats to the self. This amplification makes it more difficult for you to suppress or divert attention away from the pain.

Addressing emotional and behavioral issues also can

improve your capacity to cope with the pain itself and make it less disabling. Psychological treatment can identify and remedy emotional problems that bring on attacks of pain or make the experience more severe. Coping techniques can be preventive or used during episodes of intense pain.

A good therapist helps you rethink the pain experience. Therapy helps you identify particular problems and devise a treatment strategy. It can be helpful to identify and separate elements of the pain experience that can be pinpointed and addressed, such as improving communications with your spouse or family, rather than seeing the continuing pain as one big, overwhelming problem over which you have absolutely no control. A therapist helps you deal with the

HOW DO YOU LOOK AT PAIN?

During intense pain episodes, many people tend to look at pain as an intrusive, frustrating, stressful, or even over-whelming event. Responses such as taking narcotic medications, seeking treatment at hospital emergency rooms, isolating yourself, tensing muscles, and flooding your mind with negative self-talk are not productive, since these all contribute to the pain cycle. Other ways of thinking about pain may be more productive, as noted in Richard Hanson and Kenneth Gerber's *Coping with Chronic Pain*, par-ticularly when they are combined with positive self-statements during pain episodes. Three ways of concep-tualizing pain include:

Pain as a teacher or reminder. For some people, incidents of acute pain come as a result of physical overexertion or particular emotional stresses, such as arguments with a loved one. If you can learn from these episodes without beating yourself up, it may help you over the long term.

false assumptions that pain signals the disease is progressing, that avoidance of activity will prevent pain, and that you are helpless to control the pain. These assumptions contribute to physical unfitness, inactivity, isolation, suffering, and disability, and stop you from taking action. You also can learn to identify unconscious motivations that lead to unproductive attitudes, patterns of thinking, and self-defeating behavior. Group therapy and educational sessions can help you develop more realistic attitudes and build effective coping skills.

Coping with pain through stress management, cognitive and behavioral coping techniques, communication and assertiveness training, time management, sleep hygiene, and

Pain as an opponent. Rather than viewing pain as the victor who has already won the battle, it might be useful to view pain as a clever opponent who can't quite be defeated, but who aims to get you upset, depressed, or start taking drugs, or who wants to disrupt your life and social relationships. Channel your anger or energy into keeping this opponent at bay by not doing these things, and instead engage in healthy, long-term coping activities and preventive actions.

Pain as a survivable event. Like a surfer riding the waves or a forest animal weathering a squall, intense pain episodes can be seen as natural events with a beginning and an end. You can survive these by gliding through them without the energy-depleting tension and frustration that feed into the pain cycle.

more may be taught to you by mental health professionals, with the aim of helping you deal with the overlapping mental and emotional aspects of continuing pain.

Three Types of Therapy

Psychotherapy, cognitive therapy, and behavioral therapy are three of the methods used in pain programs to deal with the mental aspects of pain. Many combinations of cognitive and behavioral therapy are used at comprehensive pain treatment centers, since these are the fastest to teach and the easiest to apply.

Psychotherapy. Psychotherapy often is a slow process with no guaranteed results, although many individuals benefit from it. Psychotherapy, which doctors call the talking cure, is intended to address mental conflicts that underlie or accompany the experience of chronic pain. These conflicts can come from old experiences in the past, where painful feelings have been suppressed and need to be explored in the light of day. Psychotherapy can be given individually, with one person per therapist, or in a group. People dealing with cancer may benefit from psychotherapy, since it can help them address important issues such as their own mortality.

If pain is seen as a punishment for past actions, the person may feel as though the pain is a sentence imposed from the outside, and feel somehow judged by God. This may feed into feelings of helplessness and hopelessness. In these cases, a skilled therapist can help reinterpret ideas patiently, caringly, and nonjudgmentally, and help a person live with them.

Psychotherapy can help people with disorders such as migraine headaches and peptic ulcers, known as *psychoso-*

matic disorders, in which mental processes affect physical processes that trigger symptoms. *Psychogenic* disorders are those in which the physical process seems to spring directly from the mind, since doctors cannot locate a physical cause. Psychogenic disorders are believed to convert an underlying emotional conflict into a physical symptom, a compulsive preoccupation with pain, or persistent pains with no physical symptom. Psychological counseling can help sufferers of psychosomatic pain and is especially effective on psychogenic disorders. Counseling in general can help people deal with traumatic events.

"When my husband passed away, I wanted to die, and I had enough medication that I could have done it," confesses a woman who suffers from arthritis and fibromyalgia. "That's when I think you need psychotherapy. I've gotten great help from my therapist. You need somebody to talk to, to tell them things you can't tell other people. Some people won't go to a therapist, but it does help if you can let your guard down a little bit. It's good to be able to talk to somebody."

Pain can signal psychological distress. *Somatization* is a word doctors use to describe psychological problems expressed in bodily complaints. Studies have shown that somatization of psychological problems can become more frequent when individuals are under socioeconomic or political pressures or great stress, such as unemployment, migration, or feelings of powerlessness or oppression. Concepts such as somatization are different from the concept of *malingering*, a word used to describe a person who fakes a physical complaint to escape work or collect disability payments.

Cognitive therapy. *Cognitive therapy* is a relatively quick process often given in a group setting. It helps you rethink thought processes that can reinforce pain, and substitutes new and healthy thought processes. Used in most chronic pain treatment programs, cognitive therapy can be effective for problems such as mild to moderate depression, anxiety, guilt, or stress. Researchers at the University of British Columbia in Vancouver, Canada, compared two dozen studies and found that people who used cognitive therapy generally did much better than people who underwent no therapy, people using antidepressant drugs, or people who used other forms of psychotherapy or behavior therapy.

A cognitive process is a thought process. The aim of cognitive therapy is to help you consciously change negative patterns of thinking. It is well known that certain mind-sets can reinforce the perception of pain and suffering. Cognitive therapy attempts to break these unhealthy mind-sets and substitute positive statements for negative ones. "Much more happiness is to be found in the world than gloomy eyes discover," observed the philosopher Friedrich Nietzsche in *Human, All Too Human*.

David D. Burns, M.D., is a research psychiatrist and author of several popular books on cognitive therapy, including *Feeling Good: The New Mood Therapy* and *The Feeling Good Handbook*. Burns believes that distorted thinking results in negative feelings such as guilt, anxiety, and depression. It is the premise of cognitive therapy that this distorted thinking can be turned around.

Some types of distorted thinking include all-or-nothing thinking, dwelling on negative rather than positive elements of a situation, overgeneralizing, discounting the positive, jumping to conclusions, magnifying small problems into disasters, reasoning with your emotions rather than with your mind, denigrating yourself or those around you with

SETTING GOALS

One way to conquer the feeling that your life is spinning out of control is to set goals for yourself. According to the American Chronic Pain Association (ACPA), personal goals can be an important first step toward emotionally and mentally preparing you to regain control of your life. A primary benefit is that setting goals and acting on them will get your mind off your pain and onto something meaningful or useful to you.

Goals can be simple, manageable things that give you a sense of purpose. They can be as simple as getting out of bed and getting dressed every morning, beginning a program of moderate exercise or relaxation training on a regular schedule, making an effort to telephone an old friend, or beginning a hobby or a night class to study something you're interested in. According to the ACPA, goals should be:

- *Concrete and specific.* For instance, rather than a goal of getting more exercise, set a goal of walking up to ten minutes every day by the end of one month.

- *Realistic.* Take into account your personal limitations, such as physical limitations and financial limitations. Purely recreational goals, for instance, don't have to cost a lot of money.

- *Achievable.* These are goals that are within your power to accomplish. For instance, if you have been feeling depressed, simply getting out of the house for a few minutes each day might be achievable. If you are physically able to attend church or temple, but haven't gone in a while, this could be a realistic goal.

"should" and "shouldn't" statements, and blaming yourself for something that is beyond your control.

Many people with chronic pain find themselves mired in negative feelings and thought patterns, locked into self-defeating conversations inside their head that feed into the pain cycle. Cognitive therapy involves a simple, seven-step process to break out of these distorted thinking patterns. The steps are: (1) writing down how you feel about it, (2) identifying the particular event or idea that upset you, (3) identifying your own negative emotions, (4) identifying the negative thought that accompanies the negative emotions, (5) identifying the distortions and substituting more rational responses, (6) reconsidering your upset, and (7) planning corrective action.

Simply turning negative thoughts on their head also can be useful, as indicated below:

Negative: This pain is unbearable, and it will surely kill me.

Positive: This pain may be hard to bear, but I've gotten through it before, and it won't ever kill me.

Negative: I will never be able to cope with this pain.

Positive: If I take steps to help myself, I can cope.

Negative: If the doctors won't cure this disease, I'll never be able to live a normal life again.

Positive: My doctors will do all they can, and meanwhile I can work to become a person who lives a more productive life, and not a helpless invalid.

Negative: I'll never be able to run a marathon again because of this pain.

Positive: I can continue to exercise to keep myself strong and fit—maybe take a walk every day—and this will make me feel better and distract me from my pain.

Shifting your focus of attention also may be seen as a cognitive technique. Listening to music or soothing sounds, focusing on the pain sensations in an objective "scientific" manner, or calling up a happy memory or useful image or future project you'd like to complete are examples of distraction, which is covered in more depth in chapter 8 on stress.

Behavioral therapy. Behavioral therapy, also called *operant conditioning*, is commonly used in pain control centers, where it is combined with stress-reducing skills and psychotherapy. Behavioral therapies, which are now also known as health psychology, place the responsibility for controlling negative behaviors on the patient, who is ultimately most capable of managing its effects. One of the best books on controlling pain through the behavioral approach is Sternbach's *Mastering Pain: A Twelve-Step Program for Coping with Chronic Pain.*

Behavioral therapy regards pain as a conditioned response, or a behavior, that is reinforced by its own emotional, social, or financial payoffs. It often is effective in changing the patient's harmful, self-defeating behavior, and in changing the behavior of family members that reinforces pain and disability. People can fall into negative patterns of behavior quite innocently. People sometimes don't realize they actually are contributing to pain until patterns are broken and improvement occurs. Behavioral therapy can help change the negative behaviors associated with chronic pain to help diminish excessive or unnecessary disability.

Certain patterns of behavior are regarded as pain behaviors. These include the heavy use of painkilling medications, slow and guarded physical movements, expressions of pain with body language, and withdrawal from normal social encounters

BEHAVIOR THERAPY

Behavioral therapy works according to three principles outlined by Fordyce:

- Behavior is largely a function of its consequences
- Behavior followed by positive or rewarding consequences will be maintained or increased in rate
- Behavior which is followed by neural consequences will diminish or drop out altogether

or activities. Pain behaviors feed into depression and other unpleasant emotions, and they can intensify suffering.

The excessive use of analgesic drugs, for instance, is reduced or eliminated in pain management programs. Physical fitness is increased, and emotional turmoil and stress also are reduced. People with chronic pain often live a sedentary lifestyle that includes guarded movements, which result in more avoidance of activity and a downward cycle of inactivity and pain. Withdrawing from social contact, becoming irritable or unresponsive, avoiding activities you once enjoyed, or exaggerating your grunting and groaning while making great demands on caregivers, co-workers, and doctors are examples of negative pain behavior that can be unlearned.

Behavioral therapists assemble baseline data about a particular patient's pain behavior, then systematically reduce it through educational sessions involving both the patient and family members. Family and friends are encouraged to practice positive behaviors that allow the patient to deal with the pain and move on with his life.

According to Wilbert Fordyce, a psychologist who pioneered the behavioral treatment of pain at the University of Washington, Seattle, the roots of certain pain behaviors are deep. Many chronic pain patients have a history of frequent and lasting pain episodes. Certain responses to pain are reinforced during childhood. For instance, a parent might give an unusually warm, nurturing response to a child in pain, or only respond to very blatant pain signals from the child. Children model their parent's behavior and can adopt poor coping skills as a result. When these children become adults, Fordyce says, they can reinforce these pain behaviors in many ways, such as an overly sympathetic response to pain complaints, or with an angry response that the pain sufferer may unconsciously want or feel he or she deserves.

Behaviors can include using a pain complaint to avoid sexual intercourse with a spouse or some unwanted work-related responsibility. A spouse who had been feeling neglected in a marriage might secretly enjoy the good treatment received because of an illness. In behavioral therapy, these are called secondary gains, psychological rewards received from pain. While it is difficult to design an experiment that proves this, a 1987 study found that chronic pain patients reported more intense pain and engaged in less physical activity if their spouses were solicitous. Another research study published in *Psychosomatic Medicine* in 1978 compared two groups of chronic pain patients who were asked to put their arms in ice water. One group's research leader expressed sympathy and suggested he was prepared to reward pain behavior. Another group's leader suggested that pain tolerance and coping would be rewarded. The patients who believed they would be "rewarded" for pain behavior withdrew their arms from the ice water substantially earlier than the second group.

In a third study of patients at high risk of developing chronic back pain, the control group was advised to "let your pain be your guide" as to activity, and to take medication "as needed," more or less conventional medical advice. A second group was asked to take medications regularly, and to exercise on a fixed schedule at a certain level of activity regardless of pain. At the end of the study, the control group was judged to be more "sick" than the group asked to do more regularly.

In his early experiments with this concept, Fordyce described how he and his colleagues fastidiously ignored the complaints of certain chronic pain patients. Doctors were instructed simply to look out the window when these patients complained. After a while, many patients decided to stop complaining and adjusted to their predicament. Doctors saw some dramatic recoveries that they had not expected.

FAMILY SUPPORT

Like people who experience chronic pain, family members often become trapped in manipulative "pain games." The person with pain might become a tyrant at home, controlling other family members with manipulative behaviors: exaggerated moaning, grunting or groaning, subconsciously playing on the caregiver's pity. While it is natural to try to help a person who suffers pain, caregivers should understand that excessive catering actually can increase a patient's awareness of the pain. Unfortunately, many responses and reactions intended to be helpful also are constant reminders of disability and helplessness.

In other cases, family members actually may impede attempts by the patient to do positive things, such as exercise. In this way, tentative attempts at self-management by the patient are sometimes rebuffed or ignored by family members seeking to "protect" the person. These behavioral games can keep the pain sufferer in a disabled mental state, unwilling or unable to make a complete, whole-hearted attempt to live the best possible life. Although it may seem hardhearted, behavioral therapists advise families not to do things for the person in pain that he or she is able to do alone. Family members can learn to praise genuine progress made toward self-management. This can include appropriate emotional support, treating the person with chronic pain as an adult rather than as a child. Organizations such as the American Chronic Pain Association have begun to offer support sessions for family members and children, and a few other organizations provide services and support for caregivers.

Family counseling can help family members address important issues and establish ground rules if needed. Participating in counseling sessions and learning to communicate honestly involves effort by all parties. If caregivers and the person in chronic pain cannot accomplish a manageable measure of rehabilitation at home by working together under a doctor's guidance, then a certified pain treatment center with a strong rehabilitation program may be the best way to go.

EFFECTIVE COMMUNICATION

People with chronic pain often do not always communicate effectively. Sometimes pain behaviors are substituted for honest communication. For instance, if your spouse gives you a nice back rub if you appear to be in pain, you may moan and groan from then on to get the back rub. When you moan and groan, you are using a pain behavior rather than directly asking your spouse for a massage.

People with chronic pain find it difficult to ask for help,

DIFFICULT MOMENTS

When you realize you've fallen into a black hole in your emotions and your mood is bleak and desperate, there are many reasons to hold on to a feeling of hope. Psychologist Richard Sternbach advises men and women who find themselves in this state to remember the following facts:

- Your current mental state is natural but temporary, and will therefore pass.
- There are many reasons to remain hopeful, such as new medical treatments being tested at this moment.
- You'll help yourself if you get up and change what you are doing to something different, preferably something that involves your body, since working your muscles and concentrating on an activity that interests you also helps your frame of mind.

---

or to refuse requests to do difficult physical tasks that they know may make their pain worse. Some may vacillate between communicating passively or not communicating at all, and aggressively lashing out at family members and health care professionals. Effective communication is a healthy, well-lighted middle path between these two rather dark extremes, and it can be learned. Good communication can actually decrease stress, raise self-esteem, and decrease the feeling of hopelessness that comes when you feel no one is listening. Communication is an important coping skill stressed in many treatment programs and by the American Chronic Pain Association.

Negative responses to the physical, mental, and financial

hardships associated with chronic pain can alienate the person who suffers pain from caregivers and family members. Resentments typically smolder for a period of time within a strained relationship before bursting into flames. A pattern of bottling up feelings and then lashing out is common in people with chronic pain. When the person in pain lashes out at loved ones, saying hurtful things, the resulting hurt feeds into a cycle of anger, frustration, and resentment. From an emotional point of view, the chronic illness of one family member affects others in the family. This can result in escalating emotional tension and stress. Family members report increased stress-related complaints and illness when a loved one suffers from chronic pain. M. E. P. Seligman's 1975 book *Helplessness* found that many family members' response to serious illness included insomnia, panic, excessive drinking, depression and other psychological complaints, increased sexual difficulties, and communication and role problems. Divorce rates are higher than normal in these families. The endless strain and emotional pressure can tear a family apart unless steps are taken to manage it.

Straightforward communication is the best way to combat the resentments and other festering emotions that build up over time. Communicating honestly with a person who cares and listens to you is therapeutic. Communications skills are useful in conversations with doctors and medical treatment specialists. Honest communication with any person can be difficult, since it requires a combination of courage, tact, and sensitivity. Rather than passively listening and then angrily lashing out at a doctor for not answering questions you have, try to ask your doctor questions in an honest, direct manner, and listen to his or her response. This can help combat feelings of isolation, helplessness, and depression.

The three basic communication styles are *assertive*, *aggressive*, and *passive*. Identify which style characterizes you, then work to improve it or to make it more effective and consistent. An *assertive* style allows you to ask for what you want or need in a positive way, avoiding the two traps of blaming other people and feeling sorry for yourself. Assertive communication avoids being either too aggressive or too passive. You claim your basic right to answer questions honestly with a yes or a no, and to express how you feel about anything of consequence. An assertive communicator might begin many sentences with the word *I,* which shows ownership of feelings or needs expressed. Ask directly for what you want or need, and repeat your request if necessary. An assertive style might include your setting a definite time to deal with a particular problem, and following through to work on it or solve it without being put off. You aim for a "win-win" situation in this way.

An *aggressive* style also may allow you to get what you want, but often at another person's expense. People who speak aggressively often begin sentences with the word *you.* They try to make choices for other people, and they manipulate. They interrupt others and listen only to what they want to hear, practice one-upmanship and intimidation, and must have the last word. They frequently use the words "always" and "never," and they often feel a sense of "getting even" as they act. An aggressive communication style vents anger, but other people may feel humiliated, hurt, and angry after you've stopped talking. You create a "win-lose" situation by communicating in this way, and you may ultimately turn people away from you.

A *passive* style is overly self-deprecating. You aim to please other people even at great personal cost to yourself. You may hold back ideas, thoughts, feelings, and needs that you have in deference to others. You may manipulate passively by exhibiting a pathetic "poor me" attitude. You allow others to choose what, where, and when for you. You often give up after the first request. If you communicate in this way, you may feel anxious or vaguely disappointed with the result. Ultimately, you may find yourself resenting the person with whom you've been communicating.

Experts agree that the best way to communicate is with an *assertive* style. This is eye-to-eye communication, an exchange between equals, a "win-win" style usually respected by other people. People who communicate assertively often appear confident and dignified, and they feel good about the

THE SIGNAL BREATH

Participants in the chronic pain management program sponsored by the Department of Veterans Affairs in Long Beach, California, are taught a quick coping response called the signal breath. Used anytime, it is a signal to stop and think. It can provide some control over episodes of intense pain, anger, or emotional distress and may lead to wiser or more rational responses.

The signal breath is a deep inhalation that is held for a few moments, then released slowly. At the moment the breath is exhaled, you say or think a cue word or short phrase such as "relax" or "take it easy." At the same time, you scan your body for areas of muscle tension and release the tension with your breath.

Using the signal breath may lower your level of tension at crucial points, and it can give you time to stop and think about what is happening and how you will react.

exchange afterward. Communicating assertively allows you to ask for what you want, and to take responsibility for your own actions, so you automatically feel better about yourself. You avoid the muscle tension that seems to accompany aggressive and passive communications styles. If you're angry, take a deep breath and think for a minute before you speak. Beginning sentences with "I feel . . ." rather than "You should . . ." is a good place to start.

Although words are important, most communication actually takes place through body language. Body language that accompanies an assertive style finds people leaning forward as they speak and making eye contact. Aggressive body language can include adopting an aggressive posture, making threatening gestures, or raising your voice and shouting as you talk. A passive communication style can be accompanied by cowering body language or manner. Holding yourself tightly coiled or with your arms folded hard across your chest, staring coldly out the window, sends a nonverbal message that tells the world "Keep away." Smiling, winking, laughing, kissing, hugging, or touching another person in a caring, loving way sends a positive nonverbal message.

SEXUAL ACTIVITY

Sexual activity is a mild stress reliever that can decrease the physical and emotional aspects of pain. If sex is enjoyable, it can result in a good night's sleep. Sexual activity can be a pleasant if temporary diversion from pain, frequently causing it to disappear for a while. A study in Chicago's Cook County Hospital found that arthritis patients, after having sex, were completely free of pain for several hours. Another study at Rutgers University found that women could tolerate as much as 75 percent more pain when they were experiencing sexual pleasure.

Sexual problems are not uncommon in chronic pain. Several studies have linked pain with sexual dysfunction. A 1987 study of patients with low back pain found that more than two-thirds of respondents reported a deterioration in their sexual lives, including disinterest, physical incapacitation, and fear of increased pain. A study published in *Comprehensive Psychiatric Nursing* in 1975 found that only 10 to 20 percent of chronic pain clients seeking help with sexual issues had purely physical problems. A loss of sexual function can feed into a cycle of depression, anxiety, and deterioration of important relationships.

Even though it is a human need, sex isn't an easy thing to discuss for most people. Fear of failure, sexual and performance anxiety, and fear of rejection are powerful psychological factors contributing to sexual dysfunction. Physical factors such as muscle atrophy and limited joint movement—and fears associated with movement— also can contribute to sexual malaise. Prescription and nonprescription drugs can negatively affect the libido or sexual function, as can alcohol, marijuana, and even tobacco.

Medical doctors often are reluctant to ask questions about sex, and patients usually aren't eager to bring these matters up. Education, marital counseling, open and direct communication between partners, and behavioral sex therapy with the spouse's participation can help resolve problems. National organizations such as the American Association of Sex Educators, Counselors, and Therapists, and the American Association of Marriage and Family Therapists (see the appendix at the back of this book) can refer you to therapists in your area.

You can learn ways to compensate for the physical aspects of sexual dysfunction. For instance, for a person with arthritis whose hip and sacroiliac joint motion is limited, a side-to-side position during intercourse may be better than the missionary position for either partner because it relieves

STEPS TO MANAGE PAIN

In his book *Mastering Pain*, psychologist Richard Sternbach outlines the following twelve steps to coping with chronic pain:

1. Accept the fact of having chronic pain.

2. Set specific goals for work, hobbies, and social activities toward which you will work.

3. Let yourself get angry at your pain if it seems to be getting the best of you.

4. Take your analgesics on a strict time schedule, and then taper off until you are no longer taking any.

5. Get in the best physical shape possible, and keep fit.

6. Learn how to relax, and practice relaxation techniques regularly.

7. Keep yourself busy.

8. Pace your activities.

9. Have your family and friends support only your healthy behavior, not your invalidism.

10. Be open and accessible with your doctor.

11. Practice effective empathy with others having pain problems.

12. Remain hopeful.

stress on these joints and allows for more relaxed lovemaking. The timing for sexual activity can be adjusted; many chronic pains flare up at night but decrease around noon and the middle of the afternoon, which may be the best time for lovemaking. Advance preparation such as the application of moist heat, a warm bath, or range-of-motion exercises may help loosen joints and facilitate intercourse. Mild aerobic exercise also can help improve endurance and physical stamina. Water-based lubricants can help women prepare for intercourse. Vibrators may be used from time to time, but sex therapists say they should not be used to avoid other forms of sexual stimulation involving another person.

Sex is not the only way of saying "I love you." Alternatives to regular sexual intercourse can include kissing, holding, hugging, caressing, massage, oral sex, masturbation, and other mutually pleasurable physical expressions of love.

Psychological and social factors contribute to the experience of chronic pain in an important way. Depression, anxiety, anger, and other strong emotions impact your personal and family life. Behavioral therapy, cognitive therapy, psychotherapy, good communication skills, family counseling, and sex therapy can help you deal with aspects of emotional or social problems and prepare you to move on with your life. Chapter 5 addresses physical conditioning, which helps relieve pain and strengthens the body and the mind.

CHAPTER FIVE

Physical Conditioning

∾ *Combating physical deconditioning with exercise, physical therapy, and some simple methods that relieve pain.*

Conservative treatments aimed at breaking the pain cycle include many forms of physical therapy, exercise, and self-administered manual pain control methods that are safe, mild, and noninvasive. Perhaps most important is exercise, which directly combats the physical unfitness that is part of the chronic pain syndrome. At multidisciplinary pain centers, physical and occupational therapists can help you become more physically fit. Achieving fitness involves finding your true physical limits, incorporating them into a program of regular exercise, and pacing your activities. Heat and cold therapy, massage, postural correction techniques, transcutaneous electrical nerve stimulation (TENS), acupuncture, and other conservative treatments all may help relieve pain.

THE IMPORTANCE OF MOVEMENT

Regular movement or exercise is a cornerstone of many chronic pain programs and a good self-management practice. The movement of our arms and legs, the beating of our hearts, even simple acts such as smiling, eating, and breathing involve the use of muscles. Our bodies were made to move every day, and moving the muscles regularly has many health benefits.

People with chronic pain often don't move around very much. For those who are in bad physical shape, exercise must be approached carefully and methodically. If movements are painful, doctors of rehabilitation medicine, osteopaths, or physical therapists may begin a fitness program gently, using special techniques to help you gradually work up to more manageable levels.

The good news is that physical fitness is a contrary factor to chronic pain. Exercise increases the level of natural painkillers such as endorphins. It reduces anxiety, depression, and stress, and helps you control or stabilize your weight. Physical fitness increases the general feeling of well-being and makes other enjoyable physical activities possible.

Conditioning the heart and lungs increases overall blood circulation and makes it easier to breathe. Fitness increases muscle endurance and flexibility. Exercise builds muscular suppleness and strength. Increased physical fitness actually raises pain tolerance. A strong, physically fit body is more able to resist painful insults and recovers more rapidly after they occur.

PHYSICAL UNFITNESS

Many chronic pain patients fall into an extremely sedentary lifestyle. Physical unfitness or deconditioning, often accompanied by musculoskeletal pain, is part of the chronic pain syndrome. A lack of physical activity helps create physical problems such as muscle atrophy, shrunken joint capsules, a weakened heart and lungs, and more. Physical inactivity reduces the body's supply of oxygen, necessary enzymes, and other nutrients. Believing yourself unable to do much useful work or to carry on familiar activities, obsessed by a thousand worries, you also may gain weight. This puts further strain on the skeleton and supporting muscles, which are already weakened from disuse.

A basic assumption at multidisciplinary pain centers is that the physical limits that patients impose on their own activities are frequently excessive, and that some disability is self-imposed. You may impose limitations on your own physical activity because of fear, depression, and other psychological or social factors. Sometimes you limit your activities because of a belief that resting and restricting activity will somehow lessen your pain. In the acute phase of your condition, your doctors may have told you, "If it hurts, don't do it." This is good advice for acute pain, because it assists healing. It usually is not good advice for chronic pain, because too much inactivity feeds into social isolation. Thinking constantly about the pain intensifies anxiety and depression. Depression itself contributes to the cycle of physical inactivity, since depression decreases your energy and your desire to participate in physical or even social activities.

Attempts to avoid pain, though helpful in the short term, may be harmful over time. For instance, painful memories associated with certain postures can lead to a constant avoidance of these postures, which atrophies the unused skeletal muscles and creates pain. Over time, avoiding particular movements actually limits your ability to move, since muscles weaken and joints shrink with disuse. Moving less and less in an attempt to avoid pain thus leads to a cycle of more inactivity and more pain. Sometimes people with chronic pain develop an irrational fear of certain activities, such as those involving their back, which leads them to avoid some activities that they actually might do without harming themselves.

Excessive drug use contributes to inactivity. Pain-relieving drugs hamper your ability to find your true physical limits, blunt normal pain sensations connected with exercise, and contribute in other ways to physical unfitness and depression. For this reason, reducing or eliminating your use of pain medications during treatment at a pain center can help you become physically fit.

FITNESS

Becoming physically fit strengthens your body, improves mobility, and may help you sleep better. Good physical fitness helps all the important interlocking systems of the body—including the digestive system, the respiratory system, the cardiovascular system, and the immune system—do their work. Each has a role in good health. Remember that physical unfitness only gets worse if you stay in bed and try not to move at all.

Every person's physical capabilities decline with age. We do have human limits. This is the reason that professional athletes in prime physical condition eventually bow out of sports at which they excel. A number of changes overtake the human body with age, but many of these may be minimized by regular activity or moderate exercise. A study reported in the *Journal of American Geriatrics* showed that when seventy-year old subjects began a program of moderate activity, their oxygen intake increased the equivalent of fifteen years.

People in chronic pain may have experienced serious injuries, surgery, or degenerative diseases that truly limit their activities. These are real limits and are not self-imposed. Finding your true limits while continuing a physical conditioning program to keep you in the best shape possible has many benefits. When you are able to do more, the quantity of your activities and the quality of your life also will improve. Learn to pace yourself. You may find you can do some things you have long avoided because you only thought you couldn't do them.

In the beginning, exercise can produce pain, since lactic acids are produced by continued muscle action. The range of muscle movements often is drastically reduced by lack of exercise. Mobility at the joint is reduced from inactivity. Even the idea of exercise is frightening to some people, since they fear inflicting further injury on themselves. Although it may be uncomfortable, exercise will not cause injury if properly supervised and if done with the appropriate quality of movement. The discomfort of exercise is beneficial in the long run and should be distinguished from the pain of chronic pain.

Under the guidance of a doctor or physical therapist, your existing physical limitations should be taken into account before you begin any program. Exercise may be advised to the point of discomfort, but never to the point of extreme pain. It's common sense to begin exercising gently, gradually building up your strength and endurance. If pain occurs during exercise and persists, discuss this fully with the physical therapist or doctor who prescribed it for you. Exercise recommended by a medical doctor, called an exercise prescription, may need to be modified from time to time.

BENEFITS OF EXERCISE

- More muscle strength
- Less body fat
- More energy
- Better breathing
- Less joint pain
- More flexibility
- Less depression
- Better memory
- Increased reasoning
- Increased self-confidence
- Better sleep
- Less chance of heart attack

A little exercise always helps, but regularity and frequency are the two most important factors in benefiting from exercise. Many pain programs have two short exercise sessions each day. Even if therapeutic exercise is begun in a pain program, exercise should be continued at home for all the emotional and physical benefits it provides. Remove all the obstacles that you can. Exercise pays off in a more fit and well-conditioned body. It increases your pain tolerance and lets you make better use of your life.

It's important to begin any program of exercise gradually, particularly if you are greatly out of shape. Physical therapists can help you launch an exercise program appropriate to you. If you begin a program on your own, of course, consult your medical doctor first.

At pain centers, physical therapists establish a baseline for your exercise sessions. Many suggest you start exercises *below* your current level of capability, working up to greater levels of fitness from there. The idea is to build on success. Progress may be charted after each session, and charting also is an excellent strategy to follow when exercising at home. Physical therapists help improve patient *function,* defined as an ability to live and work in a normal manner. Although many people frequently see pain relief as necessary before they can function, great increases in functional capacity are possible without it.

Exercise sessions are supervised at pain centers. You should be carefully taught the proper way to do each exercise, and observed to see that you're doing it correctly. The physical therapist seeks to develop good form and good exercise habits that will not lead to injury. As an aspect of behavioral therapy, bellyaching and complaining during exercise is discouraged, and encouragement is given when goals are met. Unlike other therapeutic exercises, those you learn at a pain center should not be abandoned after treatment, and should be continued at home.

Good physical therapists help you work within your limits to increase strength and stamina. Ultimately, this makes it easier for you to live a productive life even if you have some continuing pain. While increasing your fitness level, physical therapists should take your particular medical condition into account from the beginning. For instance, the pain of fibromyalgia often decreases with increased physical activity, so a program of regular exercise frequently helps decrease this pain. People with arachnoiditis, an inflamation of the spine, however, can be helped by gentle exercise, but pushing too hard actually can make the pain worse.

Physical therapy often is combined with occupational therapy, which focuses on building purposeful self-management skills. Occupational therapists work to increase your independence and ease of movement through practical methods to decrease the amount of time you spend in pain. For example, pacing and energy conservation skills can help you carry out daily activities at work or at leisure. Learning these skills and putting them to use in your life can be quite empowering.

PHYSICAL THERAPY

Under a medical doctor's supervision, the physical therapist treats chronic pain with a number of methods, depending on the ailment. Some of these are preludes to exercise therapy, and some relieve symptoms. Frequently, some trial and error is involved. Physical therapy ideally enables you to begin an integrated plan of flexibility, strength, endurance, and conditioning exercises that reduces disability and increases ability.

As an example, physical therapy for osteoarthritis can include an education in what constitutes good posture. Postural correction can take pressure off arthritic joints and affected muscles—so can using a mobility aid such as a walker or cane to take weight off hips or knees. At home, you can follow through by making sure you have proper back support in your furniture and car seats, and a firm mattress in the bedroom, since a poorly designed mattress that is too soft or too hard can intensify discomfort and pain. Overall mobility can be increased with passive movement of the joints, leading to more active exercise. Trigger-point therapy can help if muscles around the arthritic joint are in pain. These three physical therapy techniques, used in the

GOOD POSTURE

Here are some general tips on establishing good postural habits:

- *Standing posture.* The ideal standing posture is somewhere between an exaggerated "military" stance and slumping forward. The head should be balanced on the bones of the neck without straining, with shoulders relaxed. Rather than standing with your weight on your heels, rock forward until most of your weight is on the balls of your feet; this causes your head and shoulders to settle into a more balanced position.

- *Sitting posture.* If you feel stiff when you stand up, you may have poor sitting posture. This can come from uncomfortable furniture that doesn't properly support the back, or from poor postural habits. Specially designed chairs support the back, as does inserting a pillow between the chair and the small of the back. Pushing your car seat too far forward or too far back while driving can cause you to crane your head too far forward, straining the back or neck muscles. As a general rule, don't sit in any one position for a long time without taking a break.

- *Reclining posture.* Lying on your back, with your head propped up sharply for reading or watching television, can be hard on your back. Also harmful to the back is sleeping on the stomach, with your head turned to one side. The best sleeping posture is on the side, with limbs loosely flexed, using a good plump pillow thick enough to support the neck comfortably.

treatment of many ailments, can relieve pain and prepare the body for more vigorous activity.

Postural correction techniques can help with many types of joint and muscle pain, and can alleviate back or neck pain. In 1947, the Academy of Orthopaedic Surgery defined *standard posture* as a skeletal alignment in which the parts of the body are relatively arranged in a state of balance that protects the supporting structures against injury or progressive deformity. Small microinjuries, stress, and tension result from poor postural habits, which eventually compress joint surfaces, cause adaptive shortening of soft tissues, and put additional strain on ligaments and disc structures. Poor standing, sitting, or sleeping posture habits all contribute to pain. Habits such as thrusting the head forward to look at a computer monitor, watch a television screen, or read a book can increase pain. Like any bad habit, poor posture requires discipline and conscious effort to break. The first step is learning what constitutes poor posture and consciously working to correct it. Two of the better-known methods are the Alexander technique, which focuses on good posture and weight distribution, and the Feldenkrais technique, which focuses more on harmonious movement.

Passive movement basically involves the physical therapist moving or stretching particular parts of the body for you. If your normal *range of movement* has shrunk, the physical therapist slowly enlarges it with therapeutic exercises. Passive movement is sometimes preceded by heat and cold applications to reduce muscle spasms and attendant pain, or a by "spray and stretch" technique involving spraying the skin with a rapidly evaporating liquid such as fluoromethane. This cools the skin and relaxes the muscles, allowing the therapist to stretch the arm, leg, or other body part to a fuller extension. Stretching the muscle out to its original resting length is the only way to achieve long-term relief. As a rule of thumb, pain should not persist more than a minute or two after this type of stretching. Gradually, the therapist shifts over to *active movement* assisted by the patient.

Trigger-point therapy is a technique to relieve pain in sensitive knots or areas of muscle or connective tissue, which refer pain elsewhere. Trigger points can be desensitized by a number of methods, including spray and stretch, TENS, ultrasound, vibration, massage, acupuncture, or injections. With the help of an anesthesiologist, trigger points deeper in the tissue can be treated with an injection of a local anesthetic such as lidocaine, a saline solution, a corticosteroid, or sometimes dry needling with nothing injected at all. If muscular injections relieve pain that is referred elsewhere, doctors assume the muscle contains at least one trigger point. Pain relief sometimes continues even after the anesthetic wears off, but it is not understood why. The surface of the skin over sore muscles sometimes has a lumpy or knotty appearance that can be treated with a form of massage called *myofascial release.*

In addition, forms of skin stimulation such as heat treatments can be useful in relieving the pain of osteoarthritis. One fairly common treatment submerges hands into a bath of warm, soothing melted paraffin. Massage is helpful, and TENS can relieve joint pain, as can acupuncture. Chiropractic treatment is a possibility but should be approached cautiously, since manipulating the joints can irritate them and increase pain.

Many of the techniques of physical therapy, such as postural correction or heat and cold treatments, can be utilized at home on an as-needed basis under your doctor's guidance. Regular exercise is useful over the long term for arthritis and most other disorders which cause chronic pain, because exercise helps maintain joint mobility and minimizes muscle wasting.

THE BENEFITS OF EXERCISE

Stretching, conditioning, strength building, and aerobic exercise all are useful in strengthening and conditioning the body. The basic principle of exercise is to "overload" the body with a bit more work than it typically receives. You build up strength as the body adapts to the overload by becoming stronger. Exercise helps break the chronic pain cycle.

Stretching exercises, one of the gentlest forms, are useful as a starting point. Stretching muscles greatly enhances your ability to get around. A few simple stretching movements may help relieve morning stiffness and help you get out of bed. In general, stretching improves blood circulation and provides other benefits, including toning the muscles and returning them to their normal resting length, which helps prevent injuries. This helps reduce pain.

After checking with your doctor, stretching exercises may be begun at home. The American Chronic Pain Association advises that you set aside a regular time of day to do these, establishing a routine that is easy to follow. If you're somewhat out of shape, it's best to begin stretching exercises at a modest level and to gradually increase the length of your sessions. Stretch only until you feel a gentle pull on muscles rather than pain. Some slow, rhythmic background music may help you get into the swing of it. Warm-up exercises such as walking or riding a stationary bicycle for five to ten minutes at an easy pace can warm the muscles a bit, making stretching and other exercises easier.

Aerobic exercise helps condition the heart and lungs, parts of the body often in need of conditioning after periods of prolonged inactivity. Aerobic exercise is rhythmic and continuous, and increases the breathing and blood flow. About twenty to thirty minutes of continual aerobic exercise at moderate intensity helps condition the heart and lungs. Aerobic exercise increases the flow of oxygen to the muscles up to twenty-fold, and it can increase oxygen extraction by the muscles by 400 percent.

Aerobic exercise is particularly beneficial for people with back pain, fibromyalgia, and arthritis. It helps discharge muscular and emotional tension that accompany stress. Aerobic exercise wards off depression and anxiety by increasing the production of endorphins. The skeletal muscles respond to endurance conditioning—muscle mass, capillary density, and mitochondrial density all increase, as do levels of beneficial chemicals such as ATP (adenosine triphosphate), phosphorus, and creatine.

The choice of aerobic exercise should be made carefully. Walking, swimming, and bicycle riding are low-impact aerobic exercises. Walking is one of the most natural, simple, and gentlest of all aerobic exercises. Swimming is relaxing, and the water takes the weight off painful joints and muscles. Stationary bicycles are available in most gyms and can be used at home in any weather.

Conditioning exercises basically repeat an exercise at less than maximum load until the muscles involved are fatigued. Exercise bicycles, Nordic tracks, and treadmills often are used in conditioning exercises. *Strength-building* exercises are those in which the body works against a resistance to build strength. These can be provided by weight machines that may be adjusted to the individual. Exercising to music can be a helpful motivator at home or at the gym.

Note: *Your medical doctor or physical therapist may assign you an exercise prescription. If not, always obtain your doctor's approval before you begin an exercise program at home.*

Choosing an Exercise

Mall-walking programs, exercise classes, and classes in dance, yoga, Tai Chi, and more are offered in many communities and at local schools and colleges, YMCAs, or senior citizens centers. Being in bed is no excuse not to exercise, because armchair exercises are available that allow a patient to exercise even from his or her wheelchair or hospital bed.

Aquatic therapy, or exercise in water, is sometimes quite useful in the treatment of chronic pain. Aquatic therapy is very low impact and especially good for low back pain. Water is buoyant and has a natural cushioning effect. In shoulder-deep water, it is believed that the body loses 90 percent of its weight, allowing you to tolerate longer exercise sessions and sessions that are more intense. To stand up in a swimming pool, you must keep your center of buoyancy, which is your chest, in line with your center of gravity at your hips; this strengthens and increases the length of trunk stabilization muscles.

One popular public exercise program is the YMCA's Healthy Back Program. Introduced in 1976, the program addresses exercise, stress reduction techniques, and the causes of back pain. Once you finish the program, you continue it at home on a daily basis. It targets people who don't need back surgery but have chronic back pain. In the first four years of the program, the YMCA estimated that one-third of the hundreds of thousands of participants in their program had achieved complete freedom from back pain, while another 50 percent reported improvement in pain relief and greater freedom of movement.

Choose an exercise or set of exercises that you can continue. Look at obstacles that may keep you from exercising, and use your head to remove or work around them. Choosing an activity you enjoy, varying your form of exercise, exercising with a buddy, enrolling in a class, setting aside a particular time of day to exercise, rewarding yourself for accomplishing goals, and simply not allowing yourself to procrastinate are useful in maintaining your program. Keeping a chart of your progress is helpful because it gives you tangible evidence of what you've accomplished.

Select a form of exercise which you enjoy, since this makes you more likely to continue. A little exercise helps relieve tension. Even taking a walk around the block rather than sitting for a few minutes in a rocking chair may alter your frame of mind. Expect to begin exercising slowly, and build up your sessions and your strength over a period of weeks or months. Sensible, appropriate, self-directed exercise can be done at home.

At comprehensive pain treatment centers, one of the last phases in the physical conditioning process is called work hardening, a directed form of exercise that typically takes two to six weeks. As the name implies, work hardening is task specific, aiming to get the patient's muscles close to normal before returning to employment.

Pacing Yourself

An important aspect to any exercise program, or to living or working with chronic pain, is the common sense concept of pacing. Pacing helps you strike a balance among all the things you wish to do and any limits your physical condition might impose on your activity.

By the time some people with chronic pain enter multi-disciplinary pain programs, they have become sedentary and discouraged. Many don't attempt to do what they actually might be able to do with just a few simple changes in how they do them.

You can slowly take action to improve your ability to function in the world. As your physical condition improves, you may find that many things can be accomplished a little at a time, step by step, if appropriately paced.

Sometimes a balance needs to be struck between too much and too little physical activity. Both men and women have good days and bad days. On the bad days, you may wake up miserable and stiff, take a lot of pain medication, stay in bed, and not attempt to do anything. When the good days come around and you feel better, you may overexert yourself in an effort to make up for lost time. If you jump into too much activity, this may put you back in bed the next day, with more pain.

A process of trial and error is involved in pacing. Begin any activity gradually, then slowly increase your exertion. Pay attention to such details as good posture, good environmental supports such as chairs and car seats, and proper ways of accomplishing physical tasks, such as lifting, which should be done carefully and correctly with good body mechanics.

It's important to remember that you probably won't be able to do things exactly the same way, and at the same speed, as you did them before your chronic pain condition began or when you were at your youthful physical peak. This is only a fact of life. You will benefit from knowing your limits, and sometimes you may have to communicate these limits to another person. Assertively saying no when you are asked to do something you know you can't physically do does not mean you are a bad spouse, a weakling, or a slacker. Give yourself the same leeway you would give to another person who was asked to do something he or she could not safely do.

Avoid holding yourself to impossibly high standards, a dead-end street that will only frustrate you and increase your pain. You are who you are. Strike a balance you can accept, a balance between your actual limits and the demands of your life. Take breaks while you engage in any activity, or

HEAVY LIFTING

Accomplishing physical tasks such as heavy lifting requires attention to good body mechanics. Basically, this means using the body in a way that does not create additional stress or strain. A few basic tips include:

- Take your time and plan the task beforehand.
- Divide very heavy loads into smaller loads whenever possible.
- Use mechanical aids such as pushcarts, dollies, and hand trucks to help you accomplish a task.
- Use good lifting techniques, such as bending at the knees to pick up heavy loads, and avoiding twisting or turning while lifting.
- Ask for help if you need it.

accomplish the task in segments or at a slower speed. If you become so wrapped up that you forget to take breaks, there is a price to be paid. Occupational therapists advise taking steps to remind yourself that you need a break. Use a kitchen timer or an alarm clock set to remind you to stop at a certain time. Taking a break also can involve planning ahead, such as dividing a task into small segments. For instance, you might prepare your Sunday dinner a dish or two at a time, taking a rest in between. Or you might sweep or vacuum your house a little at a time, rather than doing the whole house nonstop. You might take frequent breaks while gardening, stopping to rest before you actually get tired.

When you take a break, do something different with your body, such as stretching your legs, sitting down, lying down, or standing up. Breaks may be good times to utilize stress-reducing techniques, ride your stationary bicycle for a few minutes, or do something enjoyable such as writing a letter or an E-mail to an old friend.

Pacing is an important principle in any activity, including exercise, because taking it easy allows you to build up stamina over the long term.

SKIN STIMULATION TECHNIQUES

Many skin stimulation techniques used by physical therapists also may be applied at home as a temporary respite from pain. The skin's many sensory nerves are stimulated by these therapies, which can temporarily decrease the sensation of pain. Acupuncture and many forms of skin stimulation are believed to work on the principle of counterirritation, since they combat pain by creating other sensations that close the "gates" that prevent pain impulses from traveling to the brain.

Your doctor may recommend the use of certain skin stimulation techniques at home on an as-needed basis. One advantage is that these treatments do allow the spouse or family members to become involved in your care. Ideally, this strengthens the bond between caregiver and patient, becoming a physical expression of caring or of love, which also can provide relief. Educating caregivers in these techniques gives them practical methods to use at home and can improve the quality of decision making and overall assertiveness. Skin stimulation techniques are pain control tools that can be used along with other coping techniques such as progressive relaxation and biofeedback to interrupt the pain cycle.

Skin stimulation techniques include heat and cold treatments, massage, and TENS. Acupuncture works a bit differently, but is also included here.

Heat and Cold

Heat and cold treatments can be used separately or together. A few of the high-tech methods must be applied by physical therapists, but most can be used as self-help treatments at home. Both heat and cold must be used in moderation, and they are not suitable for the relief of all types of pain. As a general rule, cold provides longer-lasting relief than heat does.

Heat treatments dilate blood vessels, bringing more oxygen to tissues that are irritated by products such as lactic acid. Heat can reduce sensitivity to pain and alleviate joint stiffness, as well as reduce gastric acidity. By rendering the collagen in cells more supple, heat makes muscles easier to move. Treatments typically are given at 104 to 113 degrees Fahrenheit at point of contact.

Applications can be in the form of a towel soaked in hot water, a hot water bottle, an electric heating pad, special hot packs, or infrared lamps. Warm liquids are especially soothing—dipping the hands in warm paraffin to relieve the pain of arthritis, for example. A long hot bath, a warm shower, whirlpool bath, or sauna can be enormously pleasurable. In hydrotherapy, heat relieves pain while the buoyancy of the water takes the stress off the back.

Topical ointments containing menthol or other substances are not technically heat treatments, but they do give the skin a "warmed" feeling. Although these ointments do not actually heat tissues, blood vessels near the skin are dilated and carry additional blood to the area, providing pain relief for muscle soreness. Lotions such as Zostrix contain capsaicin, an alkaloid found in the common pepper plant, which stimulates the release of pain-producing Substance P from peripheral nerves and reduces its synthesis. This can reduce pain, as Substance P helps transmit pain from the extremities to the central nervous system. Topical applications of capsaicin have been used to treat post-herpetic neuralgia, cluster headaches, diabetic neuropathy, phantom limb pain, and osteoarthritis.

Deep heat treatments can relieve pain underneath the skin, but the special devices used in these treatments should be operated by a physical therapist trained in their use. No deep heat treatment device should be used over cancerous areas or near the eyes.

Infrared therapy acts about one-third an inch below the skin surface and can relieve the pain of several forms of arthritis, torn muscles, and bursitis. *Diathermy* uses short-wave radio frequencies to speed up the motions of atoms and molecules in cells. It is used only in a clinical setting to elevate muscle temperatures and increase blood flow for a condition such as osteoarthritis of the knee. *Microwave therapy* utilizes electromagnetic radiation to create heat.

Deep tissue pain is sometimes treated by *ultrasound,* which directs high-frequency sound waves above the limits of the human ear to the painful area. Ultrasound works best on painful tissues heavy with collagen such as muscles, tendons, and ligaments. When used with a topical cream containing aspirin or cortisone, ultrasound helps the cream penetrate the skin. Ultrasound can be used with muscle stimulation to treat muscle spasms and fibrous tissue adhesions. *Electrogalvanic stimulation* (EGS) uses a mild alternating electrical current that causes blood vessels to dilate. Portable ultrasound and EGS units can be used at home under professional supervision.

Cold treatments aim to lower temperatures to around 59 degrees Fahrenheit at the skin. This inhibits muscle contractions or spasms, cools the muscles, slows down activities within the cells, and anesthetizes nerve fibers. Most cold treatments are self-applied, but "spray and stretch" treatments are used by physical therapists to cool the skin prior to passive exercise.

Cold compresses that can be used at home include ready-made cold packs, a plastic bag full of ice, or a bag of frozen vegetables. A sort of ice Popsicle can be made by freezing water in a small Styrofoam cup, then tearing off the top half and using the lower half to insulate the hand while ice is applied to the skin. Cold treatments can effectively relieve pain. People with circulation impairment or who are sensitive to cold should be cautious when applying cold treatments or ice massage. Any application of cold materials should be limited to a maximum of twenty minutes per hour and should be discontinued if the skin becomes pale.

Massage

Massage is probably the oldest method of relieving muscle stiffness, swelling, and pain. Not too long ago, back rubs were given by nurses as a matter of course to reduce anxiety levels in patients, but nurses are so busy these days that the practice has been abandoned. Professional *massage therapists* practice many different forms of massage, and massage can also be learned and performed at home.

Most people enjoy being massaged, either by a professional masseuse or by a friend or family member. You may massage yourself. Gently and carefully massaging aching hands, feet, and other parts of the body may relieve pain and provide a measure of physical and emotional comfort.

Massage basically relaxes tense muscles. It reduces pain by stimulating the circulation of lymph and by dilating the blood vessels and stimulating blood flow. Speeding up the blood flow to muscles helps carry away irritating biological by-products produced by inflammation, which soothes nerve endings. A study in Norway found that massage increases levels of endorphins by about 16 percent, and that endorphin levels remain high for about an hour afterward. There is some evidence that massage increases levels of serotonin, another substance that can inhibit pain.

A study at Johns Hopkins School of Medicine in Baltimore, Maryland, found that pain patients who were touched felt better—their heart rates slowed, and their ability to tolerate pain was increased. A study at the University of South Carolina in Columbia found that a ten-minute massage decreased cancer pain significantly in men, although women who were massaged found lower levels of relief. Touching is usually comforting. Hugs, embraces, kisses, and a good massage can lift the spirit, and contribute to feelings of well-being and good health.

Swedish massage, popularized by a Swedish physician almost two-hundred years ago, is most popular in the West. It involves stroking and kneading the skin, muscles, and connective tissues to relax the body. *Shiatsu massage,* which originated in Japan, utilizes finger pressure on sensitive acupuncture points, aiming to release trapped energy and induce relaxation. In an experiment with patients in chronic pain conducted at Phelps Memorial Hospital in New York City, 86 percent of patients achieved significant pain relief when they received shiatsu massage twice a week. The American Massage Therapy Association administers professional certification to massage therapists, and some states license these therapists as well. Classes, books, and videos provide instruction in massage techniques.

Even mechanical forms of massage can help relieve pain. For instance, vibrators and vibrating beds relieve pain in some people. A 1993 study of patient satisfaction found that massage, vibration, and heat were the most popular methods of relieving the pain of cancer.

TENS

Transcutaneous electrical nerve stimulation uses mild electrical impulses delivered to the skin by hand-held, battery-powered devices. It has become a popular method of relieving muscle and joint pain; a quarter of a million units are prescribed by doctors each year in the United States. TENS is believed to work by increasing endorphin production or stimulating the large-diameter nerve fibers, altering the balance of painful stimuli entering the spinal cord. For maximum benefit, TENS should be used as early as possible in a treatment program. The method works best on reasonably localized pain and usually is more effective when combined with other therapies.

Pain experts Ronald Melzack and Patrick Wall say that TENS has a cumulative effect, and that people who do not benefit may not have been properly instructed in the operation of the machine, or told how frequently to use it. Correct use usually involves placing electrodes "between the pain and the brain," or along nerve roots, pain pathways, or near trigger points. TENS devices adjust to provide a range of electrical strengths and pulses for different types of pain.

About 70 percent of people respond favorably to TENS, according to some estimates. A 1976 study of 104 chronic pain patients showed that, upon follow-up, 71 patients were able to control their pain using TENS, whereas 14 achieved no relief. A 1987 study recommended TENS for older patients with cancer pain and back and shoulder pain. TENS devices should not be used by pregnant women, by people with pacemakers, or over open wounds or certain areas of the body such as the eyes.

Acupuncture

The technique of acupuncture, an aspect of traditional Chinese medicine, has been periodically "rediscovered" since Dutch physician Willem ten Rhyne first described it in 1683. Treatment involves the insertion of fine, disposable needles for a short period of time into tiny places on the skin called acupuncture points. The needles are sometimes inserted directly into the location of pain. They may be gently twirled, or accompanied by mild electrical currents or lasers. Acupuncture should not be painful, causing only mild discomfort. Relief may come immediately or after a few minutes or hours.

Acupuncturists, who are sometimes medical doctors or osteopaths, administer treatment believed to regulate the flow of positive and negative energy along channels in the body called meridians. When the normal flows of energy are disturbed, the Chinese theory holds, physical and mental problems result unless balance is restored. *Acupressure* uses manual pressure on the same acupuncture points, and it may be practiced at home as a self-help technique.

Acupuncture is believed to relieve pain by counterirritation and to stimulate the production of endorphins. Rates of pain relief are 60 to 70 percent for many types of pain. Acupuncture is used to treat headache, backache, arthritis, neuralgia, and depression. It can improve white blood cell count, which aids immune system function, and it also can improve digestion. According to experts, osteoarthritis, bursitis, tenosynovitis, fibromyalgia, and sometimes migraine headaches also seem to respond to acupuncture.

Alexander J. R. Macdonald, an expert in the field, states that acupuncture is most effective for secondary fibromyalgia or myofascial pain. He believes it is most effective used early, accompanied by the least degenerative changes in joints or other organic disease. Even in pain clinics that see people who have a history of anxiety and depression, organic disease, and pain for many years, Macdonald says 20 to 40 percent benefit from acupuncture. He adds, however, that acupuncture is not suitable for overanxious patients, or for those with a visceral disease that can be treated with conventional Western medicine.

A 1980 study of the effectiveness of acupuncture on pain patients found a 58 percent improvement after ten months when traditional acupuncturists were given full rein in choice of technique. A study in 1987 found electroacupuncture, or acupuncture utilizing mild jolts of electricity, provided pain relief superior to TENS. A type of acupuncture in which the needle contacts the bone, known as *osteopuncture,* is sometimes useful with the arthritic symptoms of stiffness, aching, and swelling.

Acupuncture has a reputation of providing short-term, temporary relief. Melzack and Wall note that it is difficult to design good double-blind studies using acupuncture for a number of reasons, including the design of an appropriate placebo.

To locate a clinician who practices acupuncture, contact an organization such as the American Academy of Medical Acupuncture, listed in the appendix at the back of this book. A few books, such as Michael Gach's *Acupressure's Potent Points,* are available that explain the use of acupressure at home.

Physical fitness combats the extreme physical malaise that is part of the chronic pain syndrome. Physical therapy and occupational therapy can help increase overall fitness and functioning, and reduce excessive disability. Although physical conditioning is a goal of many pain treatment programs, exercise must be continued at home on a regular basis to be of long-term benefit. Heat and cold treatments, massage, TENS, and other self-help measures may help you cope with chronic pain on a day-to-day basis. Acupuncture or acupressure may also be helpful. Chapter 6 deals with an aspect of your life over which you have almost total control—your diet.

CHAPTER SIX

Nutrition

∾ *The many health benefits of good nutrition and maintaining optimum weight.*

Increasing your day-to-day quality of life by maximizing overall physical health makes life more satisfying and aids the management of pain. It's helpful to eat nutritiously and to develop a strategy to control your weight if recommended. Eating well is an important aspect of healthy living, and nutrition is one area over which you can exert control to improve your own health.

The well-established touchstones of good health and good living in general are diet, exercise, and interactions with other people. Studies have confirmed the physical and mental health benefits of these aspects of one's lifestyle, which all indirectly affect the experience of chronic pain. Many comprehensive treatment centers employ registered dietitians or nutritionists, since eating well strengthens your body and mind and makes you more able to deal with the pain that you have.

EATING WELL

Eating nutritious food as part of a well-balanced diet is of vital importance to the maintenance and enjoyment of life. Good food is one of life's primary sensual pleasures. Diet was even more important in most ancient medical systems than it is today. The Greek physician Hippocrates repeatedly stated, "Your medicine shall be your food and your food shall be your medicine."

WATER

Drinking adequate water is crucial to the proper functioning of the body. According to the National Food Consumption Survey of 1978, many Americans are mildly, chronically dehydrated. The human body is about 60 percent water, the brain is 75 percent water, and the blood is 85 percent water. Not every adult drinks the six to eight cups a day that nutritionists recommend, a normal turnover of about 4 percent of body weight. This can create a common health problem called *dehydration*, which is reversible.

Dehydration can contribute to pain and disability. Even being a little dehydrated affects your concentration, reaction time, and memory. Muscles cramp more frequently when dehydrated. Dehydration creates an electrolyte imbalance that produces weakness. The blood and lymph thicken, slightly slowing normal circulation. Good circulation is especially important in muscles that are tense or damaged by microtrauma, or in parts of the body that are inflamed, since these conditions create pain. Because blood and lymph carry white blood cells, dehydration affects immune system function.

In general, dehydration slows the natural process of transporting nutrients and oxygen to cells and carrying away waste products. Adequate water is necessary inside each body cell for chemical reactions to take place. Outside the cell, water is the principal conducting medium,

Good nutrition won't eliminate chronic pain, but it can relieve the extra stress on the body caused by poor nutrition. Eating a balanced diet strengthens the immune system, assists normal body processes, and generally reinforces good

---

a necessary major component of blood, lymph, saliva, mucus, sweat, and urine. As a rule of thumb, if you drink adequate water, a liter or more per day, your urine should be pale yellow most of the time, and you should urinate several times a day.

Dehydration is a particular problem in older people, who generally need more water than younger people. The living conditions of many older people can make it difficult to drink enough water, particularly in summer.

Bottled or filtered water, fruit juices, and decaffeinated teas are good sources, as are fruits and vegetables which are 75 to 85 percent water. Beverages containing alcohol or caffeine are diuretics and actually contribute to dehydration by increasing your urine production. High-protein foods such as meat and cheese are slightly dehydrating, as they increase ketone levels in the blood. Robert K. Cooper, director of the Center for Health and Fitness Excellence in Bemidji, Minnesota, and author of *Health and Fitness Excellence: The Scientific Action Plan*, recommends that for optimum health, you sip water frequently throughout the day, perhaps keeping a small bottle or glass handy in areas of the home where you spend the most time, rather than trying to gulp whole glasses at a time.

mental and physical health. Drinking plenty of water every day prevents dehydration, which can negatively affect every body process, and helps all body systems function normally.

It is estimated that one in four older Americans have diets low in essential fiber, complex carbohydrates, and fruits and vegetables. Low income, social isolation, and acute chronic health problems all contribute to poor nutrition in older people, as can a lack of knowledge about good eating. Poor oral hygiene and poor mental health also adversely affect one's eating patterns.

Not many clinical studies of the precise relationship between pain and diet have been conducted, but a few things are known. In general, the stress of dealing with any chronic illness burns off energy, which is created by the process of eating and digestion. People with cancer, for instance, have a need for 20 percent more nutrients than normal. Older people require less calories than younger people, but need more nutrients in their diet. Problems with digestion, absorption, and excretion can affect physical and emotional well-being. The physical unfitness that is a part of the chronic pain syndrome has a link to poor nutrition, since studies have shown that meal quality is inversely related to the level of disability.

Some people with chronic pain don't eat when they feel depressed and consequently lose weight. Fatigue and pain can lower appetite. If your movements are restricted by pain, you may actually avoid nutritious foods, such as fresh vegetables, which take longer to prepare and cook. People who take pain-relieving medications sometimes experience bouts of nausea, lose their appetite, or have other side effects that lead to weight loss. Some medications reduce the body's ability to utilize food. If you have lost more than five pounds from your optimum weight, consult your medical doctor.

Malnutrition is a medical term for severe nutritional depletion caused by a deficient diet or the body's inability to utilize food. An obvious health problem, malnutrition is an extreme condition that needs to be treated. Some form of nutritional support may be needed for patients who are hospitalized for a period of time and who can't consume an adequate amount of calories. Appetite stimulants may be available from your physician to help you regain lost weight. Below the level of clinical malnutrition, a subclinical or marginal malnutrition in which only a few nutrients are insufficient, may lead to long-term physical deterioration, or complaints of fatigue, anxiety, and depression.

Despite a widespread interest in good nutrition, American dietary habits are poor. Fast-food lifestyles are common, and cooking with fresh, nutritious ingredients has become a lost art in many homes. According to the National Health and Nutrition Examination Survey, about one-third of Americans are obese. This condition increases their risks of health problems such as coronary heart disease, high blood pressure, diabetes, sleep apnea, and osteoarthritis. According to the same survey, about one-fourth of Americans live lifestyles that are completely sedentary, and another 54 percent don't get adequate exercise.

Some individuals react to the anxiety and stress of chronic pain by nervously snacking and binging. When combined with the inactivity that is part of the chronic pain syndrome, this results in weight gain. The loss of self-image and self-esteem that accompanies weight gain can feed into depression and other psychological problems. Overweight or obesity directly contributes to certain types of chronic pain such as back pain, where reducing and stabilizing weight may alleviate pain.

In other forms of chronic pain such as migraine headaches and rheumatoid arthritis, modifying your diet can be helpful even if you haven't gained or lost an excessive amount of weight. Avoiding certain trigger foods or eating certain foods that contain beneficial substances also can influence the intensity of pain attacks.

GOOD NUTRITION

Working to eat well-balanced, nutritional meals containing an optimum mix of macronutrients like protein, carbohydrates, and fats strengthens and fortifies the body. Adequate intakes of micronutrients such as vitamins and minerals also are important, and supplementation may be advised if these levels are depleted.

The average person in the United States eats a diet that derives 40 to 50 percent of its calories from fat, which dietitians say is much too high. This is probably twice the amount of fat most people actually need, or more. The program developed by Dean Ornish, M.D. (see chapter 3), for controlling heart disease limits fat intake to 10 percent of total calories, accomplished through a diet that is basically vegetarian, since fruits and vegetables don't contain animal fat.

In addition to the health risks associated with obesity and high cholesterol, research has shown that high levels of fat tend to lower brain function in animals. Fat makes you fat, and the saturated fats, food additives, dyes, preservatives, and other chemicals found in highly processed foods are particularly unhealthy. Animal fat helps the body produce arachidonic acid, used in the creation of inflammatory substances such as prostaglandins and leukotrienes, which contribute to pain. Working to adopt a nutritious, low-fat

FOOD GUIDE PYRAMID

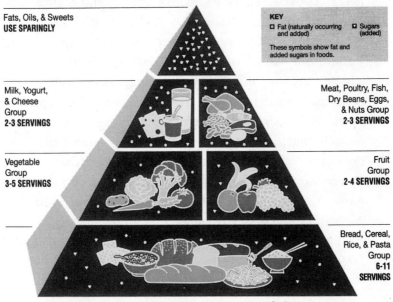

Fats, Oils, & Sweets
USE SPARINGLY

KEY
□ Fat (naturally occurring and added) ☒ Sugars (added)
These symbols show fat and added sugars in foods.

Milk, Yogurt,
& Cheese
Group
2-3 SERVINGS

Meat, Poultry, Fish,
Dry Beans, Eggs,
& Nuts Group
2-3 SERVINGS

Vegetable
Group
3-5 SERVINGS

Fruit
Group
2-4 SERVINGS

Bread, Cereal,
Rice, & Pasta
Group
**6-11
SERVINGS**

Source: U.S. Department of Agriculture/U.S. Department of Health and Human Services

What to Eat and How Much—The U.S. Department of Agriculture's Food Pyramid is a good basic guide to daily food choices. Recommendations are made on types of foods and quantities consumed. At the base of the pyramid are foods that should be eaten most frequently, expressed in servings per day.

diet containing adequate protein fortifies your body and may help you control your weight.

The Food Pyramid of the United States Department of Agriculture (USDA) is a good place to start (see figure above). USDA nutritionists recommend eating mostly plant foods such as whole grains, fruits, and vegetables, preferably in the less processed forms. Lowering the intake of fatty red meat, and especially greasy processed foods containing saturated fats and excess salt, and very sweet, sugary foods will help most people. Adding plenty of fiber-rich fresh fruits and lightly cooked vegetables, whole grains, and legumes, and drinking lots of fresh water also are beneficial. Increasing the proportion of fiber in your diet generally helps eliminate waste from your body and lowers blood pressure while adding necessary minerals such as magnesium, calcium, and potassium to the mix. Working with a registered dietitian or nutritional specialist, or carefully practicing sound principles of good nutrition on your own, can be of great benefit over the long term. If you eat a well-balanced diet, avoiding excesssive amounts of highly-processed food, you should get most of the nutrients you need directly from food. Most Americans don't eat a balanced diet, unfortunately.

Here are seven basic guidelines for a balanced diet advocated by many U.S. health organizations:

1. Eat a variety of foods.

2. Maintain an optimum weight.

3. Avoid excessive fat and cholesterol.

4. Avoid excessive sugar.

5. Eat foods with adequate starch and fiber.

6. Avoid excessive salt or sodium.

7. Limit alcohol consumption.

With chronic pain, it's particularly important to eat nutritiously, since dealing with pain requires an additional expenditure of physical and mental energy. For instance, stress depletes the body's stores of many essential vitamins. Deficiencies of the B vitamins, especially B3, B5, B6, B12, thiamine, and folacin can produce depression, apprehension, irritability, and mood swings. Adequate levels of these vitamins are essential for good brain functioning, since the brain burns approximately 25 percent of the body's fuel.

Deficiencies in the B vitamins and in minerals such as calcium, iron, copper, magnesium, and zinc can contribute to insomnia and other sleeping problems, according to Peter Hauri, director of the Insomnia Research and Treatment Program at the Mayo Clinic in Rochester, Minnesota, and author of the book *No More Sleepless Nights*.

Vitamins and Minerals

The one trillion immune cells in the human body need a good balance of nutrients even to withstand the normal ravages of age. Many Americans—particularly older Americans—are low in immune system–strengthening vitamins A, B12, C, and E, as well as selenium and zinc. A 1990 study of the diets of people over sixty-five found deficiencies in vitamins A, C, B6, and B12, and also thiamine, riboflavin, and minerals such as iron, calcium, and magnesium. Another study conducted in rest-homes found residents' bodies to be generally low in vitamin C, vitamin E, riboflavin, pyridoxine, iron, and zinc. The same study concluded that vitamin supplementation "significantly improved the biochemical parameters," bringing an important measure of immune system competence up to normal.

Research has shown a large percentage of the world's population has a low or borderline intake of necessary antioxidant vitamins A, E, C, and selenium, as well as a diet low in the trace minerals zinc, copper, and manganese, which play a role in the oxidization process. Antioxidants have beneficial effects on overall health because they inhibit the so-called free radicals that age and damage many body tissues, including those in the brain. Studies have shown health benefits in supplementing the diet with antioxidants such as vitamins C and E.

At the Shealy Institute, near Springfield, Missouri, chronic pain patients are given high levels of vitamin supplements during treatment. On discharge, patients are advised to avoid refined sugar, hydrogenated oils, processed foods, caffeine, and tobacco, and to eat between 50 and 100 grams of protein each day. In addition, they are advised to supplement their diet with a good multivitamin pill, 400 IUs of vitamin E, and 1,000 milligrams of vitamin C each day, supplements Dr. C. Norman Shealy considers safe and effective "considering the effects of smog, physical and emotional stress, and food processing."

Diet therapy can help inhibit pain. A 1987 study published in the medical journal *Pain* revealed results from a pain

SEROTONIN AND TRYPTOPHAN

Serotonin levels are low in many people with chronic pain and in people who are depressed or have trouble sleeping. Certain amino acids such as tryptophan and compounds such as acetylcholine found in high-protein foods are biological precursors to serotonin and may help increase it.

High levels of tryptophan are contained in turkey, peanuts, tuna, chicken, beef, and dairy products. Acetylcholine is found in the lecithin in foods such as egg yolks, liver, and soybeans. Milk contains a high level of tryptophan, which explains why a glass of warm milk often really helps you sleep. A high-protein meal with plenty of natural tryptophan and tyrosine may one day be proven to help mitigate certain forms of pain.

Tryptophan was popular as an insomnia remedy a few years ago. More than two dozen research studies show that 1 to 2 grams of tryptophan will induce sleep in people management program that included a diet high in carbohydrates and low in protein and fat—60 percent complex carbohydrates, 15 percent protein, and 25 percent moderate fat. Patients were encouraged to use diet exchanges to moderate food boredom; to eat foods high in fiber such as fruits, vegetables, and whole grains; to consume 8 to 10 cups of fluid per day; to eat a high-carbohydrate bedtime snack; to limit caffeine; and to set goals for controlling calories to achieve their ideal body weight. In addition to exercise, patients were urged to take a multiple vitamin and mineral supplement, plus 1 gram of tryptophan at bedtime to reduce the craving for sweets. Followed up a year later, 70 to 80 percent of the patients felt they received immediate and

---

with mild insomnia. Health food stores stopped carrying tryptophan when a batch was found to be contaminated, forcing its withdrawal from the market. In the United States, tryptophan is now available only by prescription, and is quite expensive. One prominent doctor who uses tryptophan supplements to help relieve pain says tryptophan must be taken with B vitamins to be most effective and prevent mental confusion.

In a 1976 study, increasing levels of serotonin and tryptophan helped patients lower their levels of chronic pain, which usually were of the musculoskeletal type. Another study found a diet of 80 percent complex carbohydrates, 10 percent protein, and 10 percent fat, plus 3 grams of tryptophan, reduced pain ratings from 58 to 26 on a scale of 1 to 100 in the subjects who received tryptophan, versus a reduction from 50 to 39 in the placebo group.

---

long-term benefits from the diet, and remained on the diet at least six weeks after discharge from the program. About 75 percent of patients who wanted to lose weight lost more than 2.2 kilograms, and 55 percent lost 4.5 kilograms or more. Many patients reported that following the diet seemed to decrease their pain.

Nutritious food in appropriate quantities helps us maintain optimum health, strengthens the immune system, and contributes to our overall sense of health and well-being. It is common sense that a body that is well supplied with essential nutrients is stronger and healthier, and more able to handle the physical and emotional stresses which pop up in medical treatment and in life.

OBESITY

People who suffer chronic pain often tend to gain weight. As a general rule, people who are overweight have shorter life expectancies and suffer more health problems. A 1990 study of chronic pain patients demonstrated a relationship between weight gain and decreased physical activity, a tendency to have more accidents, heightened emotional stress, and an increased sensitivity to pain. In 1993, another study suggested that people who are obese may be *more* sensitive to pain than are people of normal weight.

Obesity contributes to excessive disability, which is part of the chronic pain syndrome, and to physical unfitness, since it makes any activity more tiring. Obesity is associated with a 20 percent increase in the risk of losing physical mobility in men and a 40 percent risk in women, according to research published in 1993. Obesity or overweight often contributes to the pain of chronic back pain, arthritis, and angina. Among the more exotic complications of excess weight is a rare condition known as *neuralgia paresthetica*, in which a nerve is trapped in the front part of the thigh beneath a ligament, creating a burning, tingling pain and numbness over the anterior thigh.

Women generally store fat in the hips, buttocks, and thighs before menopause, and in the upper body after menopause. Men tend to store fat in the upper body, particularly in the abdomen. Excess weight puts additional stress on the skeleton and muscles. For example, when an overweight man with a pot belly stands up, his belly is a continuous downward drag against the skeleton and the spine. The extra weight pulls continuously against the muscles that hold the bones of the skeleton upright.

Emotional and psychological factors contribute to weight gain. When you are depressed, for instance, you may tend either to eat more and gain weight, or to lose weight. Being overweight can feed into feelings of helplessness and hopelessness, which intensify mental suffering and pain. Putting on what you consider to be a lot of additional weight can damage your self-esteem, and create psychological stress within the family circle. If efforts to lose weight are unsuccessful, psychotherapy might help. People with binge-eating disorders can be helped by supportive programs such as Weight Watchers or Overeaters Anonymous.

Stress contributes to obesity. This is why most major weight-loss programs now include an education in techniques of stress management. Weight Watchers lists stress as the major reason their clients, particularly their female clients, fail to lose weight. Weight Watchers, with branches all over the United States, holds group support sessions addressing this topic.

Purely medical issues such as the types of medications taken, other health problems, genetics, and even your previous attempts at weight loss can factor into any new effort to lose weight. Another factor is the length of time a person has suffered from pain. Following a diet to lose weight can in itself be stressful, particularly for older people. Most of the time, excess weight can be lost through gradual and sustained efforts. Losing and keeping it off is difficult, but it can be done. Interestingly, some nutritional experts believe overeating can spring from too few nutrients, and the body's drive to obtain them by eating great quantities of processed foods that are not very nutritious.

Professional *nutritionists* or *registered dietitians* can evaluate your eating patterns and help you plan a program to lose weight gradually. Diet therapy or education about what constitutes a balanced diet is included in the multidisciplinary programs that treat chronic pain. Ideally, if you saw a dietitian on your own, you would have an initial interview involving a diet history and an evaluation, followed by regular visits a few weeks apart during the time of weight loss and weight-loss maintenance. Responsible nutritionists won't recommend that you go on a crash diet, which will probably fail. They usually won't recommend that you take the trendy new diet pills, which usually work only as long as you take them and also may have long-term side effects. Unfortunately, there is no miracle cure for overweight. The best strategy is to set realistic goals and to actively take small steps every day toward reaching those goals. Making a permanent change in eating may involve substituting some healthy foods such as fruits, vegetables, and whole grains for less nutritious foods. Even a modest reduction in weight has health benefits if the loss can be maintained.

Diet therapy works in tandem with other strategies to reduce chronic pain. A study published in the medical journal *Clinical Therapy* in 1986 followed seventy-seven patients with osteoarthritis over twelve weeks of multidisciplinary treatment involving doctors, social workers, and nutritionists. At the end of three months, 80 percent had relief from the pain and symptoms, while 92 percent had improved to the extent that they could carry out the activities of daily living.

In addition to eating a nutritious, well-balanced diet, dietitians recommend up to 30 minutes of moderate but sustainable exercise per day. Exercise removes calories stored as fat in the body. One hour of exercise burns between 450 and 700 calories, a huge benefit if you are overweight. Weight lost by dieting alone includes the loss of some lean tissue, but dieting plus exercise simultaneously builds muscle and burns off fat. You burn more calories when you are physically fit, since muscles consume more calories than fat, even while they are at rest.

The following sections cover specific dietary considerations for people with back pain, arthritis, migraines, muscle pain, and other conditions.

Back Pain

Obesity aggravates lower back pain in men and women, but losing excess weight and keeping it off can lessen the stress on the body. The so-called beer belly, an accumulation of fat in the abdominal area, can greatly stress the lower back. This excess weight causes abdominal muscles to become stressed and extended, especially those stabilizing the lower spine and the pelvis. Excess weight can increase *lordosis*, or curvature of the lumbar spine; this strains the connecting ligaments and may impinge on rear joint facets, intensifying pain. In females, obesity can weaken the pelvic floor, causing referred pain to the sacrum and coccyx.

If you are overweight, you may reduce back pain if you begin a program to slowly control your weight, combining this with regular, sensible exercise to strengthen back muscles as recommended by your doctor, physical therapist, or health care team.

Arthritis

Obesity intensifies the pain of arthritis, since additional weight stresses the weight-bearing joints of the body such as the knees and hips. There is evidence that controlling your weight may help prevent arthritis. A 1992 study published in *Annals of Internal Medicine* found that women who were older and overweight could significantly lower the risk of developing osteoarthritis in their knees by losing weight. Another study of people with osteoarthritis or rheumatoid arthritis who underwent hip replacement surgery found a correlation between the degree of overweight and the extent of bone loss suffered by the patient. Working to lose weight, under a plan approved by your doctor or a registered dietitian, reduces unnecessary stress on joints.

Certain foods appear to play a role in the pain that accompanies arthritis. Eating cold-water fish often is recommended for joint inflammation. Fish is high in omega-3 and other essential unsaturated fatty acids, which create changes in the blood that inhibit the process of inflammation. Tuna, salmon, sardines, mackerel, cod, whitefish, swordfish, rainbow trout, eels, herring, squid, and halibut are all cold-water fish.

Three studies have shown that eating the fatty acids in cold-water fish can help people with rheumatoid arthritis. Other foods containing N3 fatty acids, such as corn oil and other vegetable oils, also may provide benefits. The pain of rheumatoid arthritis is sometimes intensified by certain foods. One woman saw her rheumatoid arthritis worsen when she consumed dairy products. Foods in the nightshade family more often exacerbate joint inflammation. This makes it advisable to eat zucchini, eggplant, tomatoes, bell peppers, white onions, potatoes, squash, and paprika in moderation, and to avoid foods that make arthritis worse.

Particular foods may trigger the immune and inflammatory responses associated with arthritis, or make some individuals more sensitive to painful stimuli. If you suspect that what you eat may directly contribute to pain, keeping a *food diary* or a *pain diary* listing what you eat over a period of time, and comparing your foods with your pain experiences, may help uncover food triggers. This normally is done under the guidance of a nutritional specialist, but you can do it yourself if you are fastidious.

Blood levels caused by the mineral zinc are low in some rheumatoid arthritis patients, and a few studies have shown an improved cellular immune response with zinc sulfate supplements. L-histidine, a health food supplement, may benefit patients over the age of forty-five who have active and prolonged rheumatoid arthritis.

Some people with pseudogout, a form of arthritis in which calcium crystals form between the joints, causing inflammation, find that intense exercise triggers attacks, which can be treated with medication and rest. Losing weight helps prevent these attacks.

Migraines

Migraine headaches can be brought on by certain foods, such as those containing nitrites (hot dogs, bologna, bacon, ham), nitrates, MSG (monosodium glutamate), alcohol, or the tyramine found in red wine, aged cheeses, chicken livers, or preserved fish products. Brewer's yeast, or beans or bakery goods made with brewer's yeast, cause migraines in some people.

Again, working with a registered dietitian or nutritionist can help you uncover nutritional triggers, and ultimately prevent or reduce the frequency or severity of some migraine headache attacks. People who experience migraines are often asked to keep a pain diary. This kind of record keeping helps uncover food sensitivities or unusual allergies. For instance, a few migraine sufferers have found that foods such as onions or nuts (which are not normally triggers) can bring on an attack. If a trigger food is identified, the obvious response is to lay off the offending foods to see if this helps. Not all food sensitivities will trigger a migraine all of the time, however. Depression, stress, sleep deprivation, and other factors are also triggers.

Eating more fish, which contain omega-3 fatty acids, may also help prevent migraine attacks. In one study where these fatty acids were found to be deficient among migraine headache sufferers, people experienced less frequent and less severe migraine headaches when their intake of these substances was increased by about 10 grams a day. Other studies have found deficiencies of B-complex vitamins and magnesium in migraine sufferers, with some improvements experienced when those deficiencies were brought up to normal. One study found that magnesium supplements helped women who experienced migraines during their menstrual periods.

Simply eating breakfast every day helps prevent migraines. One poll found that the majority of migraine sufferers skipped breakfast on a regular basis—something dietitians never recommend. Eating balanced meals, exercising regularly, and drinking plenty of water are helpful for migraine sufferers and for all people.

Muscle Pain

Some respected doctors believe diet therapy benefits many musculoskeletal disorders by mitigating the ischemic pain that results when blood flow to a painful area is impaired, creating oxygen starvation and pain in muscles and nerves. Michael Margoles, M.D., Ph.D., a San Jose, California, orthopedic surgeon, says that many of the 1,500 patients in his practice have taken vitamin and mineral supplements as a complementary therapy. First, supplements are used on a trial basis for six weeks to see if they have a positive effect on myofascial pain syndrome. If indicated, Margoles recommends a potassium supplement if levels are low, and perhaps a B complex with vitamins C and E, vitamin D, and supplements to insure adequate calcium and other minerals.

Authors Janet Travell, M.D., and David Simons wrote in *Myofascial Pain and Dysfunction* of a connection between myofascial pain and levels of some vitamins and minerals that affect the normal operations of the muscles. Factors included deficiencies of water-soluble vitamins such as B1, B6, B12, folic acid, and vitamin C, and reduced levels of minerals such as calcium, iron, and potassium. The authors stated that more than half of their patients required resolution of their vitamin inadequacies before they achieved prolonged pain relief. Travell and Simons theorized that vitamin deficiencies increased the irritability of trigger points by impairing the metabolism needed for muscle contraction and increasing the general irritability of the nervous system. The authors recommended a completely balanced vitamin supplement, which they said was usually safe. They cautioned, however, that the body should not be overloaded with vitamin A or other fat-soluble vitamins which can build up to harmful levels in the body.

Other Conditions

Other ailments that cause chronic pain are known to be impacted by certain aspects of the diet. There is no evidence that gastric ulcers or gastritis can be affected by diet, but avoiding cigarettes, coffee, and other caffeinated drinks can help reduce the acid reflux that often accompanies ulcers.

People with gout are often advised to reduce the consumption of alcohol and avoid foods high in purine, such as sweetbreads, fish roe, anchovies, sardines, beans, lentils, spinach, and peas.

People with Crohn's disease may suffer calorie or protein depletion, particularly of the fat-soluble vitamins, folate, and certain minerals such as iron and zinc. In addition, many Crohn's disease patients are lactose intolerant and should avoid dairy products.

The abdominal pain from chronic pancreatitis is caused by excessive alcohol consumption in 80 to 90 percent of patients. These patients often require an extremely high-calorie diet of between 2,000 and 5,000 calories per day and high in carbohydrates and protein. Supplements of vitamins A, B, K, and B12 may be recommended.

Some nutritional disorders of the nervous system are brought on by alcoholism, poor diet, or malnutrition. These include beriberi neuropathy, in which a deficiency of thiamine is present, and alcoholic polyneuropathy, in which deficiencies of thiamine, pyridoxine, niacin, pantothenic acid, biotin, and vitamin B12 can be complicating factors.

A study at Chicago Medical School showed that the amino acid phenylalanine in the dl-form blocks the degradation of painkilling endorphins and protects them, extending their life in the nervous system. Some doctors prescribe doses of this supplement, believing it helps raise the pain threshold, lifts depression, and assists in weight loss. Other doctors say dl-phenylalanine works only as a catalyst to other pain-relieving treatments, and doesn't have much effect on its own. Herbs such as St. John's wort, Ginkgo biloba, and kava kava sometimes help lift mild to moderate depression.

ALCOHOL, CAFFEINE, AND TOBACCO

Commonly used drugs such as alcohol, tobacco, and coffee all have an effect on chronic pain. Excessive use is not advised. Tobacco and coffee increase muscular tension and blood pressure and contribute to general irritability and restlessness.

Alcohol is a central nervous system depressant and an anesthetic that diminishes anxiety and sensory stimulation for a short period of time. Alcohol's effects are generally unpredictable in the short run. The use of alcohol is not an effective coping strategy for chronic pain, although an occasional drink or two with your doctor's permission may be acceptable. Long-term use (or abuse) tends to make anxiety and depression worse, and this negatively influences the perception of pain. One big problem is that alcohol can interact with medications, particularly those that depress the central nervous system, such as the opiates.

Caffeine is found in coffee, candy, tea, and most soft drinks. Caffeine also is added to some medications. A cup of coffee contains the most caffeine of any beverage, approximately 100 milligrams per cup. Caffeine is a central nervous system stimulant that constricts blood vessels in the head; its use can counteract the sedative side effects of many pain relievers. Caffeine usually is not a trigger food, but its use occasionally can trigger an acute headache by causing blood vessels in the brain to constrict. Too much caffeine may disrupt a sleep cycle and disturb restful sleep. If you are having sleep problems, dietitians often advise you not to drink beverages containing caffeine for four to six hours before bedtime.

Tobacco has been widely condemned, and most major health organizations advise smokers to quit. The nicotine in cigarettes and cigars is a powerful stimulant that increases tension, nervousness, and irritability. Nicotine tightens the muscles, making them more likely to go into spasm.

What you eat is quite important, since a balanced diet containing plenty of nutrients keeps the body strong and healthy. You have control over the foods you eat. Eating nutritiously helps you prevent malnutrition and deal with the obesity that can contribute to certain types of chronic pain. Keeping a food diary or working with a professional nutritionist or registered dietician may help you locate food triggers or improve your eating habits as part of an overall strategy to lose weight. Nutrition contributes to quality of life. Another lifestyle factor of great benefit is social support, including friends and community activities that prevent isolation, which is covered in chapter 7.

CHAPTER SEVEN

Social Support

❧ Cultivating and improving your relationships with others improves your quality of life.

The people in your social network play a role in your health. Social isolation and depression can inhibit the normal immune system response to infections and other physical threats, but expressing our humanity through conversation, love, and laughter actually makes us a bit stronger and more resilient. Social support can include relationships within a family, workplace, or even in a group of people in your community with whom you have common interests, such as a church or a support group.

Studies have shown that people who have active social relationships with family and friends live longer, healthier lives. Although the state of your health may have changed your role in the lives of other people, you may take action as much as possible to maintain your ties to family, friends, and groups of people in the community who know you and can provide support. Maintaining loving, friendly, positive relationships can help you keep a clear perspective and buoy your sense of humor. Social support lowers stress levels, which in turn lowers your perception of physical or emotional pain. Even keeping a pet can be healthy.

One of the normal effects of aging is a decreased ability to repair damage and insults to the human body, which is the job of the immune system. A compromised immune system diminishes our natural ability to fight off illness and disease, including the muscle tension and inflammation accompanying many types of pain. Proof is accumulating that negative states and emotions such as depression and anxiety can weaken the immune system and inhibit healing. The immune system is nourished, however, by simple, joyous experiences like love, friendship, affectionate touching, and laughter. By making adjustments that sweeten the quality of your life, you make continuing pain more manageable.

In 1986, in the *Journal of Chronic Disease*, John N. Morris and colleagues defined *quality of life* as "the prevention and alleviation of physical and mental distress, maintenance of physical and mental functioning, and the presence of a supportive network of informal relationships." Suffering continuing pain alone can be unbelievably agonizing and depressing, and one of life's debilitating experiences. Interacting with others in a positive way reduces the emotional pain, isolation, and feelings of depression and hopelessness that are part of the chronic pain syndrome. English psychiatrist Aubrey Lewis suggested in 1967 that simply being involved in a socially useful occupation may provide a form of protection against stress, fears, and pain.

You can take action to improve your life in this area. For many people, as in the following story, support groups can be an important adjunct to community life, provide life-affirming interactions with other people living with chronic pain, and give you an opportunity to lend emotional support to others in need.

GENE'S STORY

∾ An upbeat, older man we shall call Gene has been very active in helping other people with chronic pain who live in his area. The experience of founding and nurturing a support group has helped him live with what is now almost constant pain.

"In our support group we have people who are interested in helping themselves and their families cope with pain," Gene says, adding that people who haven't experienced chronic pain really don't understand how it feels to live with it. He points out that a support group composed of people who have "been there" is extremely helpful in the day-to-day business of living with pain. "We all know where everyone's coming from. We never talk about pain. We just discuss different aspects of how to live with it," Gene says.

Gene lives with the constant pain of arachnoiditis, an inflammation of the thin membrane that encloses the brain and spinal cord. His arachnoiditis is the result of too many back surgeries and too many myelograms (X rays of the spine which use radiopaque dye) in the past, he believes. He has accepted the fact that there is no cure in sight, but Gene hasn't given up. As he is interviewed, Gene, now eighty years old, describes his pain as being "about 22 on a scale of 1 to 10."

More than a dozen surgeries ago, Gene's ordeal began innocently enough at a golf tournament in Las Vegas. An eleven handicap golfer, Gene had played much of the three-day tournament on what he now realizes was a ruptured Achilles tendon. He experienced some heel pain, but he administered a little first aid and was back at work in his hometown the next day.

At that time, Gene was in a very enviable position. A happily married man and the father of two children, he was running a prosperous medical supply business, calling on doctors and medical groups all over the city. But the day after the golf tournament, as he was making a delivery, he heard something in his heel *snap*, and Gene fell to his knees in pain.

Gene had one unsuccessful operation on his Achilles tendon. The second, a ligament transplant, was successful, but he still had considerable pain in his heel. Five months of physical therapy helped, but the pain never really disappeared, although it did change form.

Since then, Gene has gone through six major surgeries on his back, six major surgeries on his leg, and four brain surgeries. One of the brain surgeries implanted an electrode in his brain and gave him five weeks of miraculously pain-free living. For more than a month, he recalls, he was in heaven, even venturing back on the golf course. Somehow, though, the electrode shifted a fraction of an inch out of place and the horrible pain returned.

"You name it, I've tried it," Gene says of pain-relieving techniques. He has gone through a pain management program at a major university, which he says didn't help him. He has tried hypnosis, self-hypnosis, biofeedback, magnet therapy, hydrotherapy, and many other techniques. He has had a dorsal column stimulator implanted, which provides some temporary and not particularly pleasant diversion from the pain.

Over the years, Gene has taken many types of pain-relieving drugs, including Demerol, Dilaudid, Percodan, and Percoset. "Very few of them helped. All are narcotics, and doctors are afraid to prescribe them for you," he explains. He is currently taking a low dose of morphine; his doctors are considering implanting an ambient infusion pump that can insert even lower doses of morphine around his spinal column.

Still, excruciating pain remains. Gene's sleep continues to be quite disturbed; he considers a half hour of sleep a blessing.

Although it is an ordeal, he has learned to cope with his pain, partially by helping other people cope with theirs.

Eleven years ago, Gene began looking for a support group like Alcoholics Anonymous for people in chronic pain. When he learned of the American Chronic Pain Association, Gene contacted them and started a support group. He worked hard to get the group started and keep it going for ten years. By participating in support groups run and attended by people who live with chronic pain, he has learned much about developing coping and survival skills.

"Pain is like a disease in itself, but you can't make it go away," he says. "Most of us in the group have pain that's been with us for years. To deal with it, you have to accept responsibility to help yourself and not depend on other people to do the work for you. You need an attitude of stick-to-it-iveness. And it helps to always look on the positive side. Don't think about the things you used to do, think about what you can do now.

"People suffer pain in an emotional way, and family involvement is really so important," Gene continues, adding that his wife has been particularly supportive. "It's so important to have support from your family. It's a very tough task to deal with pain without family support. When our group first began meeting, we thought of ourselves, but in recent years we've started to consider families, because the people who are living with you have to put up with a lot. We've really tried to educate them, and to explain certain things. We have to learn from each other."

Like many people with chronic pain, Gene has thought of suicide but firmly rejected the idea. He says most people in chronic pain deal with depression and thoughts of suicide. Gene's attitude is, "The good Lord put me here and the good Lord is going to have to take me. I have a lot of faith," he states. "I believe in God and in all His powers."

He observes, "So many people don't want to take responsibility for taking care of themselves, and there are very few who will take on the responsibility to help somebody else."

Gene says his commitment to the support group has given him a lot in return, and helped him take responsibility for the management of his own constant pain. He is an inspiration to many people in his support group, where he has been acknowledged for his dedication.

"The people in the group all thank me and make me feel I'm contributing something," he says. "This makes me feel like I'm not just a couch potato. I think we can all help each other."

Getting involved in meaningful activities diverts your attention from yourself and relieves stress and feelings of isolation and depression. You may want to volunteer some time to help an organization you believe in, or to help persons less fortunate than yourself in your community. Nonprofit health organizations, literacy groups, and other community service organizations welcome volunteers.

SUPPORT GROUPS

Support groups can be an important source of social support for people living with chronic pain. Support groups consist of individuals with common interests who meet on a regular basis, perhaps once every week or two weeks, to discuss common concerns. Members provide valuable emotional support and encouragement to each other. Support groups can mitigate the sense of gnawing loneliness and isolation that many pain patients feel. They can be a virtual community of sympathetic people who can immediately understand what you have gone through. Membership in most groups is free. They sometimes use a trained facilitator, but often do not.

It should be made clear that support groups are not a replacement for group therapy sessions conducted by pain clinics, which often have a fixed number of sessions and take a structured approach to teaching coping skills. Support groups are more like an ongoing coping forum, an opportunity to listen or to share your feelings. These groups can offer empathy and understanding in an atmosphere that respects your privacy and is not judgmental.

If you think a support group could help you, experts advise that you locate a support group and try going to three meetings. Contact the National Chronic Pain Outreach Association, the American Chronic Pain Association, the Arthritis Foundation, the American Cancer Society, the Wellness Community, or other groups listed in the appendix at the back of this book. Support groups also are sponsored by some hospitals, clinics, and health maintenance organizations.

Support groups help people living with chronic pain and other chronic illnesses deal with practical issues and with depression, anxiety, fear, frustration, anger, and sadness. Isolation and loneliness are familiar to people who have "been there." Group members also exchange information about nationally recognized pain clinics and pain specialists in the area. Compared to patients who go it alone, patients in support groups are less likely to overlook a potentially successful treatment option, or to continue on an unsuccessful treatment path. Each group is a bit different.

"The first time I went to one support group, twenty to twenty-five people sat around, and all they did was complain and complain," one woman observed. "I don't go in for that kind of stuff, and I didn't go back. But I did find another group six years ago, and they are wonderful. We don't just sit

SOCIAL SUPPORT

A great deal of research confirms the value of social support in maintaining good health, and longevity in general. Some of this research includes:

- A 1974 study tracked almost 7,000 Alameda County, California residents found that people with the most social connections were the least likely to die of all causes, while those with the least social connections had double the rate of mortality of their more social counterparts over a nine year period.

- A six-year study of Finnish men aged forty-two to sixty, reported in 1994, found that married men with the most friends and social ties were much less likely to die from all causes as single, divorced or widowed men with the least club or social organization participation. The men who rated their social relationships as fulfilling and nurturing also had a death rate of about half that of men who regarded those relationships as the least satisfactory.

- A study at Ohio State University College of Medicine in Columbus found that married women had higher immune function and reported fewer illnesses than women who had been separated from their husbands for up to six years. Women who felt

---

around and complain. We talk about different things. People call me. The group helps me quite a bit."

The world-famous physician Albert Schweitzer once took note of the emotional bond that exists between people who have experienced severe pain. "Who are the

they were better off divorced had better immune function than women who felt lonely.

- At Stanford University's Arthritis Self-Management Program, Kate Lorig, R.N., Dr. P.H., analyzed several hundred program participants over a four year period. While the average participant was slightly more disabled than four years previously, they reported 20 percent less pain and 40 percent fewer doctors' visits.

- A study of medical students under the stress of exams showed that those who were the most socially isolated had higher levels of stress hormones in their blood than did students who had wide social networks.

- Single men were twice as likely to die as married men over a ten year period, according to a study of more than 7,500 adults tracked over ten years by statisticians at the University of California's San Francisco Medical Center.

- A study in Prahan, Australia found that pet owners had lower blood pressure and lower levels of cholesterol than people with no pets.

members of this fellowship?" he asked. "Those who have learnt by experience what physical pain and bodily anguish mean, belong together all the world over; they are united by a secret bond." He called this group "The Fellowship of Pain."

THE POWER OF PRAYER

Some scientific evidence exists that prayer can have an effect on health, although the results are interesting but not conclusive, according to Larry Dossey, M.D., a doctor who has written extensively in this area. Psychiatrist Daniel J. Benor, M.D., surveyed 131 research studies published in English prior to 1990 and published his findings in the magazine *Complementary Medical Research*. A majority of the studies Benor examined had positive results, including fifty-six which had less than one chance in one hundred that the positive results were attributable to chance. Here is a small sampling of the research done to date in this area:

- At San Francisco General Hospital, cardiologist Randolph Byrd, M.D., randomly assigned half of a group of cardiac patients to a group prayed for by home prayer groups. Prayer groups were given patients' first names and general diagnosis, and asked to pray for them once a day. Patients who were prayed for were much less likely to require antibiotics, and much less likely to develop pulmonary edema. Patients who were prayed for did not require intubation (twelve in the control group did), and they were slightly less likely to die during the ten months of the study.

- At the Mind Science Foundation in San Antonio, Texas, individual volunteers were asked to make twenty 30-second mental attempts to calm or activate other individuals who showed signs of stress, and who were located in distant rooms but not told of the other persons efforts. As registered on a polygraph, effects were robust and consistent, and could be replicated.

- At McGill University in Canada, a healer named Oskar Estebany was asked to heal artificially created surgical wounds in mice. Estebany held the cages of the experimental group about thirty minutes a day for two weeks, and their wounds healed significantly faster than wounds on control.

- In a study published in the *Journal of Parapsychology* in 1968, ten people who were subjects in the experiment were able to inhibit the growth of fungus cultures in the laboratory by concentrating on them for fifteen minutes while four or five feet away—151 of 194 cultures responded. Several years later, the study was replicated by subjects who were located from 1 mile to 15 miles away.

- A study at the University of Redlands in Redlands, California, in 1951 divided volunteers with various life problems into three groups. Over the course of nine months, one group received psychotherapy, one group prayed for themselves every night before bed, and one group met weekly for a two-hour prayer session. Participants were given feedback from psychological tests they received during the experiment. The first group improved by 65 percent, the second group didn't improve, and the third group improved 72 percent. According to the popular book, *Prayer Can Change Your Life,* some participants in the third group achieved what the researchers called "total healing," including disappearance of problems such as stuttering, migraine headaches, epilepsy, and ulcers.

SPIRITUAL SUPPORT

A number of studies have shown that people who attend religious services on a regular basis have lower rates of anxiety and depression-related illness than people who do not. Many chronic pain patients have lost contact with their church or religious faith, psychologist Laura Hitchcock observes. Sometimes, simply going back to attend services on a trial basis can rekindle one's faith, particular friendships, or even a feeling of community.

The meaning one ascribes to pain and suffering is a spiritual aspect of pain, and it is quite important. Prayer and faith in a higher power help many people weather intense episodes of pain. Spiritual or religious feelings in general are quite diverse but can include membership in a particular denomination or faith, attending religious services, reading spiritual materials such as the Bible, praying, meditating, believing in some sort of higher power, or even having spiritual experiences that change one's life.

You can develop your spiritual self. Keeping a journal; writing, performing, or singing music; making artwork; and telling or listening to stories brings people into contact with their spiritual nature, and these experiences can be helpful or even profound. One psychologist tells the story of a patient who had no apparent spiritual resources, but who was able to connect with the spiritual side of her own nature through her dreams and her interest in Native American art and legends.

Chaplains or pastoral counselors are available at comprehensive pain clinic programs, and their services also may be sought on an individual, as-needed basis in any town. These people can be a supportive resource in any spiritual quest, which may involve an acceptance of your own human limits or your own mortality.

The meaning you attribute to your pain may have a positive effect on your perception of symptoms, how the symptoms are expressed, and the behaviors you employ to cope with it. A 1982 research study concluded that a person's ability to assign a meaning to his illness enhanced his sense of self-mastery over his medical situation. Another study in 1991 found that each patient's appraisal of the pain and the meaning ascribed to it had a greater impact on the patient than medical treatment.

As often as you can, cultivate supportive friendships, rather than isolating yourself. Continuing to engage in social activity and productive activity, and continuing to teach and learn, will mitigate stress and increase your enjoyment of life. Mingling with other people may help keep you young. Older research animals that live in stimulating environments and are given the opportunity to constantly learn actually show changes in their brains, which renders their brains similar to those of younger animals, anthropologist Ashley Montagu has observed.

Quality of life includes having meaningful social encounters with family and friends, and pursuing interests you enjoy will help you live with chronic pain. Taking action to maintain social relationships counters the debilitating effects of chronic pain, which are often increased by isolation from other people. Negative stress is a constant in any chronic illness, and the next chapter describes techniques to help relieve it.

CHAPTER EIGHT

Stress

꙰ *Stress contributes to the pain cycle, but you can learn how to relieve it.*

Whether it's a major life event that temporarily overwhelms you or a minor irritation, stress depletes your energy and your spirit. Negative stress intensifies pain and contributes to depression. Recognizing the effects of too much stress is the first step in learning how to deal with it. Techniques that control stress are taught in comprehensive pain programs, but information on these methods is available from many sources. Self-help techniques such as relaxation or breathing exercises may be practiced on the job or at home as preventive measures. Learning to control excessive stress will help you cope with pain.

Stress is as ubiquitous as it is difficult to measure and define accurately. Modern life is stressful. Negative stress, or *distress*, can originate in the body, the mind, or in outside events. A survey done in 1996 found that almost three-quarters of people surveyed in the United States said they experienced "great stress" every day. A survey of life's most stressful developments, first taken thirty years ago, was recently repeated, and the authors concluded that life has become 45 percent more stressful in the past three decades.

A major illness, a death in the family, or any number of marital, financial, or work difficulties are all life events that have a profound effect on emotional and physical health. Any life-shaking stress makes it more difficult to self-manage your pain, even if you have been doing so for some time. Even minor stresses build up over time.

When you perceive a threat, the fight-or-flight reflex to sudden or acute stress is activated. This primitive physical reflex, relayed down the autonomic nervous system, instantly prepares your body to respond. Reacting to stress causes a well-documented disturbance of hormone levels. Your adrenaline level shoots up, your heart beats faster, your blood pressure rises, your breathing quickens, your pupils dilate, your sex organs shrink a bit, and your hearing is slightly heightened. Meanwhile, a temporary shutdown of the digestive system shunts more blood to the muscles that tighten with tension. Before man became civilized, this reaction to acute stress was useful—it gave our primitive ancestors a sudden burst of physical strength, and the additional hormones and energy generated burned out during a physical response.

Chronic stress is different than acute stress, but it affects the body in a similar way. Many of the stresses of modern life are chronic and continuing, rather than sudden or acute. Under chronic stress, the body releases a chemical similar to adrenaline called cortisol. Cortisol suppresses the immune system; cortisol levels often are elevated in people who are depressed. Levels of serotonin are depleted by stress as are stores of vitamin C and the B vitamins. Stress triggers many subtle changes within the body and the mind. The muscular tension created by stress builds up unless you act to release it.

MAJOR STRESSFUL EVENTS

The Social Readjustment Scale, updated in 1997 by Thomas Rahe, M.D., and Mark A. Miller, lists life's most stressful events, which have a demonstrated link with illness. When compared to men, women reported greater stress associated with almost all the major social adjustments, with the sole exception of marriage, which was listed as equally stressful to both sexes.

Life Change	Units of Social Stress
Death of spouse	119
Divorce	98
Death of close family member	92
Marital separation	79
Fired from work	79
Major personal injury or illness	77
Jail term	75
Death of close friend	70
Pregnancy	66
Major business readjustment	62
Foreclosure on a mortgage or loan	61
Gain of new family member	57
Marital reconciliation	57
Change in health or behavior of family member	56
Change in financial state	56
Retirement	54
Change to different line of work	51
Change in number of arguments with spouse	51
Marriage	50
Spouse begins or ends work	46
Sexual difficulties	45
Child leaving home	44
Mortgage or loan greater than $10,000	44
Change in responsibilities at work	43
Change in living conditions	42

THE SYMPTOMS OF STRESS

Dealing with an impersonal medical or legal bureaucracy, driving in heavy traffic, succeeding as a parent or grandparent in difficult times, and even surviving as a worker in the competitive global economy are complicated challenges our primitive ancestors didn't face. The immediate physical response which follows acute stress isn't particularly useful these days. Because most stresses we encounter do not allow a physical release of pent-up hormones and energy, stress and tension tie many of us into tight knots of unreleased stress.

An event becomes stressful when we feel that it threatens our psychological well-being or our sense of ourselves. Some people cope well with particular types of stress, and some cope poorly. Coping strategies include trying to solve the problem, wishful thinking, avoidance, seeking social support, or blaming oneself. Obviously, problem solving and seeking social support are usually more useful and productive.

The symptoms of stress can be physical, mental, or behavioral. In *The Doctor's Guide to Instant Stress Relief*, Ronald G. Nathan, Ph.D., observes that physical symptoms of stress are often expressed in the skeletal muscles or in the involuntary nervous system, which controls breathing and heartbeat. These symptoms include headache, frowning, gritting or grinding teeth, neckache, backache, or muscle tension. Stress involving the involuntary nervous system may present symptoms such as rashes or hives, migraine headache, uneven breathing or heartbeat, dizziness, heart or chest pains, panic attacks, lowered sexual desire, or increased sensitivity to light or sound. Anxiety, worry, irritability, depression, forgetfulness, loneliness, and a feeling of being overwhelmed are among the mental symptoms. Symptoms expressed in behavior include inattention to grooming or dress, nervous habits, perfectionism, defensiveness, social withdrawal, edginess, and an overreaction to small annoyances.

Identifying these symptoms can confirm that you are under stress. This is not always obvious to the person under stress, though. Sometimes friends or family members notice that we are under stress before we ourselves are aware of it. Asking another person to tell you when you seem to be under stress can help make you aware of it, so that you may act to relieve its effects.

STRESS AS A TRIGGER

Stress is a major trigger of both physical and mental illness. The relationship of stress to migraine headaches, tension headaches, and peptic ulcers, for instance, is well documented. Many other disorders such as back pain and neck pain can be connected in some way with the experience of negative stress. Learning to use techniques that relieve stress can divert your attention from pain and lower your levels of mental and muscular tension. Taking positive action to help yourself—by doing breathing exercises, for example—fights the feeling of helplessness you may experience under certain types of stress. The action itself counteracts the physical inactivity and depression that are part of the chronic pain syndrome.

Paul Rosch, M.D., a psychiatrist and president of the American Institute of Stress in Yonkers, New York, says mental and physical stress are locked in a vicious cycle when it comes to chronic pain. By definition, he observes, any kind of pain is stressful. Anxiety and anger are emotional reactions to stress, as is the out-of-control feeling common to many who have a chronic illness. People who live with chronic pain are more likely to feel depressed. Depression and pain are a two-edged sword, one intensifying the effects of the other, since people who are depressed are more sensitive to pain. If the depression can be relieved, less pain is experienced. Proof of this is one current treatment: the short-term use of antidepressant medications such as Valium. Even patients who are not clinically depressed seem to do better on such medications, Dr. Rosch says.

Some forms of chronic back pain seem to be intimately tied into stress. Dr. Rosch points to the work of Hubert Rosomoff, M.D., chair of the Department of Neurological Surgery at the University of Miami, and John Sarno, M.D., former director of outpatient services at New York University's Institute of Rehabilitative Medicine, who are treating back pain primarily with exercise, education, and stress-reduction techniques. Dr. Sarno once surveyed his back pain patients and found that nearly 90 percent of them had a history of other stress-related complaints. This led him to develop a program dealing with back and neck problems based on education and stress relief.

The author of several books on back pain, Dr. Sarno identified what is basically a psychosomatic disorder he calls tension myositis syndrome (TMS), which produces pain in the back, shoulders, buttocks, and limbs, and sometimes other areas such as the chest. He believes many forms of back pain do not come from a herniated disc or other structural problems, as is often assumed. Rather, it comes from oxygen deprivation created by the tension from physical and emotional stress. TMS involves the constantly used postural

BACKACHE RELIEF

In one survey of the effectiveness of treatment, published in the magazine *Backache Relief*, people with back pain reported that they had received relief after working with the following types of health professionals.

Professional	Patients Reporting Dramatic Long-Term Relief (%)	Patients Reporting Moderate Relief (%)	Patients Reporting Temporary Relief (%)
Orthopedist	13	10	9
General practitioner	8	12	15
Osteopath	7	21	15
Neurosurgeon	13	13	8
Neurologist	2	2	4
Doctor of physical medicine	33	53	0
Acupuncturist	16	20	32
Rheumatologist	7	33	20
Chiropractor	14	14	28
Physical therapist	34	31	8
Dance instructor	50	40	0

muscles and the nerves that serve them; Dr. Sarno believes most back pain is basically a psychological or stress-related disorder manifesting itself as psychosomatic pain in those areas.

According to Dr. Sarno, much back pain begins with repressed anger and anxiety, which affects the autonomic nervous system, slowing down blood flow to areas of the back. The fight-or-flight reaction to stress is directed by the autonomic nervous system, which also controls the circulation of blood. Lower blood flow to the back muscles and connective tissues creates pain when muscles go into spasm, or when irritating waste materials from the metabolism of lactic acid build up. Nerves are even more sensitive than muscle to the oxygen deprivation created by lower blood flow, Sarno writes in *Mind over Back Pain*.

"The cure is knowledge," quips Sarno, who claims more than a 75 percent success rate with his patients, basically using educational seminars and follow-up sessions as needed. In two two-hour educational sessions, patients sympathetic to this approach are given insight into the causes of their disorder, then taught to take action to create changes in themselves, including the resumption of full physical activity.

Education about medical treatment can relieve stress and improve health if the proper information is delivered to the patient. A study conducted at UCLA of cancer patients with lymphoma found that those who were given procedural information about their medical treatment actually lived longer than patients who were not.

Constant, sharp, or recurring pain is stressful. The chest pain associated with angina also is associated with stressful emotions like anger, which can create a spasm in coronary arteries that restricts blood and oxygen flow. Stress-reduction techniques such as relaxation training, meditation, and biofeedback can reduce the negative impact of psychological stress. Herbert Benson, M.D., a Harvard University physician, says that 80 percent of angina attacks may be relieved by activities such as meditation or the relaxation response (see sidebar), coupled with what he calls the faith factor. Basically, the relaxation response is evoked by relaxing and focusing on

THE RELAXATION RESPONSE

Harvard University physician Herbert Benson has written several books about what he calls the relaxation response—the opposite of the stress response—which may be evoked in four steps. Coupled with a person's religious beliefs, these steps can help lower overall stress. In addition, he says research shows the relaxation response may help overcome insomnia, alleviate backaches, lower high blood pressure, and prevent hyperventilation and other health problems. The relaxation response includes the following steps:

1. Find a quiet environment.
2. Consciously relax your muscles.
3. Focus for ten or twenty minutes on a mental device such as the word one, or a simple prayer.
4. Assume a passive attitude toward intrusive thoughts.

a word that invokes your faith or spiritual belief twice a day (or whenever angina occurs) for ten to twenty minutes.

Many types of headaches and other disorders have a stress component, Dr. Rosch notes. The onset of rheumatoid arthritis is bound up with stress, as is that of fibromyalgia. In one study, more than 90 percent of women with rheumatoid arthritis reported a "significant stressful event" just prior to the appearance of symptoms. In a study of juvenile rheumatoid arthritis, where a large percent of patients came from broken homes, a major stress such as divorce or the death of a parent occurred within two years of the onset of illness in nearly half the cases surveyed. Some evidence exists that osteoarthritis also is related to stress, since the pain of arthritic joints can sometimes be reduced with stress-relieving techniques.

About half the patients in research studies of fibromyalgia believed a stressful event was linked to the appearance of their symptoms. Even small stresses such as arguing with friends and forgetting to pay bills were found in one study to intensify the severity of fibromyalgia pain, and to result in more sensitivity in trigger points on patients' bodies. Stress-relieving techniques have yielded as much as a 30 to 40 percent improvement in patients with fibromyalgia, Dr. Rosch says.

Migraine headaches and other flare-ups of pain can occur after experiencing stressful situations or events. If you can identify the situations that are stressful to you, however, you may be able to avoid them or shorten your exposure to them. This could help you achieve a measure of control over their effects and actually prevent some pain from occurring.

DIFFERENT STROKES

Many forms of stress can be experienced as either good or bad by different people. Dr. Rosch likens the perception of stress to a roller-coaster ride, in which the people sitting in the front have their hands up and are enjoying the stress of going downhill and around curves, while the people in the back are holding on tightly, teeth clenched in fear. Particular situations that create stress and trigger pain differ from person to person. What is a minor stress to one person may be a major stress to another, since every person's body, body chemistry, and emotional makeup are a bit different.

To sort things out, Dr. Rosch advises his patients to take the time to list all the things they personally find stressful. He then asks them to put these items into two lists: stresses they can personally control, and stresses they cannot control. Focusing your efforts on the former can help you minimize or eliminate stressful situations. For example, avoid individuals who create stress for you, or minimize the time you spend with them. Stresses that cannot be controlled should be recognized as such. Accepting certain unavoidable facts of life keeps you from becoming a virtual Don Quixote, forever tilting at windmills in constant frustration.

Hypnosis, biofeedback, relaxation exercises, massage, aerobic exercise, yoga, and transcutaneous electrical nerve stimulation (TENS) all relieve stress in some people. The trick is to find a method or a combination of methods that will help you. If used regularly, relieving stress can prevent or mitigate further stress and pain. However, arbitrarily imposing a stress-relieving technique on a person who doesn't like it or who finds it stressful won't work. Aerobic exercise, for instance, relieves stress, and many people enjoy it. If you begin a program of low-impact aerobics, but you dread and despise your exercise sessions, you may not help yourself much because the sessions will create more stress. Learn to listen to your body and determine if you feel better or worse after doing the activity, Dr. Rosch advises. Any strategy of stress relief must be sustainable to be effective for the person who uses it. Any strategy that works is appropriate, even those that seem quite mundane, such as taking a nap.

Trial and error may be necessary to find a stress-relieving activity that accommodates your preferences and fits into your lifestyle. Once you find one, set aside a little time on a regular basis, perhaps at certain times of day that suit you, and follow through in actually doing the activity. To strike a balance, it's a good idea to pace yourself at first. Slacking off for a few days and then throwing yourself into an exhausting attempt to "catch up" on your program simply will set you up for more stress. Achieving some success at pain relief in the initial phases of using any method is important, because success encourages you to continue.

A GOOD NIGHT'S SLEEP

Sophocles called sleep "the universal vanquisher," and for good reason. Sleep recharges our physical and emotional batteries and makes us better able to deal with the stresses of everyday life.

Insomnia, the inability to sleep, often accompanies chronic pain, as do depression and anxiety. Not getting a good night's sleep usually is stressful. Loss of adequate sleep or poor-quality sleep increases the physical stress on the body. Restless, uncomfortable sleep interrupted by pain or worry can trigger fatigue, anger, and general edginess and irritability. With less sleep, over time a certain amount of physical and mental resilience is lost, making even minor injuries or hassles seem enormously overwhelming.

It's normal to be unable to sleep for a short time on certain stressful occasions, such as the night before a final exam. Sleep disturbance usually continues for much longer after major stressful events, such as a move, financial problems, or the loss of a loved one.

People with chronic pain often have more pain at night, when there are less distractions such as television or family activity. Focusing inward at night, dreading the onset of pain, and trying to force yourself to sleep can themselves induce stress, tension, and pain. Sometimes it's useful to get up and do something fairly simple until you feel sleepy, then return to bed. Bedtime rituals, such as taking a warm bath, drinking a cup of warm milk or herbal tea, writing in a diary or reading help some people wind down and prepare for sleep.

It's interesting to note that tests conducted on subjects who felt they were getting no sleep at all found that they actually were sleeping quite a bit, but that the quality of their sleep was not completely restful. Most insomnia does cure itself over time, but practicing good sleeping habits or sleep hygiene and taking steps to reduce your stress level without the use of sleeping pills will help.

BRAIN WAVES

Many methods of stress relief, also called mind-body techniques, produce measurable physical changes in the body. Some of these changes may be measured and reflected in the speed of brain waves, rhythmic electrical patterns emitted from the brain that naturally accompany everything we do and think. The least relaxed *beta* range of fourteen to twenty-two cycles per second is created when we are wide awake and the mind is conscious of what is going on in the world. A more relaxed *alpha* state of eight to thirteen cycles per second appears when the mind is concentrating on something. The even more relaxed *theta* state of four to seven cycles per second is one in which the mind is much more withdrawn from the outside world, and we are more or less oblivious to our surroundings. Even slower is the *delta* state, in which sleep occurs.

Among its other effects on the body, the experience of stress elevates the brain into the beta range. If you can slow down your brain into alpha or theta, typical of more relaxed physical states, this will relieve stress and indirectly suppress pain.

The favorable effects of stress-relieving techniques show up in measurements of brain waves. Hypnosis, for instance, usually lowers brain waves into the theta state. Breathing and relaxation exercises pull brain activity down into theta and alpha. If you develop methods to put yourself into these more relaxed states and use them regularly, many body functions disturbed by stress and controlled by the autonomic nervous system such as heartbeat, breathing, and general metabolism can normalize. This physical and emotional normalization balances out the excitement and tension created by stress.

STRESS-RELIEVING TECHNIQUES

Exercise, good nutrition, and social encounters are invaluable in any strategy of good health, and they help relieve the physical and mental stress of inactivity, poor nutrition, and loneliness and isolation. Skin stimulation techniques also temporarily relieve pain and physical stress. Stress relieving methods discussed here include distraction, relaxation or breathing exercises, hypnosis, biofeedback, imagery and visualization, prayer, and meditation and yoga. Used regularly, these can relax tense muscles, calm the mind, and divert attention away from pain and toward a healthy, pleasurable activity. They may also make sleep easier or serve as a restful substitute for sleep.

Distraction

Anything that diverts your attention away from your pain in a useful manner can be helpful. Most of the stress-relieving techniques listed here may be considered forms of distraction.

Symptom preoccupation is common among people with any chronic illness. Those who experience constant or recurring pain can become preoccupied with their own bodies, since many serious illnesses are ambiguous diseases, of unknown origin, or not predictable, with different symptoms. Focusing on a symptom such as pain will only amplify the sensation. On the other hand, distracting yourself with an interesting or productive activity shifts the focus of your attention away. Changing your behavior in this way can be quite effective. Distraction is one way to divert attention from the negative experience of pain to more positive experiences.

Get your mind off your problems by focusing on something else of interest to you. This can be as simple as watching an engrossing TV show or movie, knitting a sweater, visiting your grandchildren, walking the dog, spending a day cooking a favorite dish, playing a musical instrument, singing, calling an old friend you haven't seen in a while, volunteering at your church or civic organization, or fishing beside a quiet mountain lake. Distraction can mean getting involved with a work project, a hobby, or a cause you really believe in.

If pain is expected to be relatively short-lived, nursing textbook author Margo McCaffery suggests you try distracting yourself with rhythmic breathing, visually concentrating on a point, singing or tapping in rhythm, listening to music or other auditory stimulation through headphones, or reading humorous books. For longer episodes, it might be useful to have several ideas in mind, so that you can move from one to another when you feel your concentration flagging. Write down the distractions you will employ prior to an episode, then consult your list when pain appears. Even rehearsing for a painful episode can help you prepare. McCaffery suggests the complexity of the distraction be related to the intensity of the pain, with suitable, relatively simple distractions for low-intensity and high-intensity pain, and more complex stimuli for the middle ranges. Trial and error is helpful in finding what works best for you.

Relaxation or Breathing Exercises

Relaxation exercises help many people deal with pain and are taught in most treatment centers because of their usefulness in combating stress and tension. It is not possible to be relaxed and anxious at the same time. Muscle tension is a common response to pain and worry, and relaxing muscles relieves this secondary tension, along with built-up psychological stress. Many people who experience chronic pain have lost their ability to completely relax, but relaxation is a skill that can be learned or relearned.

Controlled breathing techniques produce favorable changes in your brain waves by relaxing your body through techniques that deliberately change your pattern of breathing. While short, shallow breathing is characteristic of a person under stress, deep abdominal breathing is quite relaxing. Most people take from sixteen to twenty breaths per minute, but slowing it to about four breaths per minute rapidly relaxes most people.

Progressive muscle relaxation exercises also calm your mind. These involve actively tensing and relaxing different sets of muscles in a particular order, such as from your feet to your head.

Breathing and muscle relaxation techniques are often used together. Relaxation techniques can be utilized during a particular time of day—your quiet time—as preventive measures. They also can be used on an as-needed basis to combat feelings of helplessness and depression.

Autogenic training involves passive listening exercises that focus attention on various parts of the body. Developed in France and Germany, these exercises are said to be the most commonly used self-hypnotism pain control practice in the world. According to C. Norman Shealy, a neurosurgeon who uses autogenic training exercises in his pain control program in Springfield, Missouri, these exercises balance body and mind, specifically the autonomous nervous system, which is involved in stress, and the limbic system in the brain, which controls emotions. Dr. Shealy says this healthy mind-body balance can sometimes be achieved through the practice of religious faith, meditation, hypnosis, or even the use of art or music.

In the beginning, relaxation exercises may be done twice a day, or more frequently as needed. Cassette tapes that lead you through these exercises are available through music stores, bookstores, and drugstores, and by mail order.

Hypnosis

Not every person can be hypnotized, but most people who are motivated or imaginative can enter into a hypnotic trance. Despite the popular stereotype in movies, being hypnotized does not involve surrendering control of one's mind to a hypnotist. It's better to look at all hypnosis as self-hypnosis, since you must participate in the process.

Self-hypnosis is taught by most hypnotherapists, and it is yet another tool against the onslaught of pain. It can be individualized to the person. For instance, some people are more able to be hypnotized or to hypnotize themselves by using visual imagery, whereas others respond better to bodily feelings.

Hypnotic suggestion can be used to relieve physical tension, depression, symptom preoccupation, and anxiety, and to provide social reinforcement to patients vulnerable to and overwhelmed by pain. For severe continual pain, subjects can be taught to use distraction under hypnosis. For moderate pain that can be controlled by medication, people who are hypnotized can be taught to reduce their dose and clear their minds. Milder pain can be directly manipulated with the aid of hypnosis, as in making an area of the body numb.

Hypnosis is most effective for arthritis pain and cancer pain, according to pain specialist Ronald Melzack and Patrick Wall, and in general is an appropriate early treatment for organically based pain. A study conducted in 1980 found hypnosis more effective than psychotherapy for chronic pain relief, and equal to biofeedback. In some studies, hypnotism has been found more effective in reducing an experimentally induced pain than either morphine, aspirin, or an active tranquilizer.

A significant reduction in pain has been demonstrated for cancer patients who are highly hypnotizable. A study at Stanford University in 1983 used self-administered hypnosis and support groups to double the survival time of terminal breast cancer patients—and the group that used self-hypnosis showed no increase in pain levels. Another study found that doses of pain-relieving narcotics could be cut in half when hypnosis was included in treatment.

At a hospital in South Manchester, England, a research study used either hypnosis or psychotherapy to treat patients with irritable bowel syndrome. The groups that used hypnosis and self-hypnosis reported very little pain at the end of three months, whereas those that received seven 30-minute sessions of psychotherapy aimed at reducing their stress reported a smaller but statistically significant reduction in pain.

Hypnosis has been around for more than a century. In 1846, shortly before the introduction of chemical anesthesia, English surgeon James Esdaile reported an 80 percent success rate using hypnoanesthesia for major surgeries performed in India, but his discovery was lost in the hoopla over the concurrent miracle of anesthesia. The way in which hypnosis works is not completely understood, but it is believed to be a form of distraction, a method of altering the perception of pain, or possibly a stimulant to the release of endorphins in the brain.

A clinician who practices hypnotherapy can be found through the American Society of Clinical Hypnosis, listed in the appendix at the back of this book. Most hypnotists teach self-hypnosis, which may be employed at home or as needed.

Biofeedback

Biological feedback, or biofeedback, gives you a certain amount of control over your body using simple, hand-held machines attached to the body by wires that provide visual or audio "feedback" on the workings of the autonomic nervous system. Such subtle measurements of differences as small as a millionth of a volt weren't possible until recently. For many years, doctors also believed the autonomic nervous system could not be influenced or consciously controlled.

Biofeedback helps you control pain by making you aware of subtle changes in your body. Technicians show you how to use the machines, but you use the information they provide to learn to control your body in beneficial ways. Biofeedback has about an 80 percent success rate with many types of health problems. At the Menninger Foundation in Kansas, biofeedback pioneers Elmer Green and his wife, Alyce M. Green, found biofeedback can be helpful in the control of headaches and migraines, as well as in muscle tension pains. There can be a 30 to 40 percent improvement with biofeedback even in conditions such as fibromyalgia, according to Dr. Rosch.

Because biofeedback requires extended practice and mastery, it's used only for chronic pain rather than acute pain, which is of shorter duration. Biofeedback has no known side effects, but a few people are put off by the use of biofeedback machines and unable to benefit from them.

The main types of biofeedback devices are (1) *electromyographic*, or EMG, which measures the firing of the muscle fibers and the contraction or expansion of a muscle group; (2) *electrothermal*, or skin temperature measurements, usually done peripherally in the hands and feet, useful because they measure changes in blood flow that are reflected in changes in skin temperature; (3) *electrodermal*, or EDR, which measures changes in perspiration related to anxiety; and (4) *electroencephalographic*, or EEG, which measures brain wave activity.

DISORDERS TREATABLE BY BIOFEEDBACK

According to the 1984 book *Biofeedback and Behavioral Strategies in Pain Treatment*, by Alfred J. Nigel, Ph.D., here are some ailments that may be successfully treated by biofeedback:

- anxiety disorders
- causalgia
- dermatitis
- essential hypertension
- fecal incontinence
- headache (migraine, cluster, tension, mixed)
- hyperkinesis
- inflammatory bowel disease
- insomnia
- irritable bowel syndrome
- myofascial pain dysfunction
- chronic pain
- sexual dysfunction
- tic
- tinnitus
- vasoconstrictive disorders
- writer's cramp

The choice of device is important. For instance, tension headaches springing from muscle tension should be treated with devices that sense muscle tension in the head and neck. Migraine headaches, which are vascular, should be treated using heat-sensing devices such as electrothermal measurements—long ago it was learned that if you learn to raise the temperature in the fingertips, this combats migraine because you redirect blood flow from the upper body to the hands.

To locate a clinician who can teach you biofeedback, contact an organization such as the Association for Applied Psychophysiology and Biofeedback (see appendix).

Imagery and Visualization

The use of imagery and visualization to relieve cancer pain was pioneered by a radiation oncologist, O. Carl Simonton, M.D., and his wife, Stephanie Matthews-Simonton, a psychologist. They documented their methods in a book, *Getting Well Again*, which explained the techniques now commonly used in cancer treatment and other types of chronic illness. Visualization first uses relaxation techniques that put you in a quiet state of mind, then allows you to focus your imagination on images that can help you get well.

The images you employ can range from powerful guns blasting away at pain or cancer cells, to healing angels gathering around your body. The basic idea is that the imagery should seem healing to you and its power focused on your ailment. In cancer treatment, for instance, some patients visualized the rays of their radiation treatment blasting away cancer cells, or the chemicals from chemotherapy treatment leading an army of white blood cells to attack the tumor. Another image is a globe of healing white light floating over the body, comforting the area where the most muscle tension, pain, or discomfort is experienced.

If you can visualize the cause of your pain, perhaps as a bolt of electricity or an ice pick hitting a part of the body, then you can focus on transforming these images with new imagery—shorting out the electricity, pulling out or diverting the ice picks, and so forth. You may be able to transform the pain itself into numbness by imagining the painful area as a block of wood that is insensitive to pain.

Visual imaging can be learned in a comprehensive pain or cancer center, in a class in your community, or in courses taught at a location such as the Simonton Cancer Center in Montecito, California, where music therapy is also incorporated into the program. Books and tapes also can be purchased for use at home.

Prayer

Prayer is a very private experience, but it also can be extraordinarily comforting. Simply folding your hands in prayer and communicating directly with a higher power can relieve a great deal of pain and stress. Research has shown that people who are spiritually active have lower levels of depression and anxiety than people who are not. Dr. Benson observes that from a biological point of view, prayer is similar to meditation in its beneficial physical effects. He says that a belief in a higher power is useful in countering our human tendency to dread our own mortality.

For many chronic pain patients, "The Serenity Prayer," written by theologian Reinhold Neibuhr and used by many twelve-step groups around the world, has particular value in helping to sort out important life issues:

The Serenity Prayer
> God grant me the Serenity
> To accept the things I cannot change
> The courage to change things that I can
> And the wisdom to know the difference.

Reciting this prayer may help you remember that there is a difference between worries that you may address with useful actions, and worries that are beyond your control. Changes involving actions, lifestyle, and attitudes may be within your control; the effects of medical treatment on your pain may not. Worrying about things that are beyond your control is futile, and simply recognizing this can be comforting. Evidence is accumulating in support of the idea that prayer relieves stress and has many other health benefits.

Meditation and Yoga

Meditation reduces anxiety, lowering blood pressure and slowing metabolism, which increases the threshold for pain. Meditation can be used to help manage chronic pain, cancer pain, depression, and other problems.

The benefits of meditation can be found in the Eastern version called transcendental meditation, or in a simpler Westernized version called the relaxation response, popularized by Dr. Herbert Benson. Both forms of meditation induce a deep physical and mental relaxation. Both can relieve stress, relax the body, and mitigate the anxiety and fear that accompany chronic pain. Graduates of the Arthritis Self-Help Course at Stanford University, which includes the teaching of meditative techniques, have reported a 15 to 20 percent reduction in pain.

Another method that can tone and relax body and mind is *hatha yoga*, an old discipline from India that alternates controlled breathing with mild stretching exercises called postures. Yoga provides a generous, disciplined mix of two important activities—breathing control and mild exercise—which are known to help control pain. A 1993 study found that yoga can yield a greater increase in mental and physical energy than relaxation or visualization alone.

Yoga is a cornerstone in Dean Ornish's program in San Francisco to reduce heart disease without the use of surgery or drugs, instead employing diet, exercise, and stress reduction. In the Ornish program, yoga has the highest correlation with success of the modalities used.

Yoga gently builds strength, balance, and flexibility. It usually provides a workout that makes you feel better afterward. You should check with your doctor before doing yoga, however, since it is exercise, and some yoga poses involve unusual positions. Yoga classes are available in most communities, and yoga can be learned and practiced at home with the aid of tapes and books.

Other Methods

Music therapy is employed formally and informally to relieve pain. In a study at the University of Nebraska Medical Center in Lincoln, chronic pain patients were given musical tapes to listen to; patients reported significantly less pain while listening to music. Other studies have shown that listening to music can reduce the amount of medication taken by hospital patients up to 30 percent. Music can help chemotherapy patients feel less nauseous, and it benefits some people with insomnia. Listening to music you find sedating helps catapult the brain into a relaxed alpha state.

Music therapist Joey Walker suggests that music is most distracting when you choose the music, perhaps matching it to your mood. For best results, Walker suggests you hum or sing words if there are lyrics, tap your foot or fingers to the beat, or think of pleasant memories associated with the music. Playing an instrument or singing (or learning to do so), or attending concerts or recitals are enjoyable therapeutic activities.

Humor therapy sometimes takes the form of humor carts at cancer treatment centers and hospitals. Pushed from room to room by brigades of off-duty clowns in greasepaint and full regalia, these carts make the rounds to good effect. A good belly laugh is similar to exercise in that it stimulates the immune system, releases painkilling endorphins, and lowers blood pressure. The late Norman Cousins wrote a best-selling book entitled *Anatomy of an Illness*, in which he described how he used laughter and large doses of vitamin C to help him overcome the effects of ankylosing spondylitis, a form of arthritis.

Hunter D. "Patch" Adams, M.D., the humor-loving physician whose life was the basis for a popular movie in 1999, observed in his book *Gesundheit!* that laughter has been proven to decrease cortisol secretion, increase oxygenation of the blood, lower heart rate and blood pressure, and relax muscles. Laughter is a good antidote to stress. A good sense of humor is a foundation of good mental health, Adams believes, an effective social lubricant which is vital in healing not only individuals, but also communities and societies.

In one experiment, scientists measured the levels of immune system proteins in a group of people before and after they watched videos of a stand-up comedian, and found that immune factors rose higher after subjects watched the comedy routine. Researchers discovered a higher level of virus-fighting antibodies in students with a good sense of humor when compared with a group of less jovial students. In 1922, Harvard University psychology professor William

McDougall explained: "First, laughter interrupts the train of mental activity; it diverts or rather relaxes the attention. Secondly, the bodily movement of laughter hastens the circulation and respiration and raises the blood pressure, and so brings about a condition of euphoria or general well-being which gives a pleasurable tone to consciousness." It's healthy to laugh at the human comedy, at life's little foibles, and even, every once in a while, at yourself.

Aromatherapy uses massage oils, or fragrances in the air or in bathwater, to influence your mind. The primitive nerve endings stimulated by aromas connect to the brain, where they may affect emotions, moods, memories, and creativity. Pure essential oils are the best. Although the hundred-odd aromatic plant smells affect individuals differently, lavender may help with sleep, headaches, and depression; vanilla may be calming; peach may decrease anxiety; lemon may stimulate appetite; and rose may be helpful for food, headaches, nausea, and insomnia.

In two studies of interest, researchers at Memorial Sloan–Kettering Cancer Center in New York City gave one group of patients heliotropin, which smells similar to vanilla, to help them relax before undergoing magnetic resonance imaging (MRI) tests. The group that smelled the heliotropin experienced less anxiety than the group who did not experience the pleasant scent. Researchers at Duke University in Durham, North Carolina, released a subtle scent into one car in a New York City subway line, and found that aggressive acts such as shoving and pushing declined as much as 40 percent.

Dance therapy is therapeutic movement that brings the body into harmony with itself. One study published in the magazine *Backache Relief* found that 50 percent of people said they experienced dramatic long-term relief through dance therapy, and another 40 percent achieved moderate long-term relief from their pain.

Writing down how you feel about stressful or traumatic events may have some benefit. Research studies at Southern Methodist University in Dallas, Texas, showed that students who discussed or wrote down their feelings about traumatic events lowered their stress levels, decreased their utilization of medical services, and strengthened their immune systems. James Pennebaker, M.D., head of the university's research team, observed that "failure to confide traumatic events is stressful and associated with long-term health problems."

A BALANCED LIFESTYLE

Stress may be relieved by a well-balanced lifestyle focused as much as possible on productive or enjoyable activity, and away from sickness and preoccupation with pain. Learning how to communicate assertively helps relieve stress and combats negative emotions such as anger, helplessness, and depression. Setting reasonable goals for yourself, allowing adequate time to accomplish them, and rewarding yourself afterward, may prevent you from feeling overwhelmed by the presence of pain.

Although major stresses such as a death in the family are beyond our power to control, many minor stresses are within our control. If you think your bedroom is drab and dismal, for instance, you might take action to brighten it up, such as bringing in a bouquet of colorful, fragrant flowers, or hanging a colorful calendar on the wall.

Setting aside time for enjoyable activities is important, too, particularly if those activities are among those that can help relax you. Time management skills can help relieve stress. Pursuing a hobby or a particular interest is relaxing and will help prevent the inactivity, isolation, gloomy feelings, and obsessive focus on pain.

Because stress and tension often make the pain experience even worse, it makes sense to take action that relieves stress. Recognize the symptoms of stress and learn to prevent it. Whether you use distraction, relaxation exercises, hypnosis, biofeedback, or any other strategy, taking positive action to help yourself can lower pain levels intensified by stress. Develop an arsenal of stress-relieving techniques and utilize them on a regular basis. It takes a commitment of time and energy to utilize these techniques, so choose something you like. The next chapter deals with one of the major medical weapons against pain—pain-relieving drugs—which should be used judiciously when treating... chronic pain.

CHAPTER NINE

Drugs

ᑳ *Drugs can relieve pain, but they also can become part of the chronic pain syndrome.*

Pharmacological drugs are the most common form of pain control in the United States, and one of the oldest in the world. Many new drugs have been developed to treat particular conditions in the past few decades, and a great many are used in the treatment of various types of chronic pain. Drugs are usually a short-term solution, however. The use of too many drugs and drug combinations is harmful and considered part of the chronic pain syndrome. Drug use can be reduced to great benefit. This chapter surveys the drugs used to treat chronic pain, the methods used to deliver them, and precautions and considerations regarding their use as part of an overall pain control strategy.

Drugs that relieve pain are called *analgesics*. In addition, several other types of drugs, sometimes called adjuvant drugs, are employed in many situations and provide a measure of relief. Drugs are faster and more convenient to use than other pain treatments and provide short-term relief. Pharmacological drugs are cost-effective when compared to other methods of treatment such as surgery. Drugs mostly treat the symptoms, rather than the root causes of pain. Drugs must be used judiciously for a number of reasons. These include the long-term side effects possible from even the mildest pain-relieving drugs and drug combinations, and the possible danger of drug addiction.

It's important to note that cancer pain and chronic benign pain are treated differently with respect to drugs. Cancer pain usually presents as acute pain and often is treated quite effectively with drugs, including strong painkilling drugs such as morphine. Most multidisciplinary programs that treat chronic benign pain aim to withdraw you gradually from as much medication as possible as part of the process of learning to live with some chronic pain. A systematic effort to reduce the use of painkilling drugs, in combination with behavioral therapy, is not particularly useful for the treatment of *acute* pain, which includes most of the pain aris-ing during cancer treatment. This aspect of behavioral therapy—which considers the inappropriate use of medica-tions and medical services as pain behaviors—is generally most effective on types of chronic benign pain for which a physical cause, or a physical cause proportionate to the pain experienced, cannot be found.

Keep in mind that drugs are not the only way to cope with pain. People with all forms of pain can benefit from safe, simple self-help techniques such as cognitive therapy, exercise, relaxation training, or biofeedback covered in pre-vious chapters. Even if stress-relieving techniques don't allow you to throw away your pain pills completely, they can help you reduce the amount of drugs you need to control pain.

All drugs have benefits and risks, and these can be explained to you by the doctor who prescribes them, or by a pharmacist. The most obvious benefit of drugs is pain relief or

SLEEPING PILLS

Sleeping pills are only a temporary solution to insomnia, and other methods of sleep hygiene such as exercising and keeping a regular sleep schedule usually are better solutions over the long run for people with chronic pain.

Sedatives that have been used for years include barbiturates, Quaaludes, Doriden, and other drugs that provide only short periods of relief. After they have been used for two weeks, sleep actually is worse than before the medications were prescribed, according to Edward Covington, M.D., director of the pain program at the Cleveland Clinic Foundation. Newer drugs from the benzodiazepine group, such as Dalmane and Restoril, are useful for longer periods of time, but not indefinitely.

A problem with drug-induced sleep is that your sleep doesn't revert to the way it had been before. "Rebound insomnia" occurs after the drug is discontinued, and may greatly impair sleep for a period of time, especially if alcohol is consumed in the evening. Sedatives depress normal dreaming, and in rebound insomnia dreaming can return in the form of nightmares for a time.

the control of symptoms such as depression or lack of sleep. Occasionally, the use of drugs may mask the real source of pain and prevent a clear diagnosis of your problem. All drugs have side effects, and some are quite serious. These include toxicity at certain levels, which can be treated by a knowledgeable doctor, and the sometimes overstated risk of *drug addiction*, or *drug dependence*, which is a risk with opiates, minor tranquilizers, and sedatives taken over a period of time.

Pharmacological drugs can affect sexual function, sleeping patterns, and body functions such as appetite, digestion, and elimination. After using a stronger pain-relieving medication for a period of time, you can develop a *tolerance* to its effects, which leads to the need for greater and greater doses. Switching to another medication in the same class may temporarily counteract this effect. The possibility of side effects increases if drugs are taken long term, and redoubles if several medications are combined. This danger is especially great for patients who are physically compromised with additional medical problems, such as weak kidneys or high blood pressure. Thousands of people die from overdoses of prescription drugs in the United States each year, many of them elderly people.

Older people often suffer chronic pain, and as a group they are the greatest consumers of prescription drugs. The U.S. Food and Drug Administration estimates that 80 percent of adults over the age of sixty-five have at least one chronic condition that requires long-term therapy, usually including drugs. According to a 1984 study, about 25 percent of the elderly take three or more medications daily. Older people are at particular risk for either over- or undermedication because of normal age-related changes to their bodies, such as decreased drug absorption and slower metabolism, distribution, and excretion of drugs. Drug dependence is widely perceived as a problem with many drugs, particularly the opiates, but drug addiction as a result of medical treatment is uncommon in older adults.

There is a recognized relationship among chronic pain, substance abuse, and mental disorders, although the ways in which they overlap are not clear. Certainly, substance abuse is a major problem in chronic benign pain. A study in 1979 by the Mayo Clinic found that 24 percent of chronic pain patients were addicted to prescription drugs, and another 41 percent were classified as drug abusers. A high percentage of substance abusers—24 percent of opiate addicts in a 1982 study—also were found to be depressed. For this reason, many chronic pain treatment programs gradually wean the patient from all analgesic drugs, or work to put them on a low, steady dose of the mildest possible medication that effectively knocks the edge off the pain.

REDUCING THE USE OF DRUGS

Many people enter pain treatment programs taking a great number of painkilling nonprescription and prescription drugs, including various types of narcotics. People in constant pain can become psychologically dependent on painkillers, even if the drugs really don't do a good job of controlling the pain. Doctors prescribe them and "good" patients take them, sometimes in enormous quantities. People with chronic pain can take as many as a dozen different prescriptions, all with different and overlapping mental or physical effects, including some that could not possibly mitigate their pain. Painkilling drugs, especially the powerful narcotic drugs, often are still prescribed on an as-needed basis, written *pro re nata*, or *p.r.n.* This is suitable for acute pain and pains that come and go, such as those experienced after major surgery, and certain pains associated with cancer. It is not appropriate for chronic pain.

The overuse of medications affects the way you act and how you think about yourself and the world, and contributes to fatigue, mental confusion, sleeplessness, depression, sexual problems, and more. We've all been conditioned to expect that medications relieve acute pain, and they often do. Chronic pain is different. Even the strongest drugs can't relieve all pains in all people, and medications can't be used indefinitely without consequences.

Most comprehensive chronic pain treatment centers gradually reduce the use of drugs as a part of the treatment. This is often accomplished by the use of a "pain cocktail," which mixes together all the drugs you are taking with sweet-tasting syrup, so you will not realize the quantities of drugs being taken. Then, over a period of weeks, dosages of drugs are very gradually reduced. Ultimately, you are placed on regular doses of the mildest possible analgesic, usually just enough to knock the edge off the pain. Mild analgesics such as aspirin do not have the same tolerance problems as stronger drugs, and they don't cause addiction or mental clouding.

In treatment centers, this slow drug withdrawal occurs at the same time that your overall physical fitness is increased, your diet improved, and new coping strategies and stress-relieving techniques learned. According to Edward Covington, M.D., director of the pain program at the Cleveland Clinic Foundation, many people find that they become more optimistic and less irritable, sleep better, have a stronger sex drive, and have a better sense of humor when they are withdrawn from habit-forming drugs.

The advantage of taking the lowest possible dose of pain-relieving medication on a regular basis (rather than when pain appears) is that you level out the peaks and valleys of everyday pain. Keeping a certain level of a mild pain-relieving drug in your bloodstream *prevents* monstrous flare-ups of pain. Your doctor also may retain the stronger drugs for emergencies to relieve very severe or breakout pain.

If you reduce your intake of drugs, your mind may clear considerably, and you may more easily sense your current physical limits and pain threshold. This clarity helps you build your strength and learn other methods to control or manage your pain. You may overcome your irrational fear that you will be in unbearable pain without medications, and you may suffer less depression. When gradually withdrawn from medications under medical supervision, many people with chronic pain are able to stop taking analgesics altogether. Although it often surprises them, many patients have reported that they experience less pain when they are taking fixed doses of mild pain relievers, or no drugs at all, than when they took several different drugs at the same time, including stronger drugs on an as-needed basis.

Drug addiction can be easily treated in a controlled environment. Success outside a hospital setting or treatment center must involve abstinence, however. Organizations such as Alcoholics Anonymous or Narcotics Anonymous can be helpful in maintaining abstinence or sobriety even if your addiction is to prescription drugs, because they provide a program tailored to treat addiction and plenty of group support and encouragement. Learning and mastering good coping skills can stop you from running to the medicine cabinet during episodes of intense pain.

REGULAR DOSES

As a general rule, the right dose of any medication is that which provides the most relief with the least side effects. For acute pain, a doctor will begin the dose at a low level and gradually raise it until the drug proves effective. The dose is then reduced back or titrated to a level where it controls pain with fewest side effects. Doctors currently believe that regular doses are best for persistent pain and result in less overall drug intake.

Working in tandem with medical doctors are *nurses,* the most constant presence in a medical situation. Nurses administer medications, educate patients, collect and analyze data, and keep records. They monitor ongoing situations, communicating with your doctor if a particular treatment doesn't appear to be effective. The best nurses give you a chance to express your anxieties and fears, and offer compassion, assurance, and support. Good nurses are a treasure and are a prime source of reassurance and practical advice.

In a hospital, receiving medication as needed frequently involves the patient having to notify a nurse at the onset of pain, and an anxious wait for the medication to be delivered. Receiving medication on schedule can be a problem in the hospital, since nurses sometimes skip night medications if the patient is not awake, preferring to let them sleep. As a result, when the effectiveness of the medication wears off, the patient may wake up in pain in the middle of the night. If you are being given medication around the clock, and you *want* nurses to wake you up for your evening medication, nursing textbooks suggest placing a brightly colored card in the medication Kardex that states, "Please wake patient for nighttime doses of analgesic—per patient request."

Although most nurses are quite good at what they do, many were taught to evaluate pain based on the acute pain model. Among other things, the acute model holds that all patients in pain have observable signs and symptoms such as grimacing and rapid heartbeat. The acute model works for postsurgical pain and most cancer pain, but many types of chronic pain do not follow the acute pain model and are not accompanied by observable physical signs. Therefore, you may need to state clearly and assertively how you feel more than once to get the attention of the doctor or nurse.

Nurses do report problems to doctors. Do not make the mistake of complaining to your nurse, then telling your doctor, "I'm fine." If you attempt to be a "good patient" in this way, doctors may discount what you have previously told the nurse, and make their own judgments about the extent of your pain.

LONG-TERM USE

Prescribing medication as needed generally is not a good long-term strategy, although it often accompanies prescriptions for narcotics. As a patient, if you wait until the pain is peaking, this creates a need for a larger dose of medication to knock it down. One component of this rising pain is the withdrawal symptoms actually experienced by the patient, because he or she tries to hold off on the drugs (particularly narcotic drugs) until the pain becomes unbearable. As Richard Sternbach, author of *Mastering Pain,* explains, part of what many people experience as chronic pain actually springs from the withdrawal symptoms from the narcotic that they are not taking regularly. Eventually, the overuse of drugs becomes part of the chronic pain syndrome because, over time, larger and larger doses are necessary to control pain.

In most cases, breaking this escalating cycle is of great benefit because it clears your mind, puts you in touch with your body, and positions you to move forward with your life.

In other cases, medications must continue to be a part of the treatment picture—one tool, but not the only one, you have at your disposal to help control pain.

Medications relieve pain, but some take effect rapidly, while others need to be taken for a period of time to become effective. Every person's body chemistry is a bit different, making the effects of particular medications slightly unpredictable. Some people need smaller or larger amounts than average to control pain. The way a medication affects you should be reported to your doctor, particularly if results are not as expected.

All medications should be taken as directed, with an eye to possible side effects. How and when you are expected to take the medicine should be explained clearly by your doctor, as should the possible side effects. A doctor who prescribes you medication should know all the other medications you are taking—even over-the-counter drugs, vitamins, allergy pills, and alcohol, since these can interact with certain drugs. When you see a new doctor, present him with a list of the medications you are taking if you can, even if he doesn't ask. Ideally, only one doctor should be prescribing drugs for you.

From a medical doctor's point of view, another problem with prescription drugs is that patients sometimes don't take them, or don't take them as directed. Of the 750 million prescriptions written by doctors in the United States each year, it is estimated that only about one-third are taken as prescribed, one-third are only partially taken, and one-third are never filled. The Bayer Institute of Healthcare Communication in West Haven, Connecticut, estimates the cost to society of this type of treatment avoidance at $100 billion a year in lost productivity, hospital admissions, and other costs. According to a 1994 study, people with arthritis have a 55 to 71 percent record of prescription underuse, while 40 to 50 percent of high blood pressure medications and diabetes medications are underused. A patient's belief that the drug won't help them, concerns about side effects, and cost are all factors in the nonfilling of prescriptions, according to a study by the American Association of Retired People.

Pharmacists can explain to you the effects of particular medications. When you pick up a prescription, ask the pharmacist for the *package insert* that accompanies the medication—this lists possible side effects and pertinent information about the drug. Other sources of information about prescription drugs are medical reference books such as *Physicians' Desk Reference, The Merck Manual,* and *About Your Medicines,* available in the reference section of many libraries.

Note: Any side effects that your doctor advises you to report, and certainly any unexpected side effects that trouble you, should be reported to your doctor immediately or as recommended. Your medical doctor is always your best source for information about particular medications.

TAKING YOUR MEDICINE

The vast majority of medications used in the treatment of chronic pain or cancer pain are taken orally, usually in the form of pills or capsules, or sometimes in liquid form. Many prestigious medical organizations, including the American Medical Association, the American College of Physicians, and the World Health Organization (WHO), suggest that oral medications be the first choice for most patients, unless you cannot tolerate medications in this form or the pain is more complex or severe. Benefits of taking medicines orally include their low cost, the ease with which they can be used, and their availability in time-release form. Morphine and many other drugs are available in tablets and other forms.

Pain-relieving medications may be taken in the form of skin patches, suppositories, or nose sprays. All these are *systemic*, that is, they are not localized to any one part or region of the body. Systemic medications may be delivered as shots—*subcutaneous* injections given under the skin, *intramuscular* injections into the muscles, or *intravenous* (IV) injections into veins. Although a medical doctor, an osteopath, or a dentist must prescribe prescription drugs, most can be taken at home. Shots are often given by a nurse or medical assistant, but some of them also can be given at home.

QUESTIONS TO ASK ABOUT MEDICATIONS

Here are some questions to ask your doctor or pharmacist about prescription drugs:

- What kind of medicine am I being prescribed?
- When and how should I take it?
- When should I not take it?
- Exactly what will this medicine do?
- What are its possible side effects?
- What should I do if I experience side effects?
- How might it interact with other medications I take?
- How do I know if it's working?
- Should I avoid certain foods or beverages while taking it?
- How long should I continue taking it?

Regional anesthetics relieve pain in a particular area, such as that served by a particular nerve or nerve root, and they are injected or infused. Regional anesthesia may be given one injection at a time, for diagnostic or other purposes, or as multiple infusions.

Nerve blocks are injections that block sensation in the area served by a particular nerve or group of nerves. Temporary nerve blocks may be used for diagnostic purposes or for pain treatment. For instance, both causalgia and reflex sympathetic dystrophy often are diagnosed using anesthetic blocks to the sympathetic nerves. If pain is not relieved, the diagnosis is wrong. According to Verne L. Brechner, M.D., past director of the UCLA Pain Management Clinic, if the pain relief lasts about as long as the anesthetic is expected to last, then patients are candidates for a surgery called a sympathectomy, which can relieve the pain of these conditions. If relief significantly outlasts the expected effects of anesthesia, or pain returns with less intensity, patients can be helped by biofeedback or supportive psychotherapy, Brechner says. Temporary nerve blocks such as facet joint blocks using steroids are part of the diagnostic procedure for arthritis and not used for pain relief, according to Ben Shwachman, M.D., a Los Angeles anesthesiologist.

Regional anesthetics may be delivered as *epidurals*, injected directly into the hard outer layer of the spine, called the dura. They may be given as *spinals* and injected directly into the spinal space itself. These anesthetics should be administered by an anesthesiologist trained in the latest and best injection techniques.

For more severe pains, pain-relieving drugs may be delivered systemically. Surgically implanted infusion pumps can be used on patients dealing with cancer or severe intractable pain, or for delivering chemotherapy medications over a period of time. Drugs also may be delivered regionally using other devices implanted into the body that infuse medication near particular nerves of the spine for more effective and targeted pain relief.

SPECIFIC DRUGS THAT RELIEVE PAIN

From a pharmacological point of view, these are the major categories of drugs used in the treatment of pain.

- *Analgesics* block pain transmission through the nervous system. Most widely used for pain relief, they include opiates such as morphine. Sometimes included in this category, or in a separate class, are the milder *anti-inflammatory* drugs, including *nonsteroidal anti-inflammatory drugs* (NSAIDs) such as aspirin, and steroid drugs called *corticosteroids,* which reduce inflammation in the body.

- *Muscle relaxants* relieve pain by causing tense or contracted muscles to relax. They inhibit the motor nerve signals that produce spasm or contraction.

- *Psychotropic drugs* such as antianxiety drugs, antidepressants, and major tranquilizers primarily affect mood and other psychological functions. They reduce stress and the perception of pain.

- *Anticonvulsants* relieve the pain of trigeminal neuralgia, itself triggered by excessive nerve activity.

Pain relief through drugs may be a trial-and-error process, with a succession of different drugs at different doses tried before the proper relief is found. If one drug isn't working,

FIGURE 9.1   THE WHO THREE-STEP ANALGESIC LADDER

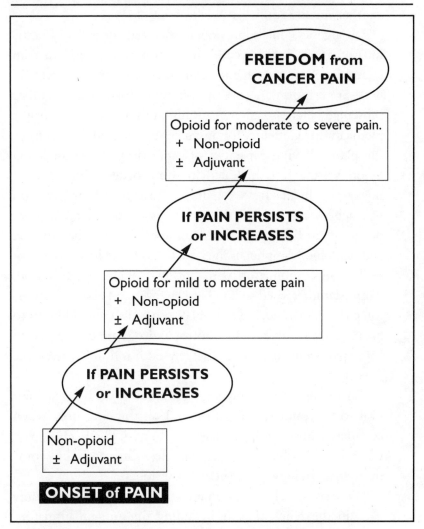

Loosely based on The World Health Organization's analgesic ladder that advises using the mildest drugs first, perhaps with adjuvant therapy, and employing stronger drugs as needed.

most doctors will try to raise or lower the dose, or switch to another medication.

Analgesics, including opiate-derived drugs and anti-inflammatory drugs, are the most commonly used in pain treatment. Some analgesic drug formulations, however, in both prescription and over-the-counter form, include other substances such as caffeine, antihistamines, and psychotropic medications. Caffeine, for instance, is believed to reinforce the pain-relieving capacities of other drugs by constricting blood vessels. It is included in some drugs prescribed for migraine headaches. Medical treatment for tension headaches can involve the prescription of an antianxiety drug such as Fiorinal, which combines aspirin, a barbiturate, and caffeine. Amphetamines such as Dexedrine are prescribed in combination with opiates to help elevate mood. Antihistamines, used to combat hay fever and colds, can reinforce the pain-relieving powers of other drugs, in addition to having sedative effects. Psychotropic drugs are considered to have pain-relieving properties in addition to their basic effects.

In the beginning, any strategy should plan to give a fair trial to the mildest drugs first, and up the ante only when adequate pain relief has not been achieved. The WHO's pain relief ladder, advising such strategies, illustrates this commonsense strategy of medicinal pain relief.

Described below are some of the drugs most commonly used in the relief of pain, including the anti-inflammatory drugs and opiates, and less frequently used adjuvant drugs such as muscle relaxants, psychotropic drugs, and anticonvulsants. This is *not* a complete list of all drugs used in the treatment of pain.

Anti-Inflammatory Drugs

Inflammation is a natural defensive reaction of body tissues to damage. Inflammation results in redness, as blood vessels dilate and then swell. The swelling puts pressure on pain-sensing nerve cells. Inflammation also causes the release of chemical compounds such as *prostaglandins* at the site of damage, and these substances both cause pain and lower the pain threshold, making the body more sensitive to pain. Anti-inflammatory drugs inhibit this response by blocking the synthesis of the irritating chemicals that create pain and diminishing the inflammation itself. The mildest are almost always taken in tablet or liquid form.

Anti-inflammatory drugs may be divided into two classes, nonsteroidal anti-inflammatory drugs and corticosteroids.

NSAIDs. The mildest pain relievers have the cumbersome but descriptive name of nonsteroidal anti-inflammatory drugs (NSAIDs). These include well-known drugs such as aspirin, a drug derived from the active ingredient in the bark of the willow tree, which was a popular home remedy for pain a century ago. NSAIDs inhibit inflammation but have some effects on the central nervous system. They are effective pain relievers, particularly for pain that is not severe. Tolerance and addiction are not problems with these drugs. They can effectively lower fever and alter pain perception, which is why so many are sold over the counter.

NSAIDs are sometimes prescribed for muscle pain, spinal pain, disc problems, tension or vascular headaches, chronic paroxysmal hemicrania (the NSAID indomethacin often relieves these types of headaches almost immediately), osteoarthritis, infectious arthritis, gout, pseudogout, bursitis, neuropathy, peptic ulcers, pelvic inflammatory disease, and other conditions.

Aspirin and ibuprofen are among the most popular of the NSAIDs, often prescribed to relieve the pain and inflammation of arthritis, for instance, although they do nothing to the painful joint. Acetaminophen is also prescribed for pain relief, although it has no effect on inflammation (and therefore has little use in relieving the pain associated with a joint inflamed by arthritis). Pain relief may require some trial and error with particular NSAIDs on the part of your doctor.

Some NSAIDs are used in specific ways. In the treatment of vascular headaches, for instance, ergotamine, which constricts arteries, is relatively mild and usually is most effective if taken orally at the beginning of an attack. It's available in inhaler form. It is taken under the tongue or rectally, along with an antinausea drug. In treating cluster headaches, ergotamine often works best as an intramuscular injection or as a preventive taken before bedtime. Ergotamine for vascular headaches requires a careful dose adjustment and should be avoided by pregnant women, people with high blood pressure, and people with cardiovascular problems. Methysergide is another NSAID used in the treatment of vascular or cluster headaches, but it has serious side effects.

Almost a hundred million prescriptions for NSAIDs are filled each year. Most work fairly quickly, although they may require repeated doses over a period of days to achieve their full effects. About a dozen drugs in this group are commonly used.

Caution: Side effects can occur even with the mildest anti-inflammatory drugs if they are taken in excessive amounts or over a long period of time. Aspirin and ibuprofen can irritate the stomach or inhibit the formation of blood platelets needed in blood clotting. Acetaminophen can damage the liver or kidneys if taken too long in excessive amounts, particularly when mixed with alcohol. In 1997, the Arthritis Advisory Committee recommended to the FDA that all NSAID labels carry a warning about the possible risk of gastrointestinal complications.

Corticosteroids

Corticosteroids are hormones produced in the cortex of the adrenal glands. Commonly known as steroids, they are the second major category of anti-inflammatory drugs. Steroids relieve pain because they block the synthesis of prostaglandins, but they have a number of potential side effects including the suppression of the natural immune response. Steroid drugs are either derived from natural sources or chemically produced. Normally, three to four steroid treatments per year is considered the maximum. Like other drugs, steroids contain symptoms rather than cure the problem.

Epidural steroids injected into the outer membrane of the spinal cord can be used to relieve low back pain. Small quantities of steroids, along with a local anesthetic such as procaine or lidocaine, also can be administered in trigger-point injections to relieve myofascial or joint pain. Corticosteroids can be used to treat some diseases that result in inflammation such as rheumatoid arthritis. Nerve compression caused by growth of a cancer is treatable with steroids, as are temporal arthritis, temporomandibular joint (TMJ) problems, gout, bursitis, some forms of neuropathy, shingles, and Crohn's disease. Steroids can be utilized with other drugs; shingles, for instance, can be treated with both corticosteroids and antiviral drugs. Used as adjuvant drugs for cancer pain, steroids can enhance the effects of other drugs and improve appetite. In all cases, steroids should be used sparingly and judiciously.

Steroids are most effective in relieving pain when the duration of symptoms is less than three months. One study found 83 to 100 percent effectiveness on patients with symptoms for less than three months, 67 to 81 percent effectiveness between three and six months, 44 to 49 percent effectiveness between six and twelve months, and 46 to 58 percent effectiveness on patients with symptoms lasting longer than a year.

Response to steroid injections can take several days—one study found 37 percent of patients responded within two days, while 59 percent responded between four and six days, and another 4 percent improved after six days. Given these statistics, it's a good idea to wait a week to see if the treatment has had an effect, then determine if subsequent injections can continue to help.

Oral steroids usually are not used in the treatment of chronic pain. One exception is polymyalgia rheumatica, for which the most effective current medical treatment at this time is steroids taken in tablet form.

Caution: Corticosteroids have many side effects. These can include acne, redistribution of fat in the body, excessive swelling or edema, increased diabetes or osteoporosis, agitation, insomnia, abrupt mood changes, and the growth of facial hair, as well as stomach irritation and ulcers. Because steroids inhibit immune system function, they can leave you vulnerable to infections. They also speed up protein metabolism, and continuous applications can cause protein to "eat up" muscle and connective tissue.

Opiates

Opiates, or narcotics, are analgesic drugs derived from the opium poppy. They have been used as a medical therapy at least since the time of ancient Rome. Laudanum was a popular remedy in sixteenth-century Europe, and many pure and manufactured forms of opiate drugs have been developed in the past century.

Opiates relieve pain because they are chemically similar to the body's own endogenous pain relievers, such as the endorphins. They affect the central nervous system, specifically the limbic system of the brain, where emotions are generated, usually lowering emotional anxiety into something akin to blissful euphoria. In general, opiates are the strongest pain relievers, relieving more kinds of pain than anti-inflammatory drugs, although they usually are not effective on neuropathic pain. When combined with other substances, opiates can increase pain relief. One commonly used drug, Percodan, combines the narcotic oxycodone with aspirin.

Once given only through hypodermic needles, opiates are now available as pills, in long-acting patches, as suppositories, and in liquid form. Pills are the simplest and the most convenient, but smaller doses are necessary if the drug is administered by other means. For instance, 300 milligrams of morphine in pill form is equal to 100 milligrams taken intravenously. Only 10 milligrams of the same drug produces the same pain relief if it is delivered via a spinal implant device directly to the central nervous system, where the same relief is achieved with thirty times less medication.

Opiates often are administered in a hospital or hospice situation by nurses, or sometimes by the patient using patient-controlled anesthesia (PCA). *Patient-controlled anesthesia,* as the name implies, gives the patient some control over IV infusions of pain medication. The patient presses a button or bar to give himself or herself more pain medication. Several studies have shown that people use less medication, have a diminished perception of pain, and have shorter hospital stays when this method is compared to more common modes of delivery, such as an IV drip infusion, which requires that a nurse be called when additional medication is needed for breakthrough pain.

A 1986 study of bone marrow transplant patients showed that those who controlled their own painkilling medication used one-third less morphine than those given morphine by nurses. Some doctors emphasize that a certain amount of dignity is retained because patients don't have to act as if they're in acute pain by screaming or grimacing to get medication. At pain clinics, asking for medication is also considered a pain behavior.

The use of opiates is highly regulated and restricted in the United States, mostly to acute pain after surgery and to terminal cancer cases. Writing in *Scientific American,* pain specialist Ronald Melzack, a professor at McGill University in Montreal, Canada, cited research conducted at Royal Victoria Hospital in Montreal, which specializes in palliative care. Oral morphine resulted in excellent pain control in 95 percent of patients, Melzack wrote, and they did not require rapidly escalating doses of the drug. Although the dose of

narcotic drugs does have to be adjusted because some tolerance develops, little actual addiction is found in cancer
patients, he says. When narcotics are no longer necessary, the
dosage can be gradually reduced to prevent withdrawal
symptoms, which usually are mild even with abrupt discon-
tinuance if used for medical purposes. One widely circulated
estimate is that only about .01 percent of cancer patients
become addicted to narcotics during treatment.

In treating cancer, an approach involving pain prevention
is wise, Melzack says, because both pain and the fear of pain
are a patient's greatest source of suffering. Prevention of pain
involves keeping a certain amount of drug in your bloodstream at all times by taking medication on a regular
schedule. Eighty to 90 percent of cancer patients treated with
a preventive approach achieve relief, Melzack claims, and
those report that their discomfort is bearable or gone. About
half the remainder get relief when other therapies are added.

Opiates are used in the treatment of a few other disorders that cause chronic pain, including Crohn's disease, or in
very mild form to treat the pain of shingles, post-herpetic
neuralgia, or gouty arthritis. The writing of prescriptions is
regulated by each state, and laws are not consistent from state
to state. In some states, doctors who prescribe narcotics must
write prescriptions in triplicate and send one copy to a state
agency that monitors the use of addictive drugs, a procedure
that intimidates many doctors.

Any blanket policy regarding drugs such as narcotics has
difficulty in allowing for the worthy exceptions. One pain
specialist recounts the case of a twenty-six year old athlete
who had sustained a major spinal injury. His doctor found
that continual low doses of oral morphine worked miracles

for this young man, who had gone back to work and had made plans to marry. When a regional medical board looked over the doctor's records, however, the members accused the doctor of prescribing narcotics for too long. The board asked the doctor to stop prescribing morphine for this particular patient. The doctor reluctantly complied, and the young man fell into a depression and lost his job, and his marriage plans dissolved as a result of his renewed pain.

Types of Opiates. Opiates may be subdivided into two types, opioid agonists, which mimic the effects of natural substances like opium, and opioid agonist-antagonists, whose effects are different.

Opioid agonists include morphine and codeine, which are derived from natural opium. Morphine was one of the first drugs synthesized from opium and remains the drug against which all other analgesics are measured. Opioid agonists include partly synthetic compounds such as heroin, hydromorphone (Dilaudid), oxycodone (Percodan), hydrocodone (Vicodin), and oxymorphone (Numorphan). Opioid agonists also include synthetic drugs such as methadone, leverphanol (Levo-Dromoran), meperidine (Demerol), and propoxyphene (Darvon or Dolene).

Opiate agonist-antagonists include drugs such as buprenorphine (Buprenex), butorphanol (Stadol), nalbuphine (Nubain), and pentacozine (Talwin).

Caution: Opiates often affect bodily functions such as digestion and elimination, since they decrease the production of stomach acids and delay the passage of food through the bowels, resulting in constipation. The best doctors will prescribe a laxative at the same time they prescribe an opiate. Other common side effects include nausea and vomiting.

Opiates also can reduce coughing, depress the rate and depth of breathing, dilate blood vessels, and occasionally cause itching. The use of opiates may produce feelings of discontent or anxiety.

Muscle Relaxants

Muscle relaxants relieve pain by relaxing muscles that are in painful spasm or that serve as trigger points that refer pain to other parts of the body. Muscle relaxants suppress pain by inhibiting relay points along the central nervous system. They can reinforce the effectiveness of other treatments such as transcutaneous electrical nerve stimulation (TENS) or physical therapy. Muscle relaxants are used to treat muscle pain, spinal pain, tension headaches, TMJ problems, tic douloureux, and other conditions.

Those used in the treatment of pain include carisprodol (Soma), cyclobenzaprine (Flexeril), methocarbamol (Robaxin), and orphenadrine citrate (Norflex). The muscle relaxant baclofen can be used to inhibit nervous system activity.

Caution: Muscle relaxants should be taken only for a few weeks, since there is a risk of increased tolerance after lengthy periods of use. Most make you light-headed or drowsy at first, so don't drive a car or operate dangerous machinery until you know the effects. It's not recommended to combine the use of muscle relaxants with alcohol, barbiturates, or narcotics. If your physician is considering prescribing these drugs, make sure you tell your doctor all other medications you take, since many types of medicine can increase normal side effects. Side effects can include dryness of the mouth, dizziness, blurred vision, and constipation.

Psychotropic Medications

Psychotropic, or "mind-turning," medications are drugs that affect psychic function, behavior, or experience. Sometimes used in the treatment of chronic pain, these drugs include antianxiety drugs or minor tranquilizers, antidepressants, and antipsychotic drugs or major tranquilizers.

Antianxiety medications inhibit neuron activity by attaching to receptors in the brain stem. They reinforce the action of a neurotransmitter called gamma-aminobutyric acid, or GABA, which reduces the level of stimulation in parts of the brain and decreases the feeling of anxiety. They lower the intense emotion associated with pain and the desire to escape it. Used on a short-term basis, they may help you sleep. They're most effective in relieving muscle pain, probably because they reduce muscle tension, but are sometimes employed to treat spinal pain, tension headaches, irritable bowel syndrome, and other disorders. Long-term use for a condition such as tension headaches can result in *rebound* headaches if the drug is discontinued.

Antianxiety drugs include many in the benzodiazepine group, including diazepam (Valium), alprazolam (Xanax), chlordiazepoxide (Librium), clonazepam (Klonopin), cloraxepate (Tranxene), lorazepam (Aivan), and oxazepam (Serax). In addition to these, meprobamate (Miltown or Equanil), which reduces anxiety and relaxes muscles, may be prescribed along with analgesics, or in a form combined with aspirin as Equagesic.

Caution: Antianxiety drugs should be used only for a few weeks, since tolerance can build up and they can become habit-forming. Side effects can include drowsiness, diminished coordination, and dizziness.

Antidepressant drugs are used to treat conditions such as clinical depression, which often accompanies chronic pain. Levels of important neurotransmitters like serotonin or noradrenaline are reduced both in depression and in chronic pain; antidepressants allow these neurotransmitters to remain a bit longer in the synapses between neurons, or to break down, which chemically relieves depression. Antidepressants also can relieve pain directly but must be taken for two or three weeks before they become effective. Doses that relieve pain are generally lower than those used to relieve depression, and these drugs can be taken in low doses without losing their efficacy.

Antidepressants are used to treat muscle pain, spinal pain, migraine, neuropathic pain, phantom limb and stump pain, post-herpetic neuralgia or shingles, and a few other disorders. Some commonly used antidepressants include fluoxetine (Prozac), tricyclics such as amitriptyline (Elavil), desipramine (Norpramin), doxepin (Sinequan, Adapin), and the chemically similar drugs maprotiline (Ludiomil) and trazodone (Desyrel). Other antidepressants include monoamine oxidase inhibitors such as isocarboxazid (Marphan), phenelzine (Nardil), and tranylcypromine (Parnate).

Caution: Side effects of antidepressants can include drowsiness, mouth dryness, constipation, dizziness, heart palpitations, fainting, weight gain, and mental agitation. Some increase the chance of epileptic seizures. Monoamine oxidase inhibitors can react with a great variety of other drugs and foods, which can trigger high blood pressure.

Major tranquilizers are sometimes prescribed for chronic pain, usually when other medications have failed to provide relief for problems such as the burning pain of nerve damage.

They are also prescribed to control the nausea experienced during chemotherapy for cancer. These tranquilizers include chlorpromazine (Thorazine), thioridazine (Mellaril), fluphenazine (Prolixin), and methotrimeprazine (Levoprome).

Caution: Major tranquilizers have many potential side effects, including loss of nervous system control, and are less frequently prescribed for pain than are antidepressants. When taken over a long period of time, they can produce *tardive dyskinesia*, characterized by facial tics and other uncontrollable movements.

Anticonvulsants diminish the abnormal brain neuron activity that causes epileptic seizures. Carbamazepine or phenytoin can be prescribed with other medications to relieve the pain of trigeminal neuralgia and glossopharyngeal neuralgia, which are characterized by bursts of abnormal neuron activity. Anticonvulsants also are involved in the treatment of peripheral neuropathies, phantom limb pain and stump pain, and post-herpetic neuralgia, where they can prevent a recurrence of pain. Anticonvulsants used to relieve pain include bamazepine (Tegretol), phenytoin (Dilantin), and valproic acid (Depakene).

Caution: Side effects of anticonvulsants include drowsiness, nausea, dizziness, blurred vision, and in rare instances, disorders of the blood. Phenytoin can produce an overgrowth of the gums called *gingival hyperplasia*. Like many medications, these should not be taken by pregnant women and are associated with birth defects.

OTHER DRUG TREATMENTS

Many other drugs are employed in the treatment of conditions and diseases that cause chronic pain. These are used to directly treat particular aspects of the disease, and this treatment may indirectly relieve pain. Only a few are described, and not all are always used to treat the conditions listed below.

Medications commonly employed to treat angina include *vasodilators* such as nitroglycerin tablets, dissolved under the tongue. Nitroglycerin opens the arteries and can prevent as well as mitigate heart attacks. Calcium channel blockers and beta blockers are employed in the treatment of angina; they work by reducing strength and speed of the heartbeat itself, which reduces the need for oxygen. Beta blockers and other adrenegic blockers that inhibit noradrenaline are used in the treatment of neuropathy, and sometimes for frequent vascular headaches.

For rheumatoid arthritis, so-called *remittive* drugs can stop or slow down destruction of joint tissues, but they require a long period of time to take effect and have serious side effects that should be carefully monitored. Remittive drugs include compounds of gold in the form of gold sodium thiomalate, which is injected, or auranofin, which is taken orally. Penicillamine, an antibiotic, sometimes works when gold doesn't. Antimalarial drugs such as chloroquine and hydroxychloroquine are available. Immunosuppressants, including some chemotherapy drugs used to treat cancer, are sometimes used when other remittive drug treatments have failed.

Systemic lupus erythematosus, one of several autoimmune diseases associated with pain in the joint area, is treated with many of the medications used to treat rheumatoid arthritis. Psoriatic arthritis often is treated with methotrexate, a chemotherapy drug.

Infectious arthritis is treated with antibiotics and other medications. Antibiotics such as tetracycline are used to combat Lyme disease. Pelvic inflammatory disease is treated with antibiotics and pain-relieving drugs.

Long-term control of gout often utilizes a combination of drugs that inhibits uric acid production and assists in its elimination. Drugs such as allopurinol, probenecid, and sulfinpyrazone can be prescribed for life.

For reflux esophagitis, liquid antacids provide relief, counteracting the stomach acid in the esophagus. Medications such as cimetidine (Tagamet) or rantidine (Zantac) and famotidine (Pepcid) can reduce the accumulation of stomach acids.

Bulk-forming agents, or *anticholinergic* drugs such as propantheline (Pro-Banthine) and dicyclomine (Bentyl), can relieve pain from severe spasm associated with irritable bowel syndrome. For diverticulitis and Crohn's disease, anticholinergic drugs may help in some cases, although if infection is present, antibiotics will be needed.

In the treatment of peptic ulcers, the overuse of aspirin or other NSAIDs to control pain can itself trigger a ulcer attack. Medications to combat this include antacids such as aluminum hydroxide and magnesium hydroxide. Histamine-2 blockers such as cimetidine (Tagamet) reduce stomach acid, which can erode the protective mucus coating the stomach. Sucralfate (Carafate) isolates ulcers by forming a protective coating over them, indirectly reducing pain. Misoprostol (Cytotec) reduces stomach acid and counteracts the power of NSAIDs to inhibit stomach mucus production, but it is not recommended for pregnant women.

For women afflicted with endometriosis, an inflammation of the mucous membrane lining the uterus, medications containing particular hormones normally are tried first in conjunction with birth control pills combining estrogen and progestin, or with progestin alone. Danazol, a synthetic testosterone, is sometimes used. Hormone therapy typically continues for several months, and possible side effects include weight gain, edema, tenderness, and acne. Danazol can cause a mock menopause, in which menstruation stops entirely.

Drugs are a major weapon in the daily battle against pain, and they are effective and usually quick to take effect. Drugs also are only a short-term solution, however, since many people with chronic pain benefit from reducing their drug intake to the minimum and combining drug therapy with other methods that relieve pain. Painkilling analgesic drugs, anti-inflammatory drugs, muscle relaxants, and psychotropic drugs can be used to treat pain, although the drug or drugs selected depends on many factors, including your diagnosis and your doctor's assessment of your pain. More radical treatments include surgery, the subject of chapter 10.

CHAPTER TEN

Surgery

Surgery is a treatment of last resort, but it has a place in the treatment of pain.

In certain cases, surgery may be necessary to relieve pain. Impressive new procedures using miniature surgical equipment, videocameras, radio waves, lasers, and more have been developed in recent years. The implanting of drug pumps and other pain-relieving devices sometimes allows superior relief than any other means. Entire joints or portions of arteries are routinely replaced. A few surgeries relieve very intractable pain for a period of time, and most surgeries are faster, less invasive, and more effective than ever before. Surgery is an established medical treatment, but in the world of chronic pain it is reserved for use in only a few types of cases. The utmost caution is necessary in considering surgery, since it is not reversible and can impede future treatments.

Because it is an invasive procedure and carries the risk of infection and damage to healthy tissue, surgery is normally a treatment of last resort. As a general rule, it should be considered only after all other possible conservative treatments have failed. Most important, the physical cause of the pain should be carefully diagnosed as one that has a realistic chance of being helped by a particular surgery.

Although some surgeries have high short-term success rates, the long-term rate of success with some surgeries is not impressive. Certain surgeries are reserved almost exclusively for the treatment of terminal cancer pain, but they can provide significant periods of relief when their use is indicated. The treatment of terminal cancer pain is discussed in more detail in chapter 11.

Before you agree to any surgery, the risks and benefits should be carefully explained to you by your doctor. You and your family should understand what the surgery can accomplish, what it can't accomplish, the probability of short- and long-term success, and what side effects or complications may be experienced as a result. Make sure you or your caregivers understand the risks and benefits before agreeing to surgery. Ask questions. If you don't understand the answers you receive, keep assertively and politely asking until the surgery and its effects are explained to you in language you can understand. Drawing up a list of questions in writing prior to talking with the doctor is helpful.

Ideally, the surgeon should be experienced in performing the type of surgery being recommended. Some surgeries are relatively rare, and if you must undergo one of these, seek out a surgeon who has done a number of them with good results.

Minor surgeries, on the one hand, are those that are not considered to involve a risk to life. Major surgeries, on the other hand, are important and serious operations that do involve a risk to life. Relatively simple surgical procedures are used to implant drug delivery systems. Implanting a dorsal column stimulator a more complex surgery can provide pain relief for selected patients after appropriate screening

QUESTIONS TO ASK BEFORE ANY SURGERY

In his book, *The Pain Game*, C. Norman Shealy, M.D., suggests that any patient considering surgery should have his or her doctor satisfactorily answer the following questions:

1. Why is this operation "necessary"?

2. What are the risks of death and complications?

3. What are the risks without surgery?

4. Are there alternative courses of treatment that don't involve surgery? What are the chances with those?

5. What are the chances that the surgery will do what it is supposed to do?

and medical tests. Surgical procedures are employed on certain back and spine problems, or for joint replacement in arthritis. Certain procedures or surgeries are used to treat angina. As a last resort, surgery can be useful in very severe forms of highly painful nerve malfunction caused by either injury or disease, such as tic douloureux, causalgia, or phantom limb pain.

Surgery that relieves pain typically blocks parts of the nervous system involved in pain transmission. Temporary nerve blocks are not surgical procedures, since their effects are temporary and are accomplished with anesthetics, but they can be valuable tools in diagnosing the causes of pain and assessing whether a particular surgical procedure might work. Certain severe cases may require a more prolonged nerve block, which employs surgery, chemicals, lasers, heat or cold, or other methods to break the sensory nerve connection at a strategic point. A less radical block is aimed at the sympathetic nervous system and can be effective in relieving some types of chronic pain.

The most severe form of permanent nerve block, also known as ablative surgery, can be an effective treatment of last resort. These surgeries are reserved for people with terminal cancer who experience intractable pain that cannot be relieved by other means. It should be emphasized that permanent surgical nerve blocks are almost never helpful on the difficult-to-diagnose and difficult-to-treat conditions that cause chronic nonmalignant pain, as opposed to cancer pain.

In this chapter, the simplest surgeries are discussed first. These include the implantation of drug delivery systems, dorsal column stimulators, various surgeries employed to treat spinal pain and arthritic joint problems, and sympathetic blocks and ablative surgeries.

IMPLANTED DRUG DELIVERY SYSTEMS

The implantation of a drug delivery system such as a portable infusion pump usually is performed without complications. It is reserved for cancer patients and patients for whom all other treatments have failed.

Implanted drug delivery systems can be superior to manual delivery of painkilling medications in a number of ways, since they are convenient, portable, and relieve pain with less medication. Anecdotal information from nurses is that terminal cancer patients on pumps generally have longer survival times than patients on drip morphine. However, these devices are expensive, and an implanted pump requires a level of commitment from the patient and the patient's support network to be most effective.

Six types of systems are currently available, including mechanically activated pumps and totally programmable versions. The pump should be appropriate for the patient. In the case of cancer patients, the decision to implant a pump is based on how long the patient is expected to live. Where life expectancy is two or three months, pain control with a pump is superior; where life expectancy is one month, an implanted epidural device such as a port usually is chosen. Some pump devices allow patient-controlled anesthesia (see chapter 9), which research shows actually reduces the amount of medication patients use.

Intraspinal drug delivery, using a drug pump and catheter, is a more complex surgery because it installs a system that delivers medication to particular parts of the spinal nervous system. Intraspinal delivery allows pain-relieving drugs to be placed near particular spinal cord receptors; medication is refilled by percutaneous injection, and amount and timing of medications are adjusted via an external programmer. Much smaller doses of narcotic medications are effective, consequently reducing side effects. When patients for this procedure are carefully selected, more than 50 percent experience good to excellent pain relief, according to Leon G. Robb, M.D., a pain specialist who heads the Robb Pain Management Group in North Hollywood, California.

Before a pump is implanted, preliminary trials using spinal opioids are required. The patient should be completely off medications at the time of the test. Since not all pain is relieved by narcotics, the trials should achieve success in the form of significant pain relief on two separate occasions. The preliminary trial should lower pain more than 50 percent, with a duration of twice the half-life of the agent, or 8 to 12 hours for morphine. If the trial is not successful at producing long-lasting analgesia, the procedure should be reconsidered, as it is quite expensive and has its drawbacks.

SPINAL COLUMN STIMULATION

Once several surgeries have failed and no further surgery is indicated, an alternative is an implanted dorsal column stimulator. The Health Care Financing Administration, which funds Medicare, has approved the procedure as a last resort for people with chronic, intractable pain when other treatment modalities are unsuitable or contraindicated.

In some cases, pain relief can be quite dramatic. Dr. Robb tells of a patient whose husband had accidentally injected her in the sciatic nerve with antinausea medication, resulting in neuralgia so severe she couldn't put her foot down on the floor. "She came into my office on crutches and walked out without them," he recalls, after she was implanted with a spinal cord stimulator.

Spinal cord stimulation involves the surgical implantation of a device that allows the patient to stimulate particular spinal nerves with mild doses of electricity, producing pain relief by "short circuiting" pain impulses. Epidural electrodes, an extension, and a power source are implanted into the body. Spinal cord stimulation is now an accepted treatment for failed back surgery syndrome, adhesive arachnoiditis, peripheral causalgia, and ischemic pain. In the book *Pain Medicine*, another authority, P. Prithvi Raj, M.D., a professor of clinical anesthesiology at the UCLA School of Medicine, writes that spinal cord stimulation also can be effective on reflex sympathetic dystrophy; phantom limb pain; radicular pain associated with epidural fibrosis; spastic torticollis; nerve root problems involving the neck, chest, abdomen, and extremities; and peripheral pain associated with post-herpetic neuralgia.

Dorsal column stimulation was first employed around 1967 by C. Norman Shealy, M.D., a neurosurgeon who investigated it after studying Ronald Melzack and Patrick Wall's gate control theory of pain (see chapter 2). The dorsal column is the only place in the body where the beta nerve fibers are separate from the C-nerve fibers. Dr. Shealy's first experimental results were promising but not predictable, mainly due to the unreliability of electronic equipment available at that time.

The first stimulator devices had high failure rates, but improved technology has produced high-frequency, low-amp products that rarely fail, as well as parts coated with Teflon and other materials that aren't rejected and don't break down in the body. Technological advances have allowed greater success with carefully selected patients—more than 50 to 70 percent of those who did not respond to more conservative treatment and surgery will experience good to excellent pain relief with spinal cord stimulation, according to one study that followed up on patients who received this treatment after two to five years. Tests to locate appropriate nerves for implantation, and a trial period with a temporary stimulator (also surgically implanted), lead up to the procedure itself, which affects pain impulses transmitted from the peripheral nervous system.

Cancer patients; patients with peripheral neuropathy, serious psychological dysfunction, and substance abuse behavior; and patients who receive secondary emotional or financial gain from pain should not be candidates for this procedure, according to Dr. Robb.

BACK AND NECK SURGERY

Surgery has been used to treat back and neck pain, but it is an extreme measure. It should be employed only after pain has become chronic, after conservative treatments have failed a complete and reasonable trial, and if a physical exam and imaging techniques establish that a disc disorder is the primary source of pain. Objective evidence of increasing damage to nerves and structural tissues needs to be definitively established by electrical tests or neurological examination.

Note that failed back surgery syndrome is one of the complaints often seen in pain clinics. Of all patients who have a disc removed to control sciatic pain, for instance, only about 60 percent achieve complete pain relief. When back surgery is not successful, the pain often becomes worse. Failure rates increase as additional surgeries are performed.

Spinal surgery usually is performed by an orthopedic surgeon or a neurosurgeon. Surgery near the cervical vertebrae in the upper part of the spine should be done by a neurosurgeon because of the high risk of damage to the spinal cord in this area. The most common surgery for low back pain is for disc protrusions with intractable nerve root irritation that gets worse. If spinal stenotic lesions that narrow the borders of the spinal canal containing the nerves interfere with nerve root function, a bony-decompression operation to remove bone could help with pain and function related to the lesions. The best results from surgery are from problems involving a protruded invertebrate disc plus spinal stenotic lesions.

The most common back surgeries include a *discectomy*, or the removal of a herniated disc between the vertebrae, along with a *laminectomy*, or the removal of part of the vertebral posterior arch. It is necessary to remove part of the vertebrae for the surgeon to get to the disc area. The aim of these surgeries is to lessen pressure on nerve roots from a bulging disc, or pressure against the nerves from some of the surrounding vertebrae that are composed of bone.

A laminectomy removes bone and therefore weakens the vertebrae from which the bone is removed, so an additional procedure called a *spinal fusion*, which fuses the affected vertebrae together, is sometimes employed. This procedure inserts small pieces of bone into the disc area; the fragments knit together, or fuse, with adjacent vertebrae to make that portion of the spine solid and immovable. Spinal fusion

BEFORE SPINAL SURGERY

In their Consumer Reports book, *The Fight Against Pain,* Charles B. Stacy, M.D., Andrew S. Kaplan, D.M.D., and Gray Williams Jr. set forth the following three criteria, which should be met before you agree to spinal surgery:

1. Physical examination and imaging techniques such as a computerized tomography (CT) scan or magnetic resonance imaging (MRI) scan have determined that a disc disorder is the primary source of your pain.

2. Conservative measures of treatment such as physical therapy, medications, and so forth have been given a reasonable trial in your case and failed.

3. Objective evidence of increasing damage to nerves and structural tissues has been established by electrical tests or neurological examinations.

operations are not commonly done today, although some doctors advocate them for intractable pain of traumatized or degenerative invertebrate discs.

Less invasive surgical procedures of this type include a *microdiscectomy*, which uses very small instruments seen through a special microscope to remove the disc. A *percutaneous discectomy* uses a hollow needle containing a cutter, inserted into the disc, cutting the disc tissue into small pieces that are removed with suction through the needle itself, usually used to remove the extended part of a herniated disc that hasn't ruptured. This procedure cannot remove an entire disc. An experimental technique that can cause allergic reactions, *chemical nucleolysis* injects a digestive enzyme into the disc to dissolve it.

It's important to remember that the overwhelming majority of back ailments can be treated conservatively. Back and neck problems have an established relationship with stress, and relieving stress can greatly mitigate pain. Conservative treatments should always be employed as a first-line treatment. Two weeks of conservative treatment is considered the minimum to see if those modalities help improve the problem, and longer trials also yield good results. Statistically, most people improve without surgery at about the same rate after two or three years, with either conservative treatment or back surgery. One expert, William Harsha, M.D., has estimated that less than 3 percent of lower back pain problems are favorably affected by surgery.

JOINT REPLACEMENT

One of the more successful surgeries employed is that to replace a joint lost to arthritis or other diseases such as osteoporosis. The joint is replaced through a surgery called

arthroplasty, in which an artificial joint or prosthesis composed of artificial parts made of materials such as titanium is
inserted and fastened into the appropriate location. This is a
radical intervention, as opposed to conservative treatments
such as physical therapy. Joint replacement is major surgery.
It requires a hospital stay and a period of recuperation.
Unlike the open joint surgeries done in the past, arthroplasty
is most commonly done with an *arthroscope*, a special type of
endoscope, or tube-and-optical system, through which interior
parts of the body can be viewed. Total hip arthroplasty and
total knee arthroplasty in particular can be quite successful in
terms of relieving pain of deteriorating joints. Artificial joints
are not strong enough to support strenuous athletic activity,
and they must be replaced after several years' use, but many
people who undergo these surgeries can return to basically
full-functioning lives.

Infection is the major concern during and after these
surgeries and is the most common reason they are not successful. Long-term survival rates of the prosthesis approach
95 percent ten years after the surgery, and close to that after
fifteen years, according to Kenneth D. Brandt, M.D., director
of the Multipurpose Arthritis and Musculoskeletal Diseases
Center at the Indiana University School of Medicine.

Another type of surgery done for arthritis, an *osteotomy*,
allows the surgeon to shave away bone spurs, or *osteophytes*,
as well as fibrous tissue that may have formed in the joint
as a result of internal bleeding. This procedure can temporarily relieve pain and improve the mobility of the joint,
but it does not provide permanent relief, since new spurs
may form and bone degeneration and inflammation may
continue or reappear.

For rheumatoid arthritis, a surgical procedure called a

synovectomy surgically removes some of the thickened synovial membrane surrounding a joint, temporarily improving mobility and slowing inflammation. Joint replacement also can be considered for rheumatoid arthritis if damage is severe.

CORONARY ARTERY SURGERY

For advanced coronary artery disease, of which the pain of angina is a symptom, two types of surgical treatment are employed to clear or repair arteries near the heart that are beginning to clog.

A *coronary angioplasty* involves the insertion of a thin tube with a plastic balloon attached to the end. The tube or catheter is maneuvered into the coronary artery or other affected arteries, then briefly inflated, in effect stretching out the artery to allow more blood flow. This provides better but temporary circulation for a period of time, and the procedure may be repeated. About 40 percent of one group of patients who had this procedure done on leg arteries had a recurrence within a year. New procedures involving lasers, or radiation, are being tested in experimental trials but are not yet approved for use.

Coronary bypass surgery is major surgery costing upward of $30,000, and it has a number of significant risks and complications. This surgery requires a general anesthetic, and basically bypasses a blocked artery or arteries by inserting a length of vein from the leg.

SYMPATHETIC BLOCKS

Cutting or blocking some of the sympathetic nerves that are part of the autonomous nervous system is a procedure known as a *sympathectomy*. Groups of sympathetic nerve ganglia exit the spine at particular locations on the base of the

neck, the middle of the back, or the lower back. Nerves exit-
ing at these locations serve specific regions of the body.
While it is a serious procedure, interrupting the sympathetic
nervous system is less harmful and longer-lasting than ablative procedures on sensory nerves. The pain-relieving effects
of a sympathectomy last a bit longer because sympathetic
nerves take longer to regenerate than sensory nerves.

A *pharmacologic blockade*, temporary nerve blocks using
injections of small amounts of morphine or Pentothal, can be
used to diagnose or detect causalgia, and show whether or
not a sympathectomy might be beneficial over the long
term. A sympathectomy should not be attempted unless
anesthetic blocks have repeatedly proved successful.

The procedure is performed by injecting chemicals
into certain sympathetic nerve ganglia, or sometimes by surgically cutting nerves. The most effective sympathetic blocks
are done with the aid of a fluoroscope, a type of X ray device
that helps assure pinpoint accuracy.

A sympathectomy can help relieve pain from some disorders, particularly those stemming from nerve injury such as
causalgia and reflex sympathetic dystrophy. For the pain aris-
ing from some cancers such as cancer of the internal organs,
blocks of the sympathetic nerves can be helpful. For phantom limb or stump pain, blocks of the sympathetic ganglia
sometimes relieve pain for a period of time.

Another surgery for phantom limb or stump pain
removes imperfectly regenerated nerve endings called *neuromas*, which have formed at the site of the amputation, but
removing these surgically is of dubious benefit over the long
run, since the surgery can lead to the formation of new ones.
Surgery also is done to remove bone spurs that may have
formed at the site of the amputation.

TEMPOROMANDIBULAR JOINT (TMJ) DISORDERS

For TMJ disorders, surgery should also be considered only as a last resort. Surgery may be an option if the disorder arises from a structural defect that might be corrected, if that defect is painful and debilitating, and if all other treatments have failed. Not all TMJ surgeries are successful, and the possibility of damage to the facial nerves and the use of general anesthesia during surgery pose considerable risks.

Arthroscopic surgery guided by a miniature microscope, videocamera, and miniature instruments can remove chunks of extraneous tissue from the TMJ area, which can relieve pain and restore mobility in some patients. A *disc plication* pulls a dislocated articular disc back into place and sutures it into position; a surgeon also repairs a disc by sewing it shut if it has become perforated. Sometimes the entire disc is removed. *Orthognathic* surgery can correct hereditary or severe malformations of the jawbones; bones are sliced apart and repositioned to heal symmetrically. In very severe cases, the entire temporomandibular joint can be replaced, a procedure similar to hip replacement surgery.

ABLATIVE SURGERIES

Ablative surgery cuts or permanently blocks one or more sensory nerves. This blocks sensation from the parts of the body serviced by that nerve or nerves. Ablative surgery can relieve the pain of terminal cancer that cannot be relieved by medications or other means. With one clear exception—tic douloureux—ablative surgeries are reserved for terminal cancer patients without long life expectancies. Certain nerve blocks are used more frequently than others—for example, an injection into the nerve center of the abdomen is used to block the pain resulting from pancreatic cancer.

The benefits of ablative surgery for cancer patients typically last only a few months, since the nerve endings knit back together, bringing a return of the pain or other unpleasant sensations. Note that surgery which relieves cancer pain also can extend the life expectancy of the patient who receives the surgery, because the patient experiences less pain.

The risk of ablative surgery is that it may destroy motor nerves as well as sensory nerves, creating a loss of motor function that may not return even when sensory nerves regroup. A lasting numbness, coupled with a loss of sensory function from the affected area, could mean that an affected area like an arm or leg could ultimately become useless.

Thirty years ago, distinguished physician John Mullan, M.D., chairman of the Department of Neurology at the University of Chicago, noted that one operation, called a percutaneous cordotomy, alleviated pain in cancer patients if their lives didn't extend beyond six to twelve months, but had little benefit for chronic pain patients who survived for years. The authors of many medical textbooks firmly recommend against the use of ablative surgical techniques that cut nerves to the brain or in the brain to treat noncancerous pain.

A technique called *neurolysis* has largely replaced open surgery. Neurolysis is often performed by an anesthesiologist; it involves the insertion of needles, preferably using a fluoroscope to guide their placement, which must be precise. The tip of the needle may carry a laser beam, it may be heated or frozen, or chemicals such as phenol or alcohol may be used to create a lesion on the nerve, which blocks sensation.

Peripheral neurolysis is reserved for patients with limited life expectancy or with recurrent or intractable pain, even after a series of temporary anesthetic blocks. In some cases of intractable pain, neurolysis is an effective treatment. Pain specialist John Bonica, M.D., says complete relief was achieved in 63 percent of patients with head and neck cancers using peripheral neurolysis, and moderate pain relief was achieved by 31 percent, although the remaining 6 percent received little pain relief.

Thermal treatments utilize radio frequency that coagulates the nerve. It creates a temperature over 45 degrees centigrade, and works in seconds.

Cryolysis or *cryoanalgesia* involves freezing a portion of the nerve using liquid nitrogen to create a nerve lesion. It is used for facial pain, thoracic pain, spinal pain, as a facet rhizotomy for low back pain and lumbar disc syndrome, and for pelvic pain and peripheral nerve pain. Vascular damage can occur, as can unattended motor nerve damage, although patients frequently recover. Pain relief from this procedure is not predictable—it can last from three to a thousand days.

Neurolytic drugs are chemicals such as alcohol, phenol, or hypertonic saline. They require extremely precise targeting of the needle onto the nerve, and careful control of the volume and concentration of chemicals used.

Surgery or neurolysis can take one of several forms:

Rhizotomy

Literally "root cuts," rhizotomies are sensory nerve blocks made close to the spinal cord where, at certain locations, motor and sensory nerves separate to enter the spinal cord at different points or locations. These are difficult operations. Because many nerves are bundled together, additional nerves may be destroyed, resulting in permanent numbness, paralysis, or other complications. They are most commonly used to relieve cancer pain, although they are an accepted treatment for tic douloureux.

One type of rhizotomy is performed at the dorsal root entry zone just inside the dorsal horns, located in the middle of the spine where peripheral nerves join with the central nervous system. The procedure targets the outermost layers of the dorsal horns where pain-sensing nerves concentrate. This rhizotomy deactivates central as well as peripheral nerves; since central neurons seldom regenerate, the treatment, where indicated, is more likely to provide lasting pain relief.

With proper selection of patients with cancer pain, facet blocks of the spine allowed 54 to 65 percent of patients to gain immediate relief, while 20 to 30 percent experienced relief for more than six months, according to Dr. Raj.

Tic Douloureux

A rhizotomy utilizing radio frequency waves or glycerol can be used to treat tic douloureux, or trigeminal neuralgia. This is the only widely accepted use of an ablative procedure for noncancerous pain. The rhizotomy is performed on the trigeminal nerve, a cranial nerve which has three branches. The procedure has a high success rate on tic douloureux and glossopharyngeal neuralgia, a similar condition. The procedure is sometimes employed to treat cluster headaches, but it has the risk of producing hearing loss or vertigo.

Radio frequency coagulation results in 85 to 90 percent relief, with a 7 percent risk of suffering irreversible numbness in the face. Rhizotomies utilizing chemical injections are rapid procedures and can be done on an outpatient basis.

One medical authority estimates that 65 percent of patients experience pain relief after one injection, while 85 percent experience relief after two. Symptoms can return, however. Anesthetic blocks of the affected nerves are sometimes successful, although drug treatments using anticonvulsant drugs are the first-line therapy for this problem.

A surgery known as a *microvascular decompression of the nerve root,* or Jannetta's procedure, is currently a surgical treatment of choice for tic douloureux. Jannetta's procedure isolates the compressing nerve close to the brain stem; a small sponge or pad made of shredded Teflon felt is inserted between the blood vessel and the nerve to relieve compression and pain. Microsurgery can be used to remove pressure on the blood vessel, but it requires an incision at the base of the skull. Because the affected area is close to the brain stem, this surgery poses risks, especially for older patients. Like most other surgeries, it is considered a last resort, suitable only for hardier patients.

Some doctors are experimenting with rhizotomies for other types of noncancerous pain. For neck pain, a radio frequency rhizotomy can be employed to raise the temperature of tissues around inflamed spinal and neck nerves, killing the pain-sensing nerves. Mark Lodico, M.D., of the Allegheny General Back Institute in Pittsburgh, Pennsylvania, says this procedure can be an effective treatment for whiplash pain, and that the majority of his patients have experienced between 50 and 100 percent pain relief.

Cordotomy

Severing a portion of the spinal cord is called a *cordotomy.* A cordotomy blocks certain pain pathways along the spinal cord, called *spinothalamic tracts,* which carry sensations of pain from the body up the spinal cord to the brain. Severing a spinothalamic tract on one side of the spinal cord effectively deadens the other side of the body from the point of the block down to the feet.

A cordotomy can relieve pain effectively for a period of time. If the patient outlives the limited effectiveness of the surgical procedure, however, there is the risk of not only of the return of pain, but also of sleeplessness and permanent numbness. It is reserved for advanced cancer pain that extends over a good portion of the body and therefore involves a number of peripheral nerves, or for unilateral lower extremity or flank pain. The pain relief from a cordotomy is limited to a period of months. The procedure is difficult to repeat. It can endanger other pathways in the spinal cord, such as those controlling the bladder, the bowel, and the legs. Incontinence, impotence, or weakness can follow a cordotomy. Because of the side effects, spinal opioids are usually a better alternative.

A *myelotomy* is another surgical procedure that provides pain relief to terminal cancer patients. It involves splitting the spinal cord lengthwise.

Surgical techniques to block pain by severing connections closer to the brain are sometimes used for cancer pain, especially pain that radiates from the head or face. These are not always successful. At the present time, blocks of the peripheral nerves or tracts along the spine are more successful.

Other forms of ablative surgery, the *thalamotomy* and *cingulotomy,* are no longer employed. Another surgery called a *mesencephalotomy* occasionally is used for cancer patients in Europe, but rarely employed in the United States, as it carries the risk of serious complications.

Surgery should be employed only as a last resort, since its results are long lasting and usually can't be reversed. Surgeries carry risks not encountered in conservative forms of treatment, but they can be effective in relieving certain forms of pain if their use is clearly indicated. As a patient, you should carefully weigh the risks and benefits of any surgery before you agree to it. Surgery is most often employed in the treatment of cancer pain, which is the subject of the next chapter.

CHAPTER ELEVEN

Cancer Pain

ᔊ *More than 90 percent of cancer pain can be relieved by relatively simple means.*

Unlike other forms of chronic pain, cancer pain should almost always be *treated* rather than *managed*. Treatment for cancer pain may be given in the hospital along with medical treatment, but most of the time it is given on an outpatient basis, often in the home. Although many aspects of pain treatment for cancer resemble that for chronic pain, narcotic drugs and certain pain-relieving surgeries are utilized much more often in treating cancer pain. For terminal patients, hospices can be a humane alternative in which to spend their final days.

In terms of its treatment, cancer pain is different than other types of chronic pain. Most of the time it presents as acute pain. Social issues such as "pain behaviors," addressed in the treatment of chronic pain, and legal issues such as the need to establish disability or settle lawsuits are not relevant factors in the treatment of cancer pain. In relieving the pain of cancer, the biggest single problem is the undertreatment of pain. Psychologically, as part of the experience of dealing with cancer, you must also confront your own fears of mortality. People with cancer look at the possibility of a radically shortened life, which is not an issue in chronic benign pain.

Cancer patients dread and fear the appearance of pain, suffering, and disability. This is particularly true if pain was one of the symptoms that led to the diagnosis of cancer.

MYTHS ABOUT CANCER PAIN

According to Cancer Care, Inc., a New York–based organization, and other sources, here are some myths surrounding the treatment of cancer pain:

1. Cancer pain is inevitable and untreatable.
   False: Many cancer patients never experience pain, and more than 90 percent of the pains that occur are treatable by simple means.

2. Pain is a signal that the cancer is getting worse.
   False: Pain is related not always to cancer, but often to other factors such as an infection or spending too much time in bed without exercise.

3. Pain medications should be taken only when you have pain.
   False: Pain is easier to control when it's mild rather than severe. Medication has a preventive effect if taken on a regular schedule.

4. Taking medication for pain makes you "high."
   False: Pain medications taken for pain control do not usually cause euphoria, but rather ease suffering, anxiety, and tension.

5. Medications will stop working over time.
   False: You can build up a "tolerance" to the beneficial effects of some medications, particularly the opiates

Much uncertainty accompanies cancer treatment, since both the cancer and cancer pain can change, creating fear and anxiety. Not all cancer patients, or even all terminal cancer patients, ever experience pain, however. In 1979, Kathleen Foley, M.D., of Memorial Sloan–Kettering Cancer Center in

---

and minor tranquilizers, but this can be overcome by increasing the dosage or switching to a different drug or drug combination.

6. It's better to live with pain than to complain about it.
   False: It's not a sign of weakness to complain about pain. Relieving pain will help your doctor help you, and it will give you more energy to fight cancer.

7. Side effects of medication are worse than the pain.
   False: This is not true if medications are used judiciously.

8. People who take narcotics must get shots.
   False: Most narcotic drugs are available in oral form, which effectively relieves pain.

9. Narcotic drugs make it harder for terminally ill patients to breathe.
   False: Suppression of coughing is a side effect of narcotics. *Everyone's Guide to Cancer Therapy* notes that tolerance to respiratory effects usually develops before tolerance to pain-relieving effects.

New York City, noted that one-third of terminally ill patients don't require analgesic medications at all.

The level of pain experienced depends to some extent on the type of cancer, the stage of the cancer, the cancer treatment, and the reaction of the patient to the pain. Cancer pain is not always severe. Pain specialist John Bonica, M.D., estimates that in cancer, 40 to 45 percent of patients have moderate to severe pain initially following their diagnosis, 35 to 45 percent have pain at the intermediate stages, and 60 to 85 percent suffer pain in advanced stages of cancer. Studies in 1985 and 1989 showed that cancer patients *expected* to experience pain, even though more than 50 percent of breast cancer patients, 80 percent of lymphoma patients, and 95 percent of leukemia patients do not report pain. People with advanced cancers that begin or spread into the bones or the abdomen are the most likely to experience pain.

Pain can come from the growth of the cancer. Malignant tumors can invade major organs and tissues, creating pain. Tumors can block the digestive tract or the path of blood vessels and cause a type of swelling called *engorgement*, creating oxygen starvation in tissues beyond the blocked area. Tumors can grow into healthy tissue and put pressure on nerve receptors, or cause the death of normal tissue. If tumors grow and press on major nerves, they can cause pain or loss of nerve function. Tumors can cause bone fractures or bone erosion. Any of these developments can trigger pain, as can standard medical treatments such as surgery, chemotherapy, and radiation therapy, which are used to control the cancer. And of course, some pains experienced by people undergoing cancer treatment may have nothing to do with the disease at all. If you have arthritis, for instance, the pain you may experience won't go away just because you are being treated for cancer.

THE UNDERTREATMENT OF PAIN

Although it is a medical cliché that pain won't kill you, this notion has come into question in light of some recent research. A few years ago, the late John Liebeskind, a UCLA psychologist and pain specialist, wrote an intriguing editorial in the magazine *Pain* entitled "Pain Can Kill," which examined the role of pain in compromising the immune system. Liebeskind noted studies on laboratory animals showing that the cytotoxic activity of natural killer, or NK, cells (major components of the immune system) and the growth of the cancer itself are increased by uncontrolled pain. "Evidence from laboratory experiments has begun to accumulate showing that pain can accelerate the growth of tumors and increase mortality after tumor challenge. It appears that the dictum 'pain does not kill,' sometimes invoked to justify ignoring pain complaints, may be dangerously wrong," Liebeskind wrote.

A little research on humans supports this general idea. A research study in Sweden showed that most cancer patients who committed suicide had inadequately managed pain. A 1985 study of breast cancer patients showed that NK cell activity correlated with patient adjustment, lack of social support, and fatigue/depression syndrome. Other studies have shown a correlation between mood and pain intensity.

"Undertreatment of pain and other symptoms of cancer is a serious and neglected public health problem," noted James Mason, M.D., head of the Agency for Health Care Policy and Research. "Every patient with cancer should have the expectation that pain control will be an integral aspect of care throughout the course of the disease."

Reasons often cited for the undertreatment of cancer pain include a lack of knowledge about pain control on the part of doctors, fears of addiction to drugs on the part of doctors, nurses, and patients, physician failure to properly assess the causes of the pain, not making pain control a medical priority, and patient fears and misconceptions, such as desiring to be "a good patient" by not complaining about pain.

MITIGATING PAIN

As with chronic pain, cancer pain is treated in several ways at large multidisciplinary cancer treatment centers. Treatments for pain include noninvasive physical therapies such as exercise, heat or cold treatments, massage, or transcutaneous electrical nerve stimulation (TENS). Heat or cold treatments and massage can provide soothing, temporary relief for patients with all types of pain. TENS often works effectively in well-localized cancer pains such as compression fractures of the spine, and can help lower levels of pain control medication. Acupuncture and acupressure are accepted support therapies for cancer pain.

The multidisciplinary approach includes the use of mind–body strategies such as hypnosis, visual imagery, meditation, and relaxation exercises. Hypnosis, for instance, especially self-hypnosis, has been proven useful in controlling cancer pain. Visual imagery was developed as an adjunct treatment by a radiation oncologist and a psychologist, and its practice helps many people extend life and make their quality of life better. Relaxation therapy is a first-line therapy against stress, which contributes to cancer pain. Distraction helps relieve any pain simply by getting your mind off your own body. Humor therapy, art therapy, support groups, and more are offered at many cancer treatment centers. Even something as pleasurable as listening to music has a pain-relieving effect that is rated twice as soothing as ordinary background sound. (See chapter 8 for more information on these therapies.)

Psychotherapy can help patients work through their encounter with cancer; psychologists have developed treatment models to help people address the issues that accompany the battle. Cognitive therapy can be quite useful in helping one regain a feeling of control over the flood of negative self-talk which often accompanies cancer.

Most pain that arises during cancer treatment fits the medical model for acute pain. A major difference between cancer pain and chronic benign pain is that strong analgesic drugs such as morphine are often effectively and appropriately used to treat cancer patients, even for relatively long periods of time. Implanted drug infusion pumps administer drugs that combat cancer pain (see chapter 10).

For the small percentage of cancer patients whose pain can't be controlled with stress-relieving techniques or drugs, other pain control measures can be effective. Temporary nerve blocks, for example, may be helpful in controlling pain in certain areas of the body. Longer-acting local anesthetic blocks can be repeated over a period of days or weeks, sometimes providing periods of great pain relief.

Radiation therapy is used to relieve a few types of pain associated with cancer, such as bone pain as a result of the spread of cancer into the skeleton. Radiation therapy basically stops the pain by stopping or arresting the cancer.

The most radical treatments are surgical or ablative procedures that cannot be reversed (see chapter 10). Ablative surgeries may relieve pain on patients for whom all other conservative measures have failed, and they have a place in the treatment of intractable cancer pain. Regional anesthesia or neurosurgery may help people who have trouble chewing or swallowing, blocking painful sensations and allowing them to eat better and regain lost weight.

DRUG TREATMENT

It is estimated that more than 90 percent of cancer pain can be controlled with simple means, usually pain-relieving drugs. As a rule of thumb, the proper dose of any medication for pain is one that provides the best control with the least side effects.

Cancer pain ranges from mild to severe, from constant to episodic, and its parameters may change over the course of treatment. Milder drugs are the recommended first line of defense. The World Health Organization's (WHO) ladder of treatment recommends using the mildest drugs first. Many people are surprised to learn that aspirin is the most commonly prescribed drug for cancer pain. Both WHO and the International Association for the Study of Pain recommend aspirin as the first analgesic for control of cancer pain, since it is effective and inexpensive. Mild drugs often control pain.

If one mild nonsteroidal anti-inflammatory drug (NSAID) doesn't control mild to moderate pain, your dose may be adjusted, or another mild drug in the same class may be prescribed. It is well known that certain people can develop side effects to one particular drug in a class, and these disappear if a similar but different drug is substituted.

Since mild drugs have the least side effects, including no problems with tolerance and no possibility of drug dependency, more than one may be used before that class of drugs is abandoned.

The next step on the treatment ladder are more potent pain-relievers. These include NSAIDs, which also include mild narcotics such as codeine, hydrocodone, or Percodan. NSAIDs have an *analgesic ceiling* beyond which they will no longer provide pain relief when used alone. This ceiling increases when they are used in combination with other drugs. These combinations usually are prescribed for moderate pain. They have side effects but often provide pain control when taken as directed.

If this level of medication doesn't work, stronger analgesic drugs including the most potent opiates can be used. These are available in pill, patch, and suppository form and may be injected or infused. An intravenous shot provides the quickest results but has a short period of effectiveness compared to time-release pills and other forms of delivery.

Analgesic drugs also may be supplemented in some cases with adjuvant drugs such as corticosteroids, psychotropic drugs such as tranquilizers and antidepressants, and anticonvulsants.

In certain cases, implanted ambulatory infusion pumps may be used to keep you medicated while you go about your business, but these usually are reserved for patients with advanced cancers or those undergoing chemotherapy. Infusion pumps may be preset, delivering several types of medication on schedule, while others allow for some patient-controlled medication. Some deliver drugs directly to the nerves of the spine and are suitable only for severe pain.

Narcotics

Doctors will try the milder drugs first, but morphine remains the gold standard of pain-relieving drugs. Morphine, Demerol, hydromorphone, methadone, and oxycodone are available in pill form or in oral solution, which are usually the preferred methods of administration. Some also are available in long-acting pill form whose effects normally last from eight to twelve hours. Fentanyl, a potent narcotic, can be given through skin patches.

A fear of addicting their patients leads some doctors to underprescribe stronger drugs, and some nurses to underadminister them. Dr. Bonica cites several studies that show physicians prescribe narcotics at two-thirds to three-fourths the dose actually needed to relieve pain. Unfortunately, the same studies show that nurses then underadminister by another one-third to one-half. This results in woefully inadequate control of pain and much unnecessary suffering.

A powerful negative stigma is associated with narcotics, driven by the federal government's war on drugs. As a result, these drugs are often prescribed on an as-needed basis, rather than in regular doses, which are more effective at preventing pain. Continuous or frequently recurring pains are more appropriately treated by regular timed doses. Drug *dependence* can result from the use of opiate drugs, but drug *addiction* is almost never a problem when the drugs are used for cancer pain. In addition to physical dependence, addiction has a psychological component. Less than 1 percent of patients who receive narcotics in the hospital become addicted. Those who do become dependent can be gradually withdrawn from them under medical supervision without undergoing painful withdrawal symptoms associated with suddenly stopping the medication.

DOCTOR-PATIENT COMMUNICATION

Controlling the cancer itself often relieves the symptom of pain. Oncologists who treat cancer may be primarily focused on controlling the cancer, but the pain that can accompany cancer treatment also should be directly addressed. Cancer pain sometimes changes location, duration, or intensity, and your doctor should be kept apprised of these changes. It may be helpful to have your pain evaluated on a simple 1 to 10 scale on a regular basis, or by the more comprehensive McGill–Melzack pain questionnaire. It helps if you and your family members can speak assertively to physicians and nurses, since you have a better chance of getting what you want if you ask for it.

If you are being treated for cancer and are not experiencing good pain relief, tell both your nurse and your doctor. Symptoms can change during cancer treatment. When you speak to a doctor, be prepared to volunteer the following information:

- Where is the pain located?
- How often do you have pain, and when does it occur?
- What is its intensity on a 1 to 10 scale?
- What kind of pain is it (sharp, dull, throbbing)?
- What makes the pain better, and what makes it worse?
- What methods of pain relief, or medications, have relieved your pain in the past?
- What other symptoms such as sweating and nausea accompany the pain?

If you think you will have difficulty explaining this to your doctor, write it down, or have someone else write it down. Present the written copy to the doctor, and perhaps send a copy to the hospital's ombudsman. Make a little noise if that's what it takes to get results. Your doctor must be aware that you have a problem before he or she can treat it.

TYPES OF PAIN

In treating cancer pain, an oncologist probably will order up a number of medical tests to determine the cause. About 80 percent of the pain experienced in cancer treatment presents as acute or sudden pain, according to author Richard A. Sternbach. Of these acute pain problems, he estimates that approximately half are due to metastatic bone disease, and another 25 percent are the result of a tumor contacting, pressing against, or penetrating a nerve. Not all pain experienced during cancer treatment arises from the cancer, of course, so a thorough medical examination and clear diagnosis are in order. Pain can result from something as simple as spending too much time in bed without exercise. Tell your doctor as much as you can about your pain, when and where it is experienced, how long it lasts, and as much about the quality of the sensation as possible.

Oncologists who treat cancer pain make a distinction between *somatic* pain and *neuropathic* pain, according to the book *Everyone's Guide to Cancer Therapy*, edited by Malin Dollinger, M.D., Ernest Rosenbaum, M.D., and Greg Cable. Somatic pain often arises from the skeletal muscles as opposed to the extremities or internal organs, and is effectively treated with drugs such as NSAIDs and opiates. Neuropathic or nerve pain, on the other hand, is often resistant to narcotics or may require extremely high doses. These two types of pain, unfortunately, are sometimes intertwined, making medical treatment more difficult and complex.

CANCER PAIN RELIEF

The U.S. Department of Health and Human Services publication *Clinical Practice Guidelines for Cancer Pain Management* has rated psychosocial pain relief methods based on the strength and consistency of scientific evidence to date. Well-designed, controlled studies of patients with cancer that yield consistent results are considered the best evidence that particular strategies can relieve cancer pain.

Rated "A" for best scientific evidence:

- Hypnosis
- Relaxation
- Visual imagery
- Patient education by providing sensory or procedural information

Rated "B" for consistent scientific evidence:

- Education in pain management
- Cognitive reappraisal
- Distraction, including music
- Biofeedback
- Psychotherapy and structured support
- Exercise

Somatic pains can spring from inflammations of the muscles or connective tissues, from a broken bone, as a result of some forms of bone cancer or abdominal cancer, or from an obstruction in the urinary tract or intestine. Nerve pain, or *neuropathy*, arises from the pain-sensing nerve cells within the nervous system, or some abnormality in processing pain information in the central nervous system. Neuropathic pain is of a different nature than other types of pain; sometimes an extremely light touch can trigger extraordinary pain. Nerve pain is frequently experienced from nerves in the hands and feet, which are at the far end of the nervous system; this is called *peripheral neuropathy*. Some surgical procedures, some radiation treatments, and some chemotherapy treatments such as those using the platinum-based drugs and Taxol can result in neuropathic pain that sometimes goes away. A tumor pressing on or invading nerves also might cause neuropathy.

Different types of medications are used to treat neuropathic pain. When pain cannot be controlled with narcotics, doctors sometimes try to control the pain with other types of drugs such as steroids, antidepressants, anticonvulsants, sedatives, and antihistamines. These are sometimes effective, although the mechanisms by which they relieve pain are not completely understood.

Exercise sometimes helps the pain of peripheral neuropathy, according to Denise Economou, R.N., an oncological nurse at Cedars-Sinai Medical Center in Los Angeles. Neuropathic pain in the hand can be lessened by squeezing rubber balls, and pain in the feet is sometimes controlled by rolling the feet over a rolling pin, or by using an abacus-type device for the same purpose. These exercises increase the blood flow to the site of pain. TENS sometimes helps control neuropathic pain, although it works best when pain is localized. Topical lotions such as those containing capsaicin may also help.

EMOTIONAL STRESS

Although cancer is becoming more and more of a curable disease, acute emotional suffering and stress often accompanies its treatment. Even when little physical pain is experienced, a storm of powerful feelings arises that includes fear, anxiety, depression, rage, helplessness, and hopelessness. These feelings create great emotional anguish. When pain appears, particularly if it was a symptom that led to the cancer diagnosis, emotional stress increases.

"Catastrophizing" is a condition in which the mind amplifies perceived pain, triggered by fear that it signals an oncoming catastrophe. This is fairly common with cancer patients who suffer great psychological dislocations. The fear that your life is out of control is quite common in any chronic illness, and cancer is no different. The roller coaster of powerful emotions can intensify pain, reduce pain tolerance, or make the pain less tolerable. This is a source of great emotional stress. Accordingly, exercise, stress management, and other mind-body techniques are regularly used to help treat pain at major cancer treatment centers, and they help you regain a sense of control as well as directly relieving stress and pain. The use of relaxation training, distraction, biofeedback, meditation, visual imaging, and other techniques can help control pain or reduce the amount of medication needed to control it.

Psychiatric disorders can be a reaction to a diagnosis of cancer and to the pain and disability associated with the disease. A 1983 study by the Psychosocial Collaborative Oncology Group revealed that 47 percent of all cancer patients had a psychiatric disorder, and of these, 39 percent experienced significant pain. This compares with only 19 percent of patients without a psychiatric diagnosis who experienced pain. In this study, the most common psychiatric disorders listed were depression or mixed moods.

If you feel completely overwhelmed by your life, if your behavior is self-destructive, or if you feel helpless to take action to help yourself, you may benefit from seeing a mental health professional. Psychotherapy is useful in addressing any loss of function and control, as well as the roiling emotional sea of strong feelings that accompanies cancer. Psychotherapy helps patients, caregivers, and family members work through their encounter with death and loss. Family counseling, group therapy, pastoral counseling, and support groups are enormously helpful to the cancer patient as well as to caregivers and family members. Support groups are sponsored in several cities by the American Cancer Society, the Wellness Community, and other organizations.

A DIFFERENCE IN PERSPECTIVE

People with cancer pain have a different perspective than people who are living with chronic pain, since they face a threat to the *quantity* of their days rather than their *quality*. This experience can result in a profound spiritual crisis that ultimately can lead to the acceptance of one's mortality and a greater and more spiritual perspective on the meaning of life itself.

Swiss-American physician Elisabeth Kübler-Ross studied the mental processes that accompany terminal cancer and other terminal illness. She has written that many people go through five psychological stages: denial, anger, bargaining, depression, and acceptance. In her monumental book *On Death and Dying*, she wrote, "It has been our life's work to help our patients view a terminal illness not as a destructive, negative force, but as one of the windstorms in life that will enhance their own inner growth and will help them to emerge as beautiful as the canyons which have been battered for centuries."

Western culture and Western medicine both fears and

fights the specter of death, and denies the idea of death at almost any cost. This is reflected in the attitudes of some physicians who see the death of a patient as a personal failure, and of the medical system itself, which seeks to prolong life even at the expense of its immutable human quality. According to Kübler-Ross, the denial of death is rooted in the impersonal and institutionalized character of modern death, which today almost always occurs in a hospital rather than in the home.

HOSPICES

Cancer hospices are not hospitals where medical treatment is dispensed, but rather places where terminal patients may spend their last days, receiving treatment to keep them comfortable. Most hospices are for adults, but a few cater to children who are terminally ill.

Hospices provide palliative care that seeks to relieve the patient from the worst effects of illness in their final days. They mitigate much of the agony and suffering accompanying a terminal illness, without seeking to cure it. Most hospices are more like homes than hospitals and espouse a very different philosophy than hospitals, whose employees focus on prolonging life at almost any cost. In the United States, some hospices are separate facilities, while some are administered in conjunction with hospitals, which allows medical treatment to be dispensed as needed, sometimes in the home.

The first modern hospice was created in England by Dame Cicely Saunders, M.D., and has served as a model in the wake of its humane and cost-efficient success. The hospice concept has spread to many countries, including the United States. The original mission statement at St.

Christopher's Hospice, London, states that palliative care exists for five reasons:

- To affirm life, not to hasten death
- To respect the worth and individuality of each person who comes for our care
- To offer relief from pain and other distressing symptoms
- To help patients with strong and unfamiliar emotions. To assist them to explore meaning, purpose and value in their lives. To offer the opportunity to reconcile and heal relationships and complete important personal tasks
- To offer a support system for family and friends during the patients' illness and in bereavement

Effective pain management is important in a hospice situation, since the primary focus is on keeping people comfortable by preventing pain. At St. Christopher's, the so-called Brompton mixture of morphine, cocaine, chloroform water, alcohol, and flavoring, delivered in liquid form, originally was used to treat pain. In subsequent years, the mixture has been supplanted by oral doses of morphine, the only important ingredient in the original mixture.

The health care team at most hospices includes not only doctors and nurses, but also spiritual counselors, social workers, physical or occupational therapists, and bereavement counselors. Respite care, which gives family members time off, and volunteers who help with meals and other chores are often part of the program.

The U.S. government's Medicare system approves hospice care for terminal cancer patients. Under Medicare Part A, patients who are not expected to survive more than six months and who need treatment for pain or other aspects of cancer are entitled to two-hundred and ten days of home care through hospice programs. Overall, Medicare is experiencing decreases in the use of acute care hospital services, large increases in outpatient use, and very large increases in Medicare Home Health and Skilled Nursing Facility benefits, as well as hospice. In 1990, some 98 million home health visits were authorized for people on Medicare.

Older people may fare best in a hospice situation. Of cancer deaths in hospice, one study found that people over the age of seventy-five were more likely to be free of pain and less likely to be in persistent pain than were younger patients.

Home care is another option if finances and the family situation allow it. Although it is less expensive than hospital treatment, it imposes significant burdens on caregivers and some hardships on the patient, since medical attention is not so readily available. Home care requires planning and coordination, but if accomplished, it allows the person to die at home in familiar surroundings.

Every human life has meaning. As Kübler-Ross observed, one of the constants in human life is hope, which never truly disappears.

The acute pain that accompanies cancer can be alleviated, usually by simple means. A great variety of pain-relieving treatments are available to cancer patients, who are treated somewhat differently than those with chronic benign pain. Psychological and emotional issues are important and should be addressed. Noninvasive stress-relieving and physical therapy treatments are supplemental, and drugs, radiation, and surgery also may be employed. In the relief of pain, many new treatments are under development, as explained in the final chapter.

CHAPTER TWELVE

Looking Ahead

~ Hope is a realistic frame of mind, given the great variety of medical research now under way.

Advances continue to be made in the understanding of all the factors that create pain and disease, as well as the factors that help relieve it. At this moment, thousands of research experiments are under way in the United States and around the world. Humankind probably will never achieve immortality, but the prolongation of the human life span, with the highest possible quality of life, is a reasonable goal.

On the pharmaceutical front, many new drugs are coming into use. For instance, some doctors expect rheumatoid arthritis will be wiped out with better drugs in the future, since drugs to treat this condition have become more effective over the past several years. New types of pain-relieving drugs, perhaps without the problems of tolerance and dependence associated with narcotics, may be discovered. Although opiate receptors located on the surface of nerve cells are known to be sensitive to narcotic drugs, it has been found that there actually are several different types of receptors, all of whose chemical keys are not yet known. Research in this area may lead to new classes of painkilling drugs without the drawbacks or side effects of narcotics. The medical journal

Science reported in 1998 that an experimental drug compound called ABT-594, chemically similar to nicotine, appears to provide as much pain relief as morphine, but without its side effects. An experimental new drug made of cone snail venom, introduced to the American Pain Society in 1996 by the director of the Stanford University Pain Clinic, shows promise of reducing severe pain with—so far—few side effects and no tolerance or addiction problems. Increasing knowledge of the peptides, which transmit pain signals, may yield useful new pain control medications, as may the continuing study of all the brain chemicals that have a role in the experience of pain.

Surgeons have created new and less invasive types of surgery using a vast array of new technology. Surgical techniques continue to grow safer and less invasive, incor-porating miniature equipment and sensing devices, videocameras, computers, and other high-tech innovations such as pacemakers that can prolong life. Attempts are being made to grow entire new organs from a few cells. Among the dizzying array of new procedures being tested in the United States is percutaneous transmyocardial revascularization, which uses a laser catheter to create tiny holes in the heart itself, thereby initiating the growth of new blood vessels to the heart wall and decreasing symptoms such as angina. At a Montreux Congress on Stress, in 1996, exposure to a certain frequency for fifteen to twenty minutes was shown to invigorate healthy cells while causing cancerous cells to expand and explode.

Scientists are looking at ways to increase health at the cellular level, where millions of chemical reactions take place every second. Some of the natural pain controls within the body, for instance, may involve normally occurring natural substances such as ATP (adenosine triphosphate), a chemical that stores free energy and is essential to the healing process and to the health of cells. Relatively large amounts of ATP are needed to control the constant movement of sodium, potassium, magnesium, calcium, and waste products in and out of our body's cells. Through the outer membrane of each cell, a constant electrical exchange takes place between positively charged ions of sodium, calcium, potassium, and magnesium, and negatively charged ions of chloride and phosphate. When this natural ebb and flow is drastically disturbed, the natural balance that the body seeks to maintain, called *homeostasis*, is disrupted. Correcting the disturbance in some undiscovered way might restore health at the most basic level.

More progress on treating painful disorders with electrical energy surely will be made, following up on the success of transcutaneous electrical nerve stimulation (TENS) and dorsal column stimulation. Pulsing magnets already heal previously unhealable bone fractures. To relieve certain types of muscle pain, permanent magnets are now beginning to be used, mostly as a home remedy but also by doctors of sports medicine. So-called microcurrent electrical therapy, employing subtle electrical and magnetic energies, is coming into use, based on the work of American scientist Robert Becker, M.D., Swedish radiologist Bjorn Nordenstrom, and others, creating an entire new field of electromagnetic medicine.

Dr. Paul Rosch, head of the American Institute of Stress and co-author of a book on magnet therapy, believes that the future will belong to "electroceuticals." Pulsed Signal

Therapy or PST, available in Europe and currently on the fast track for FDA approval in the U.S., is the most promising of these, Rosch believes. PST involves a bioelectric signal sent into the natural electrical field which surrounds the joint, as well as adjacent cartilage and connective tissue, according to PST expert Richard Markoll. Research conducted at Yale University School of Medicine teaching hospitals on 5,000 patients with arthritis showed the technique significantly reduced pain and disability, increased quality of life as a result of better sleep patterns, and had no apparent side effects.

The application of new GigaTENS stimulators to selected acupuncture points is in the preliminary stages, but its use on certain combinations or "circuits" of acupuncture points has been shown to increase DHEA, the so-called antiaging hormone, as well as serotonin, another substance often low in people with chronic pain. Pain Specialist C. Norman Shealy, M.D., regards acupuncture circuits as the most promising treatment possibilities on the horizon today. Electrical medicine may be the medicine of the twenty-first century.

In France and elsewhere, auricular therapy treats pain and other ailments using magnets, needles, and electricity applied to specific points on the ear that correspond to other areas of the body.

Prolotherapy, another promising new treatment modality for muskoskeletal disorders, involves the injection of sodium morrhuate, a derivative of cod liver oil, into painful irritated areas, which creates an immune reaction which strengthens weakened ligaments and tendons. Former U.S. Surgeon General C. Everett Koop, diagnosed with incurable pain at two neurological clinics, found permanent pain relief from this therapy, and wrote a book praising its benefits.

The field of psychoneuroimmunology, which examines the interplay between the mind, the emotions, and illness and health, is just in its infancy. The Cartesian model, which posits a clear separation between mind and body, is increasingly questioned. It is well known that unpleasant negative emotions inhibit the immune system, and that positive emotions such as joy and laughter may enhance it. Much useful information may be uncovered from the study of these effects, perhaps allowing a strengthened immune system a greater role in the mitigation of pain and the restoration and enhancement of good health. The biochemical forces at work in the unexplained, occasional successes of faith healing, folk medicine, and other alternative therapies may someday be understood, further refined, and put to wider use by health practitioners on particular ailments.

Research in the field of psychology and stress reduction may yield useful results. At the moment, many permutations of behavioral and cognitive therapy approaches are being used and refined at different pain clinics, and their effects studied to see if certain approaches are most useful on certain conditions and for certain types of chronic pain. Psychologists are trying to develop treatments that work effectively and quickly in an environment in which treatment costs are being trimmed. Overlapping mental and physical health problems are being treated in new ways. For instance, seasonal affective disorder, a form of depression that occurs in winter, can be positively affected by the use of goggles containing small red lights that flash at particular rhythms. Just shining a light on the back of the knee in a certain manner has been proven to influence circadian rhythms, which have a primary role in sleep. The enormous role of the mind in health continues to be explored. Some research underway at this moment may allow particular therapies to be even more individualized for particular patients or families, to yield more positive long-term results.

Nutrition is a another relatively new science, since the first of the vitamins was identified in 1912. The entire area of nutrition is being studied extensively, following up on the practical applications of what has been learned about how the body utilizes nutrients to protect itself on a cellular level. The role of particular vitamins, minerals, and as yet undiscovered natural substances needed for optimum health and to combat pain and other health problems, is still in its infancy and will probably be individualized as more sophisticated testing procedures and tests are developed.

So-called alternative medicine is moving closer to the mainstream, pushed as much by popular interest as by the medical profession. Sorting out what is truly helpful from what is not will take more time. Homeopathy, dance therapy, therapeutic touch, aromatherapy, and other therapies may someday contribute more to the way we treat and manage chronic pain and perhaps help make Dr. Schweitzer's "terrible lord of mankind" extinct.

As more and more progress is made on understanding and treating chronic pain, we will benefit from both the successes and the failures of scientists and researchers. Armed with the curiosity and problem-solving abilities that characterize our race, we can expect to look at old problems in a new light tomorrow.

Resources

Many resources exist in the United States and Canada that provide specific information on pain-related topics. A number of government and nonprofit organizations are listed here, as are various support organizations for particular conditions. Addresses, telephone numbers, and Internet addresses are listed as available.

Medical Organizations
Dealing with Pain

Pain Organizations

American Academy of Pain Management
13947 Mono Way, Ste. A
Sonora, CA 95370
(209) 533-9744
aapm@aapainmanage.org

American Academy of Pain Medicine
4700 W. Lake Ave.
Glenview, IL 60025
(847) 375-4731

American Pain Society
4700 W. Lake Ave.
Glenview, IL 60025
(847) 375-4715
www.painmed.org/header__default.htm

Institute for the Study and Treatment of Pain
5655 Cambie St.
Vancouver, British Columbia, Canada NC V5Z 3A4
(604) 264-7860
istop.org/istop

International Association for the Study of Pain
909 NE 43rd St., Ste. 306
Seattle, WA 98105
(206) 547-6409
http://www.halcyon.com/iasp

National Chronic Pain Outreach Association
7979 Old Georgetown Rd., Ste. 100
Bethesda, MD 20814-2429
(301) 652-4948 or (301) 698-5452
www.chronicpain.org

North American Chronic Pain Association of Canada
150 Central Park Dr., Unit 105
Brampton, Ontario, Canada L6T 2T9
1-800-616-7246 or (905) 793-5253
www.sympatico.ca/nacpac

Pain Relief Foundation
Rice Lane, Liverpool, L9 1AE
United Kingdom
441-(0)151-523-1486
www.liv.ac.uk/pri/

Information and Support
for Specific Medical Conditions

Chronic Pain Support Groups

American Chronic Pain Association
P.O. Box 850
Rocklin, CA 95677
(916) 632-0922
www.theacpa.org

National Self-Help Clearinghouse
33 West 42nd Street
New York, NY 10036
(212) 642-2944

Arthritis

Arthritis Foundation
1330 W. Peachtree
Atlanta, GA 30309
1-800-283-7800 or (404) 872-7100
help@arthritis.org
www.arthritis.org

Arthritis Society of Canada
250 Bloor St. East, Ste. 401
Toronto, Ontario, Canada M4W 3P2
(416) 967-1414

Back Pain

Back Pain Association of America
P.O. Box 135
Pasadena, MD 21122-0135
(410) 255-3633
backpainassoc@Fmsn.com

National Back Pain Association
53 Wolseley Rd.
Rush Green, Essex, Romford RM7 OBS
United Kingdom
01708-741080
homepages.nildram.co.uk/~backtalk/

Cancer Information and Support

American Cancer Society
1599 Clifton Rd., NE
Atlanta, GA 30329
1-800-227-2345
www.cancer.org/

Canadian Cancer Society
10 Alcorn Ave., Ste. 200
Toronto, Ontario, Canada M4B3B1
(416) 961-7223

Cancer Care, Inc.
1180 Ave. of the Americas
New York, NY 10036
1-800-813-4673 or (212) 221-3300
www.cancercareinc.org

Candlelighters Childhood Cancer Foundation
7910 Woodmont Ave., Ste. 460
Bethesda, MD 20814
1-800-366-2223

National Cancer Institute
Office of Cancer Communications
Building 31, Room 10A24
Bethesda, MD 20892
1-800-4-CANCER
www.rex.nci.nih.gov

Ontario Cancer Information Service
755 Concession St.
Hamilton, Ontario, Canada L8V 1C4
1-800-263-6750

Fibromyalgia

National Fibromyalgia Research Association
P.O. Box 500
Salem, OR 97308
www.teleport.com/~nfra

Responsible and Adequate Fibromyalgia Treatment
131 Felix Dr.
Ojai, CA 93023
(805) 646-1939
dixie.ncplus.com/~raft/

Headache

American Council for Headache Education
875 Kings Hwy., Ste. 200
Woodbury, NJ 08096
1-800-255-2243
www.achenet.org

Help for Headaches
2462 Howard Ave., Ste. 118
Windsor Professional Centre
Windsor, Ontario, Canada N8X 3V6
(519) 252-3727
www.headache-help.org

National Headache Foundation
428 W. St. James Pl., 2nd Floor
Chicago, IL 60614
1-800-843-2256
www.headaches.org

Reflex Sympathetic Dystrophy

Reflex Sympathetic Dystrophy Syndrome Association
116 Haddon Ave., Ste. D
Haddonfield, NJ 08033
(609) 795-8845
cyboard.com/rsds

Sickle Cell Anemia

Sickle Cell Disease Association of America, Inc.
200 Corporate Pointe, Ste. 495
Culver City, CA 90230-7633
1-800-421-8453 or (310) 216-6363

Temporomandibular Joint (TMJ) Disorders

TMJ Association, Ltd.
P.O. Box 26770
Milwaukee, WI 53226
(414) 259-3223
www.tmj.org

TMJ Information and Resource Center
P.O. Box 1824
Winchester, CA 22601

Trigeminal Neuralgia (Tic Douloureux)

Trigeminal Neuralgia Association
P.O. Box 340
Barnegat Light, NJ 08006
(609) 361-1014
neurosurgery.mgh.harvard.edu/tna/

Vulvar Pain

Vulvar Pain Foundation
P.O. Drawer 117
Graham, NC 27253
(910) 226-0704
www.vulvarpainfoundation.org

Other Resources

Acupuncture

Acupressure Institute of America
1533 Shattuck Ave.
Berkeley, CA 94709

American Academy of Medical Acupuncture
5200 Wilshire Blvd., No. 500
Los Angeles, CA 90036
1-800-521-2262

Alternative Therapies

U.S. Office of Alternative Medicine
P.O. Box 20907
Silver Springs, MD 20907
(888) 644-6226
www.ncbionim.nih.gov

Art Therapy

American Art Therapy Association
1202 Allanson Road
Mundelein, IL 60060
1-888-290-0878
www.arttherapy.org

Biofeedback

Association for Applied Psychophysiology and Biofeedback
10200 W. 44th Ave., No. 304
Wheat Ridge, CO 80033-2840
1-800-477-8892
www.aaplo.org

Caregiver Support

Friends Health Connection
P.O. Box 114
New Brunswick, NJ 08903
1-800-48-FRIEND
www.48friend.com

National Family Caregivers Association
9261 E. Bexhill Dr.
Kensington, MD 20895-3104
1-800-896-3650
www.nfcacares.org

Depression

Depression/Awareness, Recognition, and Treatment
National Institute of Mental Health
Rockville, MD 20857
1-800-421-4211
www.ninh.nih.gov

Diet

American Dietetic Association
216 W. Jackson Blvd., No. 800
Chicago, IL 60606
1-800-366-1655
www.eatright.org

Financial and Other

Advocacy Center for Persons with Disabilities, Inc.
2671 Executive Center Circle West, Ste. 100
Tallahassee, FL 32301

American Association of Retired Persons (AARP)
601 E St. NW
Washington, DC 20049
1-800-424-3410

Medicare Information Line
Information about Medicare, Medicare supplemental insurance, HMOs, and special programs for low-income people.
1-800-638-6833

Pharmaceutical Manufacturers Association
Provides a list of drug companies that offer free medication to people in need.
1100 15th St., NW
Washington, DC 20005

President's Committee on Employment of People with Disabilities
(202) 376-6200

U.S. Equal Opportunity Commission
1-800-872-3362

Fitness

American College of Sports Medicine
P.O. Box 1440
Indianapolis, IN 46206
(317) 637-9200

CC-M Productions (Armchair Fitness Videos)
8510 Cedar St.
Silver Spring, MD 20910
1-800-453-6280

National Organization of Mall Walkers
P.O. Box 191
Hermann, MO 65041
(314) 486-3945

Hospice

National Hospice Organization
11 Beacon St., No. 910
Arlington, VA 02108
1-800-658-8898
www.nbo.org

Humor Therapy

American Association of Therapeutic Humor
9040 Forestview Rd.
Skokie, IL 60203

The Humor Project
480 Broadway #210
Sarasota Springs, NY 12866
(518) 587-8770
www.humorproject.com

Laughter Therapy
P.O. Box 827
Monterey, CA 93940
(408) 625-3788

Hypnosis

American Society of Clinical Hypnosis
2200 Devon Ave., No. 291
Des Plaines, IL 60018-4534
(708) 297-3317

Massage

American Massage Therapy Association
820 David St., Ste. 100
Evanston, IL 60201
(847) 864-0123
www.amtamassage.org

Medical Organizations

American Academy of Hospice and Palliative Medicine
11250 Roger Bacon Dr., Ste. 8
Reston, VA 20190-5202
(703) 787-7718
www.aahpm.org

American Academy of Physical Medicine & Rehabilitation
One IBM Plaza, Ste. 2500
Chicago, IL 60611-3604
(312) 464-9700
www.aapmr.org

American Board of Medical Specialties
1-800-766-2378
ww.certifieddoctor.org

American Chiropractic Association
1701 Clarendon Blvd.
Arlington,VA 22209
(703) 276-8800
www.amerchiro.org/

American College of Occupational and Environmental
Medicine
55 W. Seegers Rd.
Arlington Heights, IL 60005
(847) 228-6850
www.acoem.org

American Society of Anesthesiologists
Pain Therapy Committee
520 N. Northwest Hwy.
Park Ridge, IL 60068
(708) 825-5586
www.asahq.org

Music Therapy

National Association for Music Therapy
8455 Colesville Rd., Ste. 930
Silver Spring, MD 10910

Nurses

Visiting Nurse Association of America
3801 E. Florida Ave., No. 900
Boston, MA 80201
1–800–426–2547
www.naa.org

Sex Therapy and Therapy

American Association of Sex Educators, Counselors, and
Therapists
435 N. Michigan Ave., No. 117
Chicago, IL 60611
(312) 644–0828

American Association of Marriage and Family Therapists
225 Yale Ave.
Claremont, CA 91711

Sex Information and Education Council of the United States
130 W. 42nd St., Ste. 2500
New York, NY 10036

Sleep Disorders

American Sleep Disorder Association
604 Second St. SW
Rochester, MN 55902
(507) 287–6006
www.asda.org

Stress

The American Institute of Stress
124 Park Avenue
Yonkers, NY 10703
(914) 963-1200
www.stress.org/

Yoga

International Association of Yoga Therapists
20 Sunnywide Ave., Ste. A-243
Mill Valley, CA 94941
(415) 332-2478

Related Reading

Medical Textbooks on Pain

Bonica, John J., M.D. *Management of Pain*, 2d ed. Philadelphia: Lea and Febiger, 1990.

Wall, Patrick P., and R. Melzack. *Textbook of Pain*, 2d ed. New York: Churchill Livingstone, 1989.

Weiner, Richard S., M.D., ed. *Pain Management*, 5th ed. Boca Raton, Fla.: St. Lucie Press, 1998.

Other books of interest

American Council on Headache Education. *Migraine: The Complete Guide*. New York: Dell, 1994.

Burns, David D. *The Feeling Good Handbook*. New York: Plume/Penguin, 1989.

Cousins, Norman. *Anatomy of an Illness*. New York: Norton, 1979.

Cowles, Jane, Ph.D. *Pain Relief: How to Say No to Acute, Chronic, and Cancer Pain!* New York: Mastermedia Ltd., 1993.

Dollinger, Malin, M.D., Ernest H. Rosenbaum, M.D., and Greg Cable, eds. *Everyone's Guide to Cancer Therapy.* Toronto, Canada: Somerville House Books Ltd., 1994.

Gach, Michael Reed. *Acupressure's Potent Points: A Guide for Self-Care of Common Ailments.* New York: Bantam Books, 1990.

Ornish, Dean, M.D. *Dr. Dean Ornish's Program for Reversing Heart Disease.* New York: Ballantine, 1990.

Sarno, John, M.D. *Healing Back Pain.* New York: Warner, 1991.

Shealy, C. Norman, M.D. *The Pain Game.* Milbrae, Calif.: Celestial Arts, 1976.

Solomon, Seymour, M.D., and Steven Fraccaro. *The Headache Book.* Yonkers, N.Y.: Consumer Reports Books, 1991.

Stacy, Charles B., M.D., Andrew S. Kaplan, D.M.D., and Gray Williams Jr. *The Fight Against Pain.* Yonkers, N.Y.: Consumer Reports Books, 1992.

Sternbach, Richard A., Ph.D. *Mastering Pain: A Twelve-Step Program for Coping with Chronic Pain.* New York: G.P. Putnam's Sons, 1987.

Internet Sites

www.centerwatch.com/RESOURCE.HTM
Lists ongoing clinical trials for chronic pain, migraine, and other diseases and conditions.

igrn.nlm.nih.gov/
Free public gateway to search databases such as MEDLINE.

www.ncbi.nlm.nih.gov/PubMed/
National Medical Library at the National Institutes of Health.

www.rxlist.com/cgi/rxlist.cgi
Extensive drug information available by name, including cautions and side effect information.

www.usp.org/toolbar/search.htm
U.S. Pharmacopoeia on-line is a searchable database of drugs and drug manufacturers.

www.ama-assn.org/aps/amahg.htm
The American Medical Association's physician locator describing the practice and qualifications of licensed medical doctors and doctors of osteopathy.

www.PAIN.com/defaultcon.cfm?direct=cl
Compilation of several hundred pain specialists in several countries by Dannemiller Foundation–World Wide Congress on Pain.

www.aash.org
The home page of the American Association for the Study of Headache, featuring information for physicians and health care professionals.

www.htinet.com/him.html
The Headache Information Network is an interactive resource offering excerpts from recorded talk-show programs or access to transcripts that may be downloaded.

www.headache2000.com
The British Association for the Study of Headache.

www.aan.com/public/pig.html
The American Academy of Neurology Patient Information Guides, listed alphabetically.

www.healthtouch.com/level1/leaflets/102429/102429.htm
Healthtouch features the complete texts of the National Institute of Neurological Diseases' publications for consumers on chronic pain, headaches, and migraine.

Glossary

Acupuncture. A traditional Chinese healing technique that involves the insertion of fine needles into particular points along the body, called meridians, with the aim of balancing vital energies. Practiced by *acupuncturists*.

Alexander technique. Postural training that can reduce pain.

Allodynia. Pain created by a stimulus that is not typically painful and below the normal threshold.

Analgesia. A medical term for a medication that relieves pain.

Anesthesia. Literally, "without feeling." A lack of feeling, such as numbness, that may be natural or induced by drugs.

Anesthesiologist. A medical doctor who specializes in anesthesia.

Anesthetic. A medication that causes a lack of sensation. *Topical* anesthetics are applied to the surface of the body and cause a lack of sensation in the area around the application. *Local* anesthetics produce a numbness in localized parts of the body and are often administered by injection near a particular nerve. *General* anesthetics cause lack of consciousness and are injected or inhaled, as before surgery.

Antidepressant. A medication used to treat depression and sometimes pain on a short-term basis.

Behavioral therapy. A psychological and social treatment strategy that aims to change unhealthy behavior that may contribute to pain.

Breakthrough pain. A sudden, intense increase or flare-up in pain levels.

Chiropractor. A specialist in the function of the spine and nervous system who manipulates the skeleton and often treats back pain.

Cognitive therapy. A psychological treatment that seeks to recognize and reverse negative, unhealthy thought patterns and change them to positive healthy patterns.

CT scan. An X-ray type technique which uses computer technology to provide very detailed information.

Dance therapy. The use of dance as restorative therapy. May be given by a *dance therapist.*

Deafferentation. A loss of sensation created by the severing or destruction of sensory nerves, which is more or less permanent.

Depression. An emotional state characterized by lack of interest in all formerly pleasurable outlets such as sex, food, friends, hobbies, and entertainment, ranging from mild to severe.

Disability or **"handicap."** A disadvantage resulting from impairment of functional limitations that prevents the fulfillment of a role that is normal for that individual, given age, sex, social, and cultural factors.

Drug addiction. Both a physical and psychological dependency on a habit-forming substance, such as a narcotic drug.

Drug dependence. A physical dependence on the effects of a particular habit-forming drug, and one that does not have a component of psychological need.

Drug tolerance. The point at which doses of some drugs lose their effectiveness, when the dose must be increased to achieve a similar result.

Dysesthesia. An abnormal and painful sensation that can occur spontaneously or in response to a particular stimulus.

Dysphoria. A mood of the emotions expressed as anxiety, distress, sadness, or depression.

Edema. A medical term for swelling.

Endorphins. Natural chemical substances that relieve pain.

Epidural anesthetic. A drug injected between the middle and lower back to deaden sensation in nerves leading to the chest and lower part of the body.

Euphoria. A happy mood of well-being or buoyant self-confidence.

Family doctor. A medical doctor now usually referred to as a *general practitioner, family practitioner,* or *internist.* Family doctors may prescribe medications and other treatments to help manage pain, or they may refer to other medical doctors who specialize in particular areas.

Hyperalgesia. An abnormal increase in the intensity of pain.

Hyperesthesia. A hypersensitivity to sensation of any kind in response to a stimulus.

Hyperpathia. A syndrome in which the pain response is exaggerated beyond normal, often produced under repeated exposure to a stimulus that initially is not painful.

Idiopathic. Coming from an unknown cause, or caused by medical treatment.

Impairment. Any loss or abnormality of psychological, physiological, or anatomical structure or function.

Inflammation. Defensive reaction of the body to damage, characterized by surface redness, swelling, and hypersensitivity of pain-sensing neurons.

Insomnia. An inability to sleep, or sleep prematurely ended or interrupted, often caused by anxiety and pain.

Invasive procedure. Any medical procedure in which body tissues are penetrated by an instrument that could cause discomfort or pain.

Massage therapy. A pain-relieving therapy that strokes or kneads the muscles with various forms of therapeutic massage. May be practiced by a *massage therapist*.

Music therapy. The use of music as restorative therapy. May be employed by a *music therapist*.

Nervous system. The entire system of nerve cells and nerves, including the brain and spinal cord, which receive and respond to stimuli.

Neuralgia. Pain in distribution of nerves.

Neuritis. A medical term for inflammation of the nerves.

Neurologist. A medical doctor who treats disorders of the nervous system, such as certain types of headaches and forms of nerve damage.

Neuron. Any single nerve cell that carries electrical impulses in one direction or the other. Each neuron contains a *cell body* that contains the nucleus, and fine branches or *terminals* at each end.

Neuropathy. A disturbance of function or a pathological change in a nerve.

Neurotransmitter. Chemical compounds flowing across tiny spaces called *synapses* between neurons, helping to transmit or suppress messages from one part of the body to another in a fraction of a second.

Nutritionists, or **registered dietitians.** Specialists who design an appropriate nutritional program focusing on aspects of diet. The purpose of the program may be to identify and avoid foods that trigger migraine headaches, to tailor a diet for specific medications, or to achieve a loss of weight.

Nociceptor. A nerve receptor sensitive to noxious stimuli that transmits the impulse. *Nociception* is the process by which a noxious stimulus is transmitted by the peripheral nervous system to the spinal cord and brain.

NSAIDs. Nonsteroidal anti-inflammatory drugs such as aspirin that relieve the pain associated with inflammation.

Occupational therapy. A therapy that helps build or restore the ability to carry out everyday tasks at home or at work.

Oncologist. A medical doctor who specializes in the treatment of cancer. *Medical oncologists* administer chemotherapy. *Radiation oncologists* administer radiation treatment. *Surgical oncologists* perform cancer surgery.

Opiate drugs. Drugs refined or chemically derived from the opium poppy, such as morphine. Also called narcotics.

Orthopedist. A medical doctor who treats disorders involving the bones or joints of the skeleton, such as spinal problems.

Osteopath. A doctor of osteopathy (D.O.) who manipulates the spine and uses other means to restore normal body functions. An osteopath focuses on the muscles, bones, and joints, and believes they should be properly balanced to assure good health.

Pain. An unpleasant sensory and emotional experience associated with damage to the body.

Pain threshold. The level of sensation at which any stimulus, such as pressure or heat, is first recognized by the body as painful.

Pain tolerance level. A medical term for the level at which pain cannot be voluntarily endured.

Palliative treatment. Treatment that seeks to mitigate symptoms but does not cure the underlying condition. Primarily given to improve the quality of life.

Paraesthesia. Sensations alongside normal ones, unpleasant and different but not painful in themselves, such as in "pins and needles" pains that occur without apparent cause.

Pathology. Something that results from a process in the body which is not normal, such as an abnormal growth or an infection.

Pharmacology. The science of drugs, including their chemical structure and how they achieve particular effects on the body.

Phasic pain. Pain that feels as if it spreads from a location along a nerve to peripheral areas served by the nerve. For example, in sciatica, caused by pressure on the sciatic nerve, the pain feels as though it is radiating down one leg.

Physiatrist. A medical doctor who specializes in physical or rehabilitative medicine.

Physical therapy. Therapeutic physical treatments for pain involving the muscles, bones, joints, and nerves, such as heat and cold treatments. Usually applied by a *physical therapist*. *Physiotherapists* and *kinesiotherapists* utilize similar techniques to help correct postural defects and other muscular and joint problems, employing conservative, noninvasive treatment techniques.

PRN. *Pro re rata in* Latin. It means to give medication "as needed."

Prognosis. A doctor's prediction of the future course of a disease and the chances for recovery.

Psychiatrist. A medical doctor who also has an advanced degree in psychology, specializing in mental health problems. A psychiatrist can prescribe antidepressant medications for short-term treatment for mental problems such as depression, which can accompany chronic pain.

Psychogenic pain. A medical term for pain that has emotional or mental causes.

Psychologist. A licensed mental health professional who practices psychotherapy or psychological techniques, including individual therapy and group sessions, but who does not prescribe medications.

Referred pain. Areas or trigger points of persisting tenderness, which "refer," or shift, the sensation of pain to other parts of the body.

Rheumatalgia. Chronic pain that comes from rheumatism.

Rheumatologist. A medical doctor who treats diseases of the joints, such as rheumatoid arthritis or other disorders of the rheumatic system.

Sciatic nerves. The body's largest nerves, which begin in the buttocks and carry sensation to most of the legs.

Side effect. A secondary, usually unwanted reaction to medication or treatment.

Somatic pain. Pain emanating from any of the body's sensory nerves, except those of the internal organs. Soma is a Greek word meaning "of the body."

Subclinical pain. Pain that has no visible symptoms.

Subcutaneous. Below the skin, as in a subcutaneous injection.

Suffering. A state of severe distress associated with events that threaten the intactness of a person and may or may not be associated with pain.

Support group. A group of people who meet on a regular basis to discuss topics of mutual interest and concern, such as how to live with chronic pain.

Surgeon. A medical doctor who performs surgery and other procedures. Surgeons may specialize in an area such as orthopedic surgery, neurosurgery, or oral surgery; some specialize in specific types of surgery for a particular disorder.

Syndrome. A group of signs or symptoms which indicate an abnormal condition.

Systemic pain. Pain that affects the entire body.

TENS. Transcutaneous electrical nerve stimulation is a treatment that relieves pain through the use of small mechanical stimulators that provide mild doses of harmless electricity.

Therapist. A person skilled in giving a particular type of treatment, usually in a specialized area of health care.

Tonic pain. Continuous pain that may fluctuate in intensity.

Topical anesthetic. An anesthetic applied to the skin, producing temporary numbness.

Trigger point. A hypersensitive area of muscle or connective tissue, usually associated with myofascial pain syndrome.

Vertebrae. The bones of the spine.

Visceral pain. A medical term for pain emanating from the internal organs, or viscera.

Index

A

A-beta nerve fibers, 70-71, 267
Ablative, surgeries, 274-279
Academy of Orthopaedic
    Surgery, 146
Acceptance of pain, 112
Acetaminophen, 246-247
Acupressure, 161-162, 286, 313
Acupuncture, 12, 20, 41, 56, 65,
    105, 147, 154, 160-162, 205,
    286, 313
        acupuncture points, 160
        effectiveness on pain,
            161-162
        experimental uses of, 304
Acute pain, 25, 66, 287
Acute versus chronic pain, 6-9,
    24-27, 60, 230, 236-237, 287
Adams, Hunter "Patch", 225-226
Adapin, 255
A-delta nerve fibers, 70-71
Adjuvant drugs, 229, 289
Adrenegic blockers, 257
Aerobic exercise, 149
Afferent nerves, 63, 67, 69
Aivan, 254

Alcohol, 183
Alcoholics Anonymous, 235
Alexander technique, 146
Allodynia, 93
Allergies, 32
Alternative therapies, 306, 314
        See also acupuncture;
            hypnosis; biofeedback;
            relaxation therapy;
            nutrition; stress-relieving
            techniques
American Academy of Medical
    Acupuncture, 162
American Academy of Pain
    Management, 36, 48, 307
American Cancer Society, 191,
    296, 310
American Chronic Pain
    Association (ACPA), 4-6, 121,
    127, 128, 148, 189, 191, 309
American Institute of Stress, 91,
    203
American Massage Therapy
    Association, 159
American Pain Society, 8, 302,
    307
Analgesic ceiling, 289

Analgesic drugs, 229, 242-253
   See NSAIDs; steroids;
      narcotics
Anger, 13, 107, 110, 134, 203-204
Angina, 74, 96-97, 206, 257
Angioplasty, 272
Anklosing spondylitis, 79-80
Anti-anxiety drugs, 254
Anticholinergic drugs, 258
Anticonvulsant drugs 242, 256,
   289
Antidepressant medications, 114,
   255
Antihistamines, 244
Anti-inflammatory drugs 245-249
Antimalarial drugs, 257
Antioxidant vitamins, 171-172
Antipsychotic drugs, 43
Aquatic therapy, 150
Arachnoiditis, 143, 187
Aromatherapy, 226-227
Arthritis, 9,10, 18, 20, 59, 72, 74,
   80-83, 149, 207, 239, 246, 247,
   257, 263, 304
      diet and, 178-179
      joint replacement, 270-272
      triggers for, 81
      types of, 80-83
Arthritis Foundation, 16, 18, 59,
   309
Arthroplasty, 271
Arthroscopic surgery, 274
Artificial joints, 271
Armchair exercises, 150
Aspirin, 157, 234, 246-247, 258,
   288

Assessment by doctor, 23
ATP, 303
Auricular therapy, 304
Autoimmune disorders, 79, 91-92
Autogenic training, 56, 216-217
Autonomic nervous system, 63,
   205

B

Back pain, workplace, 18
Back and neck pain, 8, 9, 12,
   15-20, 72, 74-80, 149-151,
   205, 245, 247, 253, 254, 255,
   263, 269
      nutrition and, 177-178
      stress and, 204-206
      surgery and, 268-270, 278
Balanced diet, 170
Behavioral therapy, 12, 15, 28,
   123-126, 230, 250, 281
Benefits of exercise, 148-151
Bentyl, 258
Benzodiazepine, 231, 254
Beta blockers, 257
Biofeedback, 12, 41, 56, 188, 209,
   219-221, 293, 314
      devices used with, 220
      pains it can relieve, 221
Body mechanics, 153
Bone marrow transplants, 250
Bone pain, 287
Bone spurs, 82, 273
      See also osteophytes.
Bradykinin, 110

Brain waves, 213–214
Breathing techniques, 216
Brompton mixture, 298
Bursitis, 84, 156, 161, 246, 247
Bypass surgery, 272

C

Caffeine, 183–184, 210
Capsaicin, 156, 294
C-nerve fibers, 70–71, 267
Carafate, 258
Caregivers role, 32, 107, 125–127,
    155, 189, 314
Cancer Care, Incorporated, 282,
    310
Cancer pain, 7–10, 19, 21, 74,
    158–159, 206, 218, 225, 230,
    233, 247–248, 273, 281–299,
    302
        causes of, 284–285, 292–294
        drug treatment of, 288–290
        emotional aspects of,
            294–296
        incidence of, 284
        noninvasive, adjunct
            therapies for 286–287,
            293
        surgeries for, 264–266, 273,
            274–279
Causalgia, 92–93, 263, 273
Causes of pain, 29–30
        See also physical pain;
            psychogenic pain; mental
            aspects of pain
Central nervous system 63–64
Chemical nucleolysis, 270
Chemotherapy, 289

Chiropractic treatment, 147, 205,
    318
Chronic fatigue, 91
Chronic pain defined, 2, 7–9
Chronic paroxysmal hemicrania,
    89, 245
Chronic pain syndrome, 11, 19,
    29, 53–55, 111
Chronic rheumatism.
        See fibromyalgia.
Cingulotomy, 279
Circadian rhythms, 305
Clinical trials, 49
Cluster headaches, 88–89, 154
Codeine, 252, 289
Cognitive strategies to control
    pain, 116–117
Cognitive therapy, 12, 15, 114,
    119–123, 293
Cold treatments, 157
Communications training, 12, 15,
    55, 127–132, 153
Conditioning exercises, 149–150
Conservative pain treatments, 44
Coping with pain, 52.
        See mental aspects of pain.
Copper bracelets, 59
Cordotomy, 278–279
Corticosteroids. *See* steroids.
Cortisol, 200. *See also* stress.
Coronary artery surgery, 272
Covington, Edward, M.D.,
    210–211, 231, 234
Counterirritation, 71, 154
Crash diets, 176

Creatine, 149

Crohn's disease, 99, 182, 247,
251, 258

Cryolysis, 276

Cytotec, 258

D

Dalmane, 231

Dance therapy, 150, 205 227

Danzol, 259

Darvon, 252

Death of spouse, 119.
See also major stressful
events.

Deep heat treatments, 154

Definition of pain, 6–7, 162

Depression, 6, 8, 13, 15, 28, 43,
54, 65–66, 68, 104, 107, 108,
110–115, 117, 120, 121, 123,
128, 129, 133, 138, 139, 149,
180, 185–186, 217, 255, 285,
295, 305, 315
getting through hard times
and, 128
stress and, 203–204
symptoms of, 113–114

Dermatomyositis, 92

Dehydration, 164–165

Demerol, 188, 252, 290

Dentists, 240.
See also TMJ disorders.

Depakene, 256

Desyrel, 255

Dexedrine, 244

Diabetes, 74, 95, 154, 167, 248

Diagnosing pain, 24
See also physical causes of
pain.

Diathermy, 156–157

Diet. See nutrition; diet therapy.

Dietitians, registered, 176, 178,
180, 315

Diet therapy, 12, 98, 99, 176–177,
315

Dimensions of pain, 68–69

Dilantin, 256

Dilaudid, 188, 252

Disability and pain, 9, 17–19,
30–31

Disability insurance, 40

Disability, reduction of, 52

Disc problems, 40, 77–80,
168–270

Discetomy, 268–269

Distorted thinking, 120–122

Distraction, 73, 214–215, 286–
287, 293

Diverticula, 98

Diverticulitis, 98–99, 257

Doctor-patient communication,
32, 37–38, 127–133, 291–292

Dolene, 252

Dollinger, Malin, M.D., 292

Dorsal column, 267

Dorsal column stimulators,
43–44, 188, 262, 266–267

Dorsal horn, 62

Doriden, 231

Drugs and pain control, 21, 45,
  229–259
    drug addiction, 231–233,
      251, 282–283, 286, 290
    drug tolerance, 289–290
    categories of, 242
    dependence, 231–233, 290
    dosages, 234–235
    overuse of, 42, 52, 210–211
Drug pumps, 241–242, 249–250,
  262, 264–266, 287, 289
Duke University, 227
Duoneal ulcers, 98
Dynorphins, 65

E

Educating yourself, how to,
  16–17, 23, 206
Education, benefits of, 2, 15, 117,
  155, 293
Efferent nerves, 63, 69
Effort headaches, 89
Elavil, 255
Electrogalvanic stimulation
  (EGS), 157
Electromagnetic medicine,
  303–304
Emotional aspects of pain, 5,
  13–16, 21, 28, 31, 68, 202–203,
  294–296
Emotional cycle of pain, 111–112
Endogenous opiods, 65
Endogenous pain controls 65
Endorphins, 65, 138, 158, 219
Endoscope, 271
Endometriosis, 100, 258–259
Enkephalins, 64
Epicetus, 101

Epidurals, 241, 247
Equanil, 254
Ergotamine, 246
Exercise, beginning a program,
  141–143
Exercise, benefits of, 5, 73, 114,
  138–151, 177, 209, 210, 231,
  293–295
    exercise and diet, 177
    pacing your activities,
      152–154
    particular benefits, 142, 210
    supervision of, 143
    types of exercise, 148–151
Exercise prescriptions, 41, 141
Exercise therapy, 12, 141–143
Extent of chronic pain in United
  States, 17–19
Evaluation and treatment of
  chronic pain, 24
Evaluation of pain by doctor,
  31–36

F

Failed back surgery, 268
Faith, 189. *See* prayer
Family issues, 55
Family support, 126–127
Fear, 13, 68, 110, 133, 139–140
Feldenkrais technique, 146
Fellowship of Pain, 193
Fenatyl, 290
Fiber, 166, 170. *See* nutrition.
Fibromyalgia, 1, 66, 74, 89–91,
  104–106, 119, 143, 149, 161,
  207–208, 219, 311.
Fibrositis. *See* fibromyalgia.

Fighting back, 103
Fight or flight reflex, 200, 205
Financial issues, 12, 28, 49, 50-51
Fiorinal, 244
Fitness, 54, 72
Flexeril, 253
Fluoroscope use, 273
Food diary, 179
Food Guide Pyramid, 169-170
Food and Drug Administration
  (FDA), 232, 247, 304
Functional pains, 75, 78-79,
  89-90
Future treatments, 301-306

G

Gastric ulcers, 98
Gate Control Theory, 15, 20,
  67-72, 102-103
Gingival hyperplasia, 256
Ginkgo biloba, 183
Gold sodium thiomalate, 257
Glossopharyngeal neuralgia, 94,
  277-278
Goal-setting, 4, 49, 121, 134
Good health, 22
Gout, 83-84, 182, 246, 247, 257
Gouty arthritis, 83, 251
Group therapy, 117

H

Harris survey, 8, 18
Headaches, 20, 65, 72, 74, 87-88,
  220, 245, 253, 254, 257.
  See also migraine headaches;
    tension headaches
Headaches, extent of, 8

Health and fitness excellence, 165
Health Care Financing
  Administration (HFCA), 266
Health history, 31-32
Health insurance, 47, 50-51
Health maintenance
  organizations (HMOs), 36
Healthy back program, 150-151
Heat treatments, 147, 155-158
Helplessness, 129
Herniated disc, 79, 204, 268-270
Heroin, 252
Hip replacement surgery, 178
Histamine-2 blockers, 258
History of pain treatment, 14
Hobbies, benefits of, 228
Homeostasis, 303
Hope, 128, 134.
    See also future treatments.
Hormone therapy, 259
Hospice, 297-299, 315, 317
Hot dog headaches, 89
How pain is perceived, 67
Humor, 12-13, 225-226, 287,
  305, 317
Hydroconodone, 289
Hydromorphone, 290
Hypnosis, 12, 41, 188, 209, 213,
  217-219, 286, 293, 317
Hysterectomy, 100

I

Iatrogenic (unknown or doctor-
  caused) complications, 24
Ibuprofin, 246-247

Imagery and visualization, 220-222, 286, 293

Immune system, 165-66, 174, 185-186, 192-193, 226, 248, 285

Immunosuppressant drugs, 257

Inactivity and pain, 54, 138-139

Indomethacin, 245

Infectious arthritis, 83, 246

Inflammation, 76

Information about chronic pain, 16-17

Infrared therapy, 156-157

Injections, 240, 241

Insomnia, 40, 65, 113, 114, 129, 167, 180, 188, 221, 248, 319
  sleep and stress, 212-213
  sleeping pills, 231
  ways to improve sleep, 210-211

Insomnia Research and Treatment Program, 171

International Association for the Study of Pain, 102, 288, 308

Intraspinal drug delivery, 265-266

Irritable bowel syndrome, 98, 254

J

Jannetta's Procedure, 278

Joint disorders. *See also* arthritis; TMJ disorders.

Joint pain, 8. *See* arthritis, benefits of exercise.

Joint replacement, 270-272, 274

Journal of American Geriatrics, 140

Journal of Chronic Disease, 186

Juvenile rheumatoid arthritis, 83, 207

K

Kava kava, 183

Klonopin, 254

Koop, C. Everett, 304

L

Lactic acid, 66

Laminectomy, 269

Laser surgery, 275, 302

Laughter, benefits of. *See* humor.

Legal issues, 31

Levo-dromoran, 252

Levoprome, 256

L-histadine, 179

Librium, 254

Life-changing events, 201

Limits of medical treatment, 58

Long-term success of treatment, 56

Lordosis, 177

Loss of control, 110

Ludiomil, 255

Lumbar fusion, 41

Lupus, 257

Lyme disease, 83, 87, 258

M

Magnet therapy, 105, 188, 303-304

Major surgery, 262

Major tranquilizers, 255-256

Malingering, 119

Malnutrition, 167

Managing pain, 7

Marie-Strumpell disease, 79–80
Marphan, 255
Massage, 71, 147, 158–159, 286
Massage therapy, 158–159, 317
Mastering pain, 123, 134, 237
Mayo Clinic, 56, 171.
Mcgill-Melzack Pain
   Questionnaire, 35–36, 291
Meaning of illness, 197
Medicaid, 51
Medical tests, 31–32, 42, 78,
   81, 187, 227.
     See also evaluation of pain.
Medicare, 50–51, 110, 266,
   298–299, 315
Medications, 27, 229–259
Medication, oral forms of,
   239–240
Medication, regular doses of,
   235–236
Medication, overuse of, 123–124
Medication questions to ask your
   doctor, 240
Meditation, 223–224
Medline, 17
Mellaril, 256
Memorial sloan-kettering, 226,
   283
Mental aspects of pain. See mind's
     influence on pain.
Methodone, 290
Methotrexate, 257
Methysergide, 246–247
Mesencephalotomy, 279
Microdiscectomy, 40, 270
Microtrauma, 76

Microvascular decompression, 278
Microwave therapy, 157
Migraine headaches, 65, 74,
   87–88, 161, 168, 208, 220
     dietary factors and, 179–181
     symptoms of, 88
Mind science foundation, 194
Mind's influence on pain,
   101–135, 232–233
Minnesota Multiphasic
   Personality Inventory
   (MMPI), 47
Minor surgery, 262
Misconceptions about pain, 38–39
Morphine, 10, 110, 230, 240,
   249–253, 273, 287–290
Motivational aspects of pain,
   68–69
MPS. See myofascial pain
   syndrome.
Multidisciplinary treatment,
   12–13, 52–53, 230.
     See also pain treatment
     centers.
Multipurpose arthritis and
   musculoskeletal diseases center,
   271
Muscle disorders, 89–92
Muscle guarding, 76
Muscle pain, 8, 76, 89–92,
   181–182, 245, 253, 255
Muscle relaxants, 242, 252
Muscle relaxation, 216
Muscle spasms, 76, 96, 184
Muscle tension, 107, 132, 217
Musculoskeletal pain, 18
Music, benefits of, 123, 224–225,
   287, 317

Myalgia. *See* fibromyalgia.
Myelotomy, 279
Myofascial pain syndrome (MPS)
  89–91, 161
Myofascial release, 147
Myths about chronic pain,
  108–109

N

Narcotics, use of, 107, 109, 210,
  232, 237, 249–253, 290, 292,
  294, 301–302.
Narcotics Anonymous, 235
Nardil, 255
National Cancer Institute, 311
National Chronic Pain Outreach
  Association, 15, 191, 308
National Fibromyalgia Research
  Association 311
National Headache Foundation,
  86, 312
National Institutes of Health, 16
National Institute of Mental
  Health, 114, 315
Neck pain. *See* back and neck
        pain.
Need for nutrients, 166–168
Negative emotions, 122
Negative thoughts, 122
Nerve blocks, 241, 263–264, 287
Nerve regeneration, 67
Nervous system, 62–64
Neuralgia paresthetica, 174–175
Neurolysis, 275–276
Neuromas, 94, 273
Neuropathy, 74, 92–94, 154, 182,
  246, 247, 255, 257, 292–294

Neurotransmitters, 62
New York University's Institute
  of Rehabilitation Medicine,
  204
Nicomachean ethics, 13
Nitroglycerin, 257
Nociception, 66
Noninvasive pain treatments, 44
Non-steroidal anti-inflammatory
  drugs. *See* NSAIDs.
Noradrenaline, 66, 93, 255
Norepinephrine, 66
Norflex, 253
Norpramin, 255
NSAIDs, 242, 245–247, 258,
  288–289, 292
Nucleolysis, 270
Numeric Pain Intensity Scale
  34–35
Numorphan, 252
Nurses, role of, 236–237, 240
Nutrition, 21, 163–184
Nutritionists, 176–177

O

Obesity, 174–177
    depression and, 175
    disability and, 174–175
    pain and, 174
Occlusal splits, 85–86
Occupational therapy, 12, 23,
  144, 151, 154, 318
Older patients, 57, 232, 299
Omega-3 acids, 178–180
Oncologists, role of 291–294

Operant conditioning. *See*
behavioral therapy.
Opiate drugs. *See* narcotics.
Opiate agonists, 252
Opiate agonist-antagonists, 252
Oral hygiene, 166
Orgasmic headaches, 89
Ornish, Dean, M.D., 12, 97,
168, 224
Orthopedic and rehabilitation
medicine, 75
Orthognathic surgery, 274
Osteoarthritis, 82, 144-147, 156,
161, 167, 270-272
Osteopaths, 205, 240
Osteophytes, 82, 271
Osteoporosis, 52, 80, 248,
270-272
Osteopuncture, 162
Osteotomy, 271
Overeaters Anonymous, 175
Overtreatment of pain, 9-10
Overweight. *See* obesity.
Overuse of drugs, 6, 9, 133, 140,
233-234.
See drug addiction;
drug tolerance; withdrawal
from drugs.
Oxygen uptake, 140

P
Pacing yourself, 134, 152-154
Pain behaviors. *See* behavior
therapy.
Pain "cocktails," 234
Pain definition of, 102. *See* acute
versus chronic pain

Pain diary, 32, 179, 180
Pain disorders, 73-100
Pain history, 34
Pain medicine, 66, 266
Pain treatment centers and
clinics, 20, 23, 29
Pain treatment programs, 46-53,
143, 151, 233-234
Pain consultants, 19
Pain management, 16, 19, 109
Pain modulating substances in
the body, 64-66
Pain relief, 34
Pain specialists, 12, 43
Pain tolerance, 39
Pain treatment centers, 12, 45-46
advantages of, 53
disadvantages of, 53
Pain treatments, types of, 44-45
Palliative care, 297-299
Pancreatic cancer, 275
Pancreatitis and diet, 182
Parasympathetic nervous system,
63
Parnate, 255
Passive movement, 144-147
Patient's Bill of Rights, 36, 48-49
Patient controlled anesthesia
(PCA), 250, 265
Patient pressure for drugs, 58
Patient, role of, 26, 34
Patient to person, 4-5
Patients with chronic pain, 19
Patient rights, 4
Pain and disability, 2
Pelvic inflammatory disease,
99-100, 258

Pelvic pain, 99–100
Pepcid, 258
Peptic ulcers, 98
Percodan, 188, 252, 289
Percoset, 188
Pericutaneous discectomy, 270
Pericutaneous transmyocardial
    revascularization, 302
Peripheral neurolysis, 276
Peripheral neuropathy, 95, 294
Peripheral nervous system 63–64
Pets, benefits of, 106, 185, 193
Pinched nerve, 79
Psychogenic pain, 29–30, 39
Phantom limb and stump pain,
    93–94, 106–107, 156, 255, 263,
    266, 273
Pharmacists, 240
Pharmacologic blockade, 273
Phenylalanine, 182–183
Physiatrists, 15, 205
Physical conditioning and pain,
    137–151
Physical deconditioning, 138–140
Physical effects of chronic pain,
    8–9, 137–151
Physical fitness. *See* fitness.
Physical limitations, 140–144
Physical pain, 61–100
Physical therapy, 23, 40–41, 78,
    85, 143–148, 205
Physical fitness, 134.
        See exercise; physical therapy.
Physical unfitness, 124
Placebo effect, 103.
Polymyalgia rheumatica, 89, 91,
    248

Polymyositis, 92
Positive thoughts, 189
Post-herpetic neuralgia, 31, 74,
    94–95, 156, 247–248, 251, 267
Post-traumatic headaches, 87
Post-traumatic pain syndrome, 92
Post-traumatic spreading
    neuralgia, 92
Posture, 144–146, 152–153, 211
Posture, tips on improving, 145
Prescriptions not filled,
    238–239, 251
Pressure point syndrome.
        See fibromyalgia.
Prayer and faith, 194–197,
    222–223
Privacy rights during treatment,
    49
Pro-banthine, 257
Prolotherapy, 304
Prolixin, 256
Pro re nata, p.r.n., 233
Processed foods 168–169
Prognosis, 48
Prostaglandins, 245, 247
Prozac, 255
Pseudogout, 84, 179
Psoriatic arthritis, 83, 257
Psychogenic arthritis.
        See fibromyalgia.
Psychological testing 47, 54
Psychogenic disorders, 119
Psychosocial collaborative
    oncology group, 295.
Psychosomatic disorders, 118–119

Psychosomatic medicine, 125
Psychoneuroimmunology, 305
Psychotherapy, 118-119, 287, 293, 296.
See behavioral therapy; cognitive therapy.
Psychotropic drugs, 242-244, 254-256, 289
Pulsed signal therapy (PST), 304

Q

Quaaludes, 231
Quality of life, 185-197
Quality of life defined, 186
Quality of life effects, 19
Questions to answer about pain, 291

R

Radiation therapy, 287
Radio frequency surgery, 276-277
Range of movement, 146
Raynaud's disease, 74
Rebound headaches, 154
Reflex sympathetic dystrophy, 9, 92-93, 266, 272-273, 312
Reflex sympathetic dystrophy syndrome association, 312
Reiter's syndrome, 83
Referred pain, 91
Reflux esophagus, 97, 258
Referrals to specialists, 57
Refusal of treatment, 49
Regional anesthetics, 241
Regulation of narcotics, 250-252

Relaxation exercises, 5, 12, 134, 209, 213, 216-217, 286
Relaxation response, 223-224
Remittive drugs, 257
Repositioning splits, 86
Resources, 21-22
Restoril, 231
Rheumatoid arthritis, 82-83, 103, 168, 178-179, 206-207, 247-249, 257, 271-272
Rheumatoid factor, 83
Rheumatoid nodules, 83
Rhyzotomies, 276-278
Risks and benefits
of back surgery, 268-270
of drugs, 230-231
of medical treatment, 36-37
of surgery, 261-263, 275
Robaxin, 253
Robb Pain Management Group, 265
Robert Wood Johnson Foundation, 13
Roles of doctor and patient, 26
Role of the mind, 101-135
Rosch, Paul, M.D., 90-91, 203-204, 206-209, 219, 303.

S

St. Christopher's Hospice, 297-298
Schweitzer, Albert, 20, 192-193, 306
Sciatica, 79
Sciatic pain, 40, 268
Sciolosis, 32, 80

Seasonal affective disorder, 305
Second opinions, 57-58
Self-defeating behavior, 123-124
Self-efficacy, 110-111
Self hypnosis. *See* hypnosis.
Self-management, 27, 29, 60,
    72-73, 126-127
Self-reinforcement, 111
Sensory nerve cells, 62.
Sensory tests, 33
Serax, 254
Serenity Prayer, 223
Serotonin, 65, 158, 172-173, 255
Setting priorities, 4
Sexual issues, 32, 113, 132-135,
    221, 232, 319
Shealy Institute, 56, 172
Shiatsu massage, 159
Shingles. *See* post herpetic
    neuraligia
Sickle cell anemia, 31
Side effects of drugs, 232,
    238-239, 302
        anticonvulsants, 256
        muscle relaxants, 253
        narcotics, 252-253; *See also*
            drug addiction.
        NSAIDs, 246-247
        psychotropic medications,
            254-256
        steroids 248-249
Side effects of surgery, 262-263
Signal breath, 131
Simonton Cancer Center, 222
Sinequan, 255
Skin patches, 240

Skin stimulation techniques,
    154-160
Sleep hygiene, 210-212, 231
Sleeping pills, 210-211
Sleeplessness.
        See insomnia.
Slipped disc, 79
        See herniated disc.
Social readjustment scale, 201
Social support, 5, 21, 185-197,
    215
Social support research, 192-193
Soma, 253
Somatic nervous system, 63
Somatization, 119
Sources of chronic pain, 24, 28.
        See also emotional aspects of
            pain; physical pain;
            mental aspects of pain;
            stress.
Spastic torticollis, 266
Spinal fusion, 269
Spinal pain.
        See back and neck pain.
Spinal cord, 77
Spinal cord stimulation, 266-267
Spinal injections, 241
Spinal stenosis, 80
Spine, 77-78
Spinothalamic tracts, 278-279
Spiritual aspects, 194-197,
    222-223
Spondylosis, 79
St. John's wort, 183
Standard posture, 146
Steroids, 59, 147, 242, 247-249,
    289, 294

Strength-building exercises, 150

Stress and chronic pain, 5, 8, 12, 15, 21, 64, 66, 75, 78, 87, 96, 116, 175, 193, 194, 199-228, 270, 305, 319

  symptoms of, 202-203

  ways to relieve, 46, 98, 114, 128, 138, 185, 209, 214-228, 295

Stretching exercises, 148

Stump pain.

  See phantom limb and stump pain.

Substance abuse, 232-233

Substance P, 66, 110, 156

Success of multidisciplinary treatment 55-57, 103

Suicide, 6, 43, 112, 285.

  See also depression.

Support groups, 12, 15-16, 104-106, 187-193, 287

Suppositories, 240

Surgery, 21, 27, 32, 45, 86, 188, 261-280, 302

Swedish massage, 159

Sympathectomies, 272-273

Sympathetic nerve blocks, 272-273

Sympathetic nerves, 93, 272-273

Sympathetic nervous system, 63

Synovectomy, 272

Synovial fluid, 81

Symptoms of depression, 113-114

Symptom preoccupation, 214

Systemic medications, 240-242

T

Tagamet, 258

Tardive dyskinesia, 256

Team approach, 11

Tegretol, 256

Tender points, 90

Temporal arteritis, 89

Temporary relief from pain, 154-160

Tension Myositis Syndrome (TMS), 204-206

Tetrocycline, 257-258

TENS, 12, 20, 40-41, 65, 71, 85, 159-160, 209, 253, 286, 303-304.

Tension headaches, 87, 220

Therapist, role of, 116-117

Therapy, benefits of 115-126

Thorazine, 156

Tic douleureux, 31, 74, 94, 253, 263, 274, 277-278, 313

Titration of drugs, 236

Thalamotomy, 279

Therapeutic exercises, 146-147

TMD disorders. *See* TMJ disorders.

TMJ disorders and treatment, 84-86, 247, 253, 274, 312-313

Tobacco use, 184

Tolerance to drug, 232

Topical ointments, 156

Tranxene, 254

Transcutaneous electrical nerve stimulation. *See* TENS.

Transmission of pain impulses, 66, 70-71

Tricyclics, 255
Trigeminal neuralgia.
   See tic douleureux.
Trigger foods, 168
Trigger points, 79
Trigger point therapy, 144,
   146–147
Tryptophan, 172–173
Types of pain, 36, 71

U

UCLA Pain Management
   Center, 241
Ulcers, 98, 182, 246, 258
Ulcerative colitis, 99
Ultrasound, 157
Undertreatment of pain, 9–10,
   13, 281, 285–286, 290.
   See cancer pain.
U.S. Department of Health
   Services, 18, 59

V

Vascular headaches, 87–88
Vasodialators, 257
Valium, 254
Vertebrae, 77–80
Vibrators, 59, 135, 159
Viscera, 95
Visceral pain 95–100
Vicodin, 42, 252
Vinegar, 59

Vitamins and minerals, 32, 59, 80,
   95, 168, 170–174, 179, 180,
   181, 182, 200, 225, 238
Vulvar pain, 313

W

Walking, 149
Water and health, 164–165
Wellness community, 191, 296
Wellness, defined, 22
Whiplash, 278
Withdrawal from drugs, 52,
   233–235, 237–238, 290
Workdays lost from pain, 8,
   18–19
Workers compensation, 41–42,
   50–51, 109
Working, benefits of, 105–106
World Health Organization
   (WHO), 22, 239, 243
Writing, benefits of, 211, 227

X

Xanax, 254

Y

Yoga, 12, 150, 209, 319
YMCA, 150

Z

Zantac, 258.